War and the Works
of
J.R.R. Tolkien

**Recent Titles in Contributions to the
Study of Science Fiction and Fantasy**

Monsters, Mushroom Clouds, and the Cold War
M. Keith Booker

Science Fiction, Canonization, Marginalization, and the Academy
Gary Westfahl and George Slusser, editors

The Supernatural in Short Fiction of the Americas: The Other World in the New
World
Dana Del George

The Fantastic Vampire: Studies in the Children of the Night
James Craig Holte, editor

Unearthly Visions: Approaches to Science Fiction and Fantasy Art
Gary Westfahl, George Slusser, and Kathleen Church Plummer, editors

Worlds Enough and Time: Explorations of Time in Science Fiction and Fantasy
Gary Westfahl, George Slusser, and David Leiby, editors

No Cure for the Future: Disease and Medicine in Science Fiction and Fantasy
Gary Westfahl and George Slusser, editors

Science and Social Science in Bram Stoker's Fiction
Carol A. Senf

Chaos Theory, Asimov's Foundations and Robots, and Herbert's Dune: The Fractal
Aesthetic of Epic Science Fiction
Donald E. Palumbo

The Novels of Kurt Vonnegut: Imagining Being an American
Donald E. Morse

Fantastic Odysseys: Selected Essays from the Twenty-Second International
Conference on the Fantastic in the Arts
Mary Pharr, editor

The Utopian Fantastic: Selected Essays from the Twentieth International
Conference on the Fantastic in the Arts
Martha Bartter

War and the Works
of
J.R.R. Tolkien

Janet Brennan Croft

Contributions to the Study of Science Fiction and Fantasy, Number 106
C. W. Sullivan, III, Series Adviser

Westport, Connecticut
London

Library of Congress Cataloging-in-Publication Data

Croft, Janet Brennan.
    War and the works of J.R.R. Tolkien / Janet Brennan Croft.
       p. cm.—(Contributions to the study of science fiction and fantasy, ISSN 0193–6875 ;
no. 106)
    Includes bibliographical references and index.
    ISBN 0–313–32592–8 (alk. paper)
    1. Tolkien, J.R.R. (John Ronald Reuel), 1892–1973—Criticism and interpretation. 2.
Literature and history—Great Britain—History—20th century. 3. Tolkien, J.R.R. (John
Ronald Reuel), 1892–1973—Knowledge—History. 4. Fantasy literature, English—History
and criticism. 5. Middle Earth (Imaginary place) 6. War in literature. I. Title.
II. Series.
    PR6039.O32Z624 2004
    828'.91209—dc22   2003060425

British Library Cataloguing in Publication Data is available.

Library of Congress Catalog Card Number: 2003060425
ISBN: 0–313–32592–8
ISSN: 0193–6875

First published in 2004

Praeger Publishers, 88 Post Road West, Westport, CT 06881
An imprint of Greenwood Publishing Group, Inc.
www.praeger.com

Printed in the United States of America

The paper used in this book complies with the
Permanent Paper Standard issued by the National
Information Standards Organization (Z39.48–1984).

10 9 8 7 6 5 4 3 2

To my husband, Duane, and my daughter, Sarah
"Of making many books there is no end."

Contents

Acknowledgments

First and foremost, I'd like to thank Kayla McKinney Wiggins of Martin Methodist College in Pulaski, Tennessee. When I mentioned how fascinating it was to apply Paul Fussell's *The Great War and Modern Memory* to Tolkien's works, she told me to stop talking and start writing. Excellent suggestion! Dr. Wiggins also read the manuscript and offered valuable advice.

I would also like to thank several people at the University of Oklahoma Libraries. The Interlibrary Loan Department helped me obtain a number of hard-to-find items. I appreciate the help of Mark Coe, who read the manuscript with an eagle eye, and the University of Oklahoma library administration, a grant from whom allowed me to make a short research trip to the Marion Wade Center at Wheaton College in Wheaton, Illinois.

I'm grateful for the good fellowship and enthusiasm of my fellow members of the Mythopoeic Society, especially Dan Timmons, David Bratman, Susan Palwick, and Bruce Leonard, who helped me refine some of my thoughts during conversations at our annual conferences and in online discussions. The community at Debbie Ridpath Ohi's "Talking Tolkien" online discussion boards also helped me work out some of my ideas; thanks especially to Turumarth, susanna, and Katarina.

Finally, I'd like to thank my family for their patience during the writing of this book. I could not have done this without their encouragement and support.

Chapter 1

Introduction

WAR AND THE ARTS

Throughout history, war and conflict have been a source of inspiration for the arts. From *The Iliad* and *The Aeneid* to Shakespeare's *Henry V*, from ancient Egyptian frescos and Aztec carvings to Picasso's *Guernica*, from the photojournalism of the American Civil War to the fantasy of *Star Wars* and the realism of *Saving Private Ryan*, war reverberates in the artistic imagination. Robert Hauptman states, "[E]ven the least prescient reader must realize the creative result of individual war-time experience. The literary artifact is not responsible for the situation; instead, the evil at last has this singular positive result" (Hauptman). But as Daniel Timmons has pointed out, "Since the Vietnam conflict, war as a subject and theme in art and literature has been suspect" ("We Few" 1). Many literary critics during the last third of the twentieth century exhibited an unthinking antiwar bias and looked only for evidence of war's psychic wounds, dismissing any idea that participation in war can also be a factor in personal maturation or a source of pride. As Joanna Bourke indicates, even those who suffer psychological damage from war often say that the "satisfaction and excitement outweighed distressing experiences" ("Effeminacy" 57). In light of this, our understanding and appreciation of many authors can be enhanced by honestly examining the role of war for both good and bad in their lives and their art, even those writers who do not make an obvious and unambiguous connection between the two.

John Ronald Reuel Tolkien is an example of an author who did not explicitly and directly refer to his war experiences in his published writing, but whose work was nevertheless strongly influenced by them. Tolkien had a complex attitude toward war, as is only to be expected from someone who lived through both the "War to End All Wars" and the soon-to-follow Second World War, and moreover made the heroic literature of the northern European medieval world his academic specialty. His fiction, criticism, and letters demonstrate a range of attitudes changing and maturing over his lifetime, in the end appearing pragmatic and rational, if regretful and pessimistic, about human nature, evil, and the inevitability of conflict. Yet Tolkien was hopeful, as befits his Catholicism, about the ultimate fate of the human soul. His personal life informed his reading, and conversely, his reading influenced how he understood and interpreted his own experiences. In this book, I aim to explore this symbiosis of action and reflection through an examination of Tolkien's biography and an investigation of the depiction of war in his works. In the end, I hope to offer an explication of Tolkien's beliefs about war and courage, bearing in mind that war is only one lens through which to look at Tolkien's work, but one that greatly enriches our reading.

Humankind has always lived in an uncertain world with the potential to be dramatically changed by a new kind of war at any time, just as Tolkien's world was. As the recent terrorist attacks on the United States have shown, we are each likely to be confronted by the need to closely examine and perhaps rethink our own attitudes toward armed conflict at least once in our lifetimes. Literature offers us a way to explore and understand alternative ways of thinking and their consequences, and science fiction and fantasy are particularly useful laboratories for such thought experiments.

The events of September 11, 2001, were not without an influence on the popularity of Tolkien's books. The timing of the release of Peter Jackson's keenly anticipated film adaptation of the first book of *The Lord of the Rings* was fortunate in a way; audiences were hungry to see a depiction of the fundamental and universal struggle of good and evil, clothed in fantastic costume perhaps, but applicable to their own lives. Some reviewers saw the movie and by extension the books as pure escapism, but other more thoughtful critics understood their significance. A writer for the *National Review*, for example, compares the movie to its source: "If the new film version of *The Lord of the Rings* is seen as a flight from reality, then it has impeccable timing; after September 11, retreating into a fantasy realm of wizards and ringwraiths sounds like a welcome diversion. . . . Yet the book . . . speaks directly to some of the most fundamental concerns of this world: the nature of evil, the lure of power, and the duty of courage" (Miller 43). A review in *Christian Century* points out that "[a]fter September 11, the movie also serves as a salutary reminder that war is not an antiseptic affair of bombs dropped from on high, but that the battle against evil is dirty and dangerous and unending" (R. C. Wood). Another critic says the film "reverberate[s] with . . . a post-traumatic resonance" (Holden). And an editorial in *Commonweal* says that in a world "poised on the brink of chaos and carnage," the popularity of the film is significant; "*The Lord of the Rings* is essentially a meditation on the origins and nature of evil," and its author was "acutely sensitive to the murderous nihilism of modern warfare" ("Of Hobbits"). Marina Warner used *The Lord of the Rings* as an example when she said, "Myths in which heroic figures are pitted in mortal combat against diabolical enemies have gained fresh energy in popular culture since [September] 11" (Warner).[1]

The movie also led to vastly increased sales for the books, and introduced them to a huge new readership, their appetite for meaty, fast-paced adventure-fantasies already whetted by the enormous success of J. K. Rowling's Harry Potter books. *The Hobbit* sold an estimated 1.1 million copies in 2001, six times its 2000 sales, and *The Lord of the Rings* sold 2.3 million copies, ten times the previous year's sales (Maryles), before the movie was even released. Houghton Mifflin expected its 2001 sales to reach eight figures (K. Campbell). In 1966, when the Ballantine paperback was released, *The Lord of the Rings* sold 2,750,000 copies, and in 1972 was still selling around 100,000 copies a year in Great Britain; "[b]y 1980, eight million copies of *The Lord of the Rings*, in eighteen languages, had been sold" (Veldman 98).

Recent "Book of the Century" and "Book of the Millennium" polls in the United States and England have placed Tolkien's *The Lord of the Rings* at or near the top of lists of books most loved by the public. The Waterstone's and Channel 4 poll in England in late 1996 was a case in point; some critics and journalists were so appalled at the results that they accused the Tolkien Society of rigging the voting (Shippey, *Century* xxii). The *Daily Telegraph* went so far as to repeat the poll with its own readers instead of the general public, and obtained the same results (Shippey, *Century* xxi). In the United States, *The Lord of the Rings* was voted "Book of the Millennium" and Tolkien "Author of the Millennium" by Amazon.com readers (*Best of Millennium*).

There must be a reason why a work is this popular and enduring, still in print and selling steadily after nearly fifty years. In spite of the whining in certain critical circles at the results of the Waterstone's poll, the votes for Tolkien as "Author of the Century" weren't artificially inflated by a conspiracy of fanatics but simply reflected the number of readers who felt that these books were of lasting value and importance in their lives. Prolific critic Harold Bloom may have his "aesthetic doubts" about Tolkien's *Lord of the Rings*, calling it "inflated, over-written, tendentious, and moralistic in the extreme . . . stiff, false-archaic, [and] overwrought" (Bloom, *Rings* 1). He may even find it so foreign to his critical sensibilities as to dismiss it as a "Period Piece" (his capitalization) in two separate essays (*Rings* 1; *Tolkien* 2). Douglas Anderson has pointed out Bloom's mistake in seeing *The Lord of the Rings* as rooted "culturally and historically" in the 1960s (137). The work is not something that was popular once and now forgotten or discredited, but something that has already spoken to several generations of readers and is likely to continue to do so. Bloom's opinions sound querulous and hollow; like Edmund Wilson in his (in)famous essay "Oo, Those Awful Orcs!" (Wilson), he seems quite unable to understand why anyone might disagree with him.

It is difficult to think of any other recent writer who has impressed so vast and loyal an audience and influenced so many other artists in different fields, from George Lucas to Led Zeppelin to the entire fantasy publishing industry. Tolkien's skill at intricate, interlaced plotting, the resonance of his images, his knowledge of the roots of language, the imaginative landscape he creates, the archetypal yet individual characters, the sense of an immense history behind everything, and the struggle between good and evil at the base of it all bring readers back over and over again. Charles Newton speculated that one of the reasons writers like Tolkien appealed even to serious readers like his students at Cal Tech was that "the heroes were mighty, their struggles large, their joys spacious, their dooms tragic" (344). Tolkien is a worthwhile subject for scholarship whether or not one finds the work itself of value, if only because of his influence on popular culture and fiction. It does not matter in the end if the critical establishment sees Tolkien as a master prose stylist or a plodding Oxford don with a tin ear for dialogue. The richness of the works has allowed millions of readers to make them part of their own personal mythology. The way the story lives in their minds is what counts.

WHY SHOULD WE PAY ATTENTION TO WHAT TOLKIEN HAS TO SAY ABOUT WAR?

Paying particular attention to war in Tolkien's works enriches our understanding not only of the works themselves but also of their historical milieu, our own relationship to this past, and our response to conflict in our own times. A recent article in *Time* recognized that Tolkien "is a poet of war, and we are a nation in need of a good, clear war story" (Grossman 94).

Examining the extent of the effect of war on Tolkien's work also sheds light on the artistic process, and reaffirms that an author may not always be completely aware of the exact influence of his personal experiences on his work. William Ready points this out in his book *The Tolkien Relation*: "Old soldiers deny that their experience has any real bearing on their future, but it does. Tolkien's war had an influence on him as strong as his childhood, although he may not know it and does deny it, for those who served in the trenches in World War I were never the same again" (12). Tolkien himself made incompatible statements about the impact of war on his writing, particularly the Second World War: "[His] statement that World War Two had no effect on the composition of [*The Lord of the Rings*] . . . contradicts an earlier view that the 'darkness' of the impending war did have 'some effect' on the writing of the work . . . critics, then, might have avoided considering the impact of the war on Tolkien's work because the author dismissed it in one place, even though he affirmed it in another" (Timmons, "Mirror on Middle-earth" 239). I think both world wars influenced Tolkien more than he may have realized.

In a recent conference presentation on *Henry V* and *The Lord of the Rings*,

Daniel Timmons listed several critics "who eloquently and intelligently support Tolkien's treatment of war." He went on to say, concerning the antiwar critics: "What I find curious is that war, as a concept, has become so generic, divorced from any specific cause, process, or results, that it's *presumed* to be wrong, in any and all circumstances. Thus, to celebrate the valour and strength of those fighting such battles appears, at the very least, antiquated, if not misguided" ("We Few" 8). It is both a critical and a historical mistake to presume that all wars are equally wrong and unnecessary. Tolkien's writing supports the concept of "just war": that when force is used for evil purposes, force must be used to resist it, and that those with the strength to do so must be prepared to fight force with force, not appeasement, accommodation, or passive resistance. Critics who feel that armed conflict is always wrong may be letting their personal distaste and discomfort with the idea of war keep them from an accurate understanding of what Tolkien is saying.

John Goldthwaite, in his book *The Natural History of Make-Believe*, is one critic who seems to willfully misinterpret the impact of the First World War on Tolkien's work, turning Tolkien's own words topsy-turvy in his personal distaste for anything that smacks of the glorification of war or of "sword & sorcery fantasy" (215):

Tolkien had survived some of the ghastliest battles of World War I; his friends had not. Nor, apparently, had his memory of the war. There is none of the observed truth of, say, an *All Quiet on the Western Front* to these clashes, even granting them their terms as make-believe. He regressed, it seems, into a compensatory dream of how a war ought to be fought, not with bodies piling up stupidly in trenches—that was all wrong, you see—but in the grand manner, with stirring rides and deeds of valor. . . . The irony must have escaped him that the make-believe swagger he was here honoring was precisely the kind of toy-soldiering that had led to the horrors of World War I to begin with. (Goldthwaite 217–18)

Goldthwaite must have dipped rather shallowly into Tolkien if he recalls the "stirring rides" but not the piles of dead at Helm's Deep, the faces of drowned warriors in the Dead Marshes, or the heads of fallen men lobbed over the walls of Minas Tirith by the orcs. He seems to have forgotten the ent Beechbone going up in flames like a torch during the taking of Orthanc, Sam's reaction to the dead Southron in Ithilien, and the nasty particulars of Merry and Pippin's days as prisoners of the orcs. Tolkien may not have spelled out the clinical details of death on the battlefield, but that was not the kind of story he was writing. As far as make-believe swagger, there is nothing in the words or acts of Aragorn or Éomer that is out of place in their societies, and in any case, all such "swagger" is balanced by the presence of the hobbits and their clear, down-to-earth view of matters.[2]

Hal Colebatch takes a clearer view of how war influenced Tolkien's vision of the way the world works: "These tales presume a world in which some sort

of conflict is an inevitable fact, which good people must be prepared to face"
(51). He sees a similar message in C. S. Lewis's Narnia books:

[C]ourage is needed against enemies in all worlds. No safer option is available and the
way will be hard, demanding and unfair. Bound up with this is the need for nobility,
and the acceptance of making unequal sacrifices if necessary. Being "nice" or closing
one's eyes to the existence of enemies does not protect one. 'Innocence' in a sense
will be violated. Part of the challenge is to accept this and face the world while retaining innocence in a more profound sense. (49)

Colebatch quotes Diana Wynne Jones, who reveals a possible reason why
antiwar critics are so hostile to Tolkien: "[T]he story dealt with people pushed
by a relentless enemy into a situation where 'the only defence can be some
form of attack' " (cited 71). This may indeed be the key; it can be uncomfortable to realize that sometimes force is a necessary response to threats
against life and freedom.

MISUNDERSTANDING TOLKIEN

Nan C. Scott, writing at the time of the Vietnam War, described three
possible conflicting and incompatible readings of *The Lord of the Rings* that
help to clarify the positions of some of the critics quoted above:

There are those who find in *The Lord of the Rings* a glorification of war and weap-
onry, a focusing upon the romantic and heroic elements of military conflict, and who,
according to their prejudices, admire or dislike the book for this reason, or who,
finding it attractive for other qualities, uneasily hedge their affections against their
consciences. At the opposite extreme are those who have made almost a cult-symbol
of Frodo Baggins, mostly the young who . . . outraged by the war in Viet Nam,
see . . . a glowing ideal in Frodo's ultimate pacifism after his return from Mordor.
(Scott 23)

Mary Ellmann was one writer who read Tolkien as glorifying war and disliked the book for that reason. She was appalled by Tolkien's use of war as
the solution to the Orc problem:

Two solutions are offered, an evil and a good. And the evil is much the better: Sauron
the Dark Lord makes the Orcs into a police force. . . . One might object that this is
to create a systematic evil where there had been only anarchic evil before. But the
savagery of the Orcs is at least inhibited by their being in uniform: they cannot eat a
suspect until he has been questioned. It is harder, at any rate, to rejoice in the good
solution. This is based, as good always was on Middle-earth, upon a straightforward
principle: the only good Orc is a dead Orc. So Legolas the Elf and Gimli the Dwarf
compete in slicing off Orc heads. (225)

Better an organized evil in uniform than its eradication? Perhaps the author was not thinking of the uniformed and organized horror of Hitler's Final Solution. Ellmann's criticism does highlight, however, the problematic nature of the Orcs; unlike any other race in Middle-earth, there seems to be no possibility of their redemption. Far from overlooking this problem, Tolkien continued to struggle to reconcile it long after the book was published.

Another writer who felt Tolkien glorified war and therefore was a pernicious influence was Douglas Stewart, writing in *The Nation* in October 1967 (Stewart). *Publisher's Weekly* had recently reported that a South Vietnamese general had begun using the Lidless Eye of Sauron as his battle emblem after reading a translation of *The Lord of the Rings* ("Tolkien Mythology Comes to Vietnam"). Stewart took this as a symbol of all that was wrong with American involvement in Vietnam, and thought that the State Department was as confused as Tolkien in positing "Good" and "Evil" as primal forces. This kind of thinking could only lead to the conclusion that the enemy must be totally destroyed, without an attempt at a peacefully negotiated coexistence. Whether or not General Westmoreland did indeed think this way, it is a simplistic rendering of good and evil in Middle-earth, where the battleground is not just external but within each character's soul as well. Nick Otty also sees Tolkien's view of war as very black-and-white and misses the subtleties; he claims unequivocally that "[w]ar is celebrated in *The Lord of the Rings*. There is none of the ambivalence about war to be found in Homer or Shakespeare" (175).

As Scott noted, there have long been readers who have interpreted Tolkien as a pacifist writer by ignoring aspects of the whole. They read Frodo's refusal to take up arms during the Scouring of the Shire as a refutation of all that went before it. An article in the *Boston Globe*, for example, implied that Tolkien was seen as strongly antimilitary when the author said, "many students in the '60s identified with the conflict of good vs. evil in *The Hobbit* and *The Lord of the Rings* trilogy, as they themselves were struggling against a promilitary establishment" (Aoki 14). Pacifism was a major component of the youth movements of the 1960s and 1970s, and it can be easy to read *The Lord of the Rings* as an antiwar book if that is all one is looking for. However, reading it as a whole, against the background of Tolkien's biography and his letters and other writings, paints a more complex picture.

Philip Helms is an example of the other extreme; in his "The Gentle Scouring of the Shire," he focused so exclusively on Frodo's pacifism as to nearly lose sight of the fact that it was armed conflict that finally freed the Shire, not passive resistance. Tolkien did indeed hold "a genuine antipathy for war as such, and for violence rather generally as a technique for resolution of problems" (23). But Helms chose his supporting quotes from Tolkien's letters very carefully; for example, from one letter to his son Michael, Helms quotes the lines about how "[o]ne War is enough for any man" but leaves out Tolkien's longing to "do something active" and his pride in being "the father of a good young soldier" (*Letters* 54–55). Tolkien may have hated war as only a veteran could, but he also felt that sometimes it was necessary to take up arms. Helms postulates an interest in Gandhi on Tolkien's part, and tries to equate Frodo and the Mahatma. Frodo and his band do initially deal with the ruffians through noncooperation, but it soon becomes clear that violence will be necessary to dislodge them. Helms puts this down to a lack of understanding of Frodo's plans for nonviolent action. However, Gandhi's methods of noncooperation and protest fasting would be unlikely to work as well against an enemy with no moral scruples, no internal rule of law, and no need to worry about the good opinion of the world, as they did against the British Raj in India in 1946 or the U.S. government in the 1960s (Phillips 101).

We can only speculate at this point about what director Peter Jackson will do with Frodo's growing pacifism and the Scouring of the Shire in the third installment of his movie trilogy (if he even includes this sequence, which is unlikely). The first two movies have already cast Aragorn in particular as more conflicted and ambivalent about fighting for his goals than originally written.

Much recent criticism is more balanced, and many writers now seem to feel that Frodo is not the only character through whom Tolkien spoke. For critics familiar with his letters and other writings, it is clear that Faramir, Aragorn, Gilraen (Aragorn's mother), Gandalf, Elrond, Éomer, and Sam (as well as others in the legendarium) also expressed his thoughts on war. In fact, a chorus of voices is needed to articulate Tolkien's views on the subject. However, even some recent critics, with access to works by Thomas Shippey, Verlyn Flieger, and others, read war in *The Lord of the Rings* shallowly. Michael N. Stanton, in his 2001 book *Hobbits, Elves, and Wizards*, devotes only a sentence or two to war: "World War I exacted a terrible cost on Tolkien's generation, and there is a sense in which *The Lord of the Rings* is an anti-war story, among the many other kinds of story it is" (4–5). He never explains this statement or gives any examples to support it. Stanton manages to almost completely avoid mentioning the two major set-piece battles of Helm's Deep and Pelennor Fields; there is no description of Helm's Deep at all, and Pelennor Fields merits only a short paragraph (77).

WHAT TOLKIEN IS SAYING

What Tolkien tries to tell us, through this chorus of voices on war, is as complex and self-contradictory as life itself. From northern myths and legends he derives the idea that stubborn courage is paramount, even in the face of impossible odds, faceless and uncountable enemies, and hopeless situations. In the end, obstinate bravery, individual action, and self-sacrifice all still mean something. Personal honor is also important, and far more important than public glory; Sam and Frodo know they must go on because it is the only right thing to do, even if no one ever knows about it. As Lois McMaster Bujold has one of her characters say, "Reputation is what other people know about

you. Honor is what you know about yourself" (293). Tied to this is the responsibility for living with the consequences of one's actions (and for a Christian like Tolkien, the consequences continue after death as well), balanced
with the ever-present possibility of eucatastrophic, redemptive grace.[3]

Tolkien also says that war is sometimes necessary and must be faced with
all one's skill and might to minimize the death on both sides. Tolkien might
not agree wholeheartedly with the ancient Greeks that "war is terrible but
innate to civilization," but he would certainly argue that it is "not always
unjust or immoral if it is waged for good causes to destroy evil and save the
innocent" (Hanson, *Autumn* xv). It is not wrong to take pride in using that
skill in a just cause, but it is not civilized to take joy in it for its own sake;
one can love that which one defends, but not the means by which one is forced
to defend it, as Faramir points out (*Towers* 280). And yet there is no question
in Tolkien's mind that war is a terrible and wasteful thing, not to be undertaken lightly or for any reason other than a truly just cause, and as a Catholic
he wished for the "universal Conversion" of the human race and an end to
war (*Letters* 78).

The melancholy, anticlimactic ending to *The Lord of the Rings* also brings
home the cruel fact that sometimes the damage of war to a person's soul is
not curable in this world. Innocence and peace of mind will inevitably be lost
in war as a necessary sacrifice, but we can and should still rage against their
loss; Tolkien's letters in particular exhibit this attitude. He reinforces the
lesson that leaders have responsibilities, including moral ones, particularly in
his criticism of *Beowulf* and in "The Homecoming of Beorhtnoth Beorhthelm's Son." And Tolkien also demonstrates that there is a place for pacifists,
like Frodo at the Scouring of the Shire, to give us hope that wars may some-
day cease and to remind us to be just and merciful in our dealings with our
enemies, for the sake of their souls and our own as well.

SCOPE

In this book, I will focus primarily on *The Hobbit* and *The Lord of the
Rings*, the major works familiar to most readers of Tolkien. I will also examine a number of other works published in Tolkien's lifetime, such as his
Beowulf essay and "The Homecoming of Beorhtnoth Beorhthelm's Son." I
will look at some posthumous works such as *The Silmarillion* and the twelve-
volume *History of Middle-earth* as well, but mainly I will use them as a way
of illustrating background for what was actually published during Tolkien's
life. Tolkien's *Letters* and Humphrey Carpenter's *Tolkien* will be my major
sources for biographical information.

I will be drawing much of my information on the world wars, classical and
medieval warfare, and war in literature from the works of three historians:
John Keegan, Paul Fussell, and Victor Davis Hanson. I owe all three my

gratitude for their clear prose style and strong opinions—not always in agreement with each other.

In writing this book, I have tried to keep in mind W. H. Auden's statement about criticism:

What is the function of a critic? So far as I am concerned, he can do me one or more of the following services:
1) Introduce me to authors or works of which I was hitherto unaware.
2) Convince me that I have undervalued an author or a work because I had not read them carefully enough.
3) Show me relations between works of different ages and cultures which I could never have seen for myself because I do not know enough and never shall.
4) Give a "reading" of a work which increases my understanding of it.
5) Throw light upon the process of artistic "Making."
6) Throw light upon the relation of art to life, to science, economics, ethics, religion, etc. (Auden, "Reading" 8–9)

I hope that this book will introduce new readers to Tolkien, convince readers of his continued relevance in our time, relate his work to that of other veteran-writers, "read" the work through the lens of war, show how he transformed his experiences into art through "Making" (or, as he called it, "Sub-creation"), and relate art to war in general.

In Chapter 2, using Paul Fussell's *The Great War and Modern Memory* as a starting point, I examine Tolkien in relation to other veteran-writers of the Great War. Tolkien is especially interesting because he avoided the ironic response of his contemporaries and instead mythologized his experiences, creating a more universally understandable work. I discuss Tolkien's war experiences and look for evidence of how he used these experiences in his writing in *The Hobbit*, *The Lord of the Rings*, and other works. I speculate on why he chose the literary form of the fairy-story to express his reaction to the war.

In Chapter 3, I look more closely at a variety of common themes in post–World War I literature, as described by Fussell in *The Great War and Modern Memory*, and show how Tolkien used these themes or sometimes transformed them. I also show how he both resembled and differed from other World War I–era writers in his treatment of these themes.

In Chapter 4, I explore the role of World War II in Tolkien's life and works, especially how his experiences as the father of two soldiers may have influenced his depiction of fathers and sons in his work. I look at how he compares to other World War II writers, particularly Thomas Shippey's list of "traumatized authors," and to World War II literary style and themes.

In Chapter 5, I examine the ramifications of military leadership, investigating Tolkien's philosophy of how a leader should lead, and how it might have been influenced by his studies in classical and northern European literature and his own war experiences. I illustrate how his philosophy is borne out by selected characters in his works, his depiction of the role of military leadership in the maturation process, and the dangers inherent in leadership.

In Chapter 6, I look at some specific military topics in Tolkien's works that might show the influence of his own World War I background: training, intelligence, signaling, and maps, and the part they play in each of the major battles.

In Chapter 7, I tie all this together by seeking to define Tolkien's philosophy of military conflict and applying it to the Scouring of the Shire and Frodo's life after the destruction of the Ring. I show that the three themes of this book—the influence of Tolkien's war experiences on his writing, the depiction of war in his works, and his philosophy of war as revealed in his fiction, criticism, and letters—are intertwined and inseparable from each other.

NOTES

1. The remarkable influence of Tolkien's work is revealed when this writer, who is unfamiliar enough with *The Lord of the Rings* to state categorically that it contains no female heroism (among other factual errors), still knows that Tolkien depicted the struggle between good and evil as a recurring and unending cycle.

2. Goldthwaite is not a particularly reliable critical voice on Tolkien; his assertion that sub-creation is "a declaration that God's creation is deficient" (219) reveals a deep misunderstanding of Tolkien's philosophy, in which sub-creation is an act glorifying God's gifts of imagination and intelligence.

3. "Eucatastrophe" is a term that Tolkien proposed in his essay "On Fairy-stories" to define the "good catastrophe" or "sudden joyous 'turn' " ("On Fairy-stories" 68) in fairy tales, and that he applied in turn to Christianity, with the Resurrection being the "Great Eucatastrophe" ("On Fairy-stories" 72).

Chapter 2

The Great War and Tolkien's Memory

"The hell where youth and laughter go"
—Sassoon, "Suicide in Trenches"

INTRODUCTION

J.R.R. Tolkien was part of a generation of Englishmen "caught in youth" during World War I. While he disliked criticism that focused on details of any author's life, he could not entirely deny the influence of his experience on his work; as he points out in the introduction to the second edition of *The Lord of the Rings*, "the ways in which a story-germ uses the soil of experience are extremely complex" (*Fellowship* 7). Tolkien famously despised allegory, and none of his works are allegories of World War I or any other war, but the impact of the Great War is evident in some of the themes Tolkien explores, and is echoed in some of the events that occur in Middle-earth. What Tolkien forged from his experiences differs greatly from the writing of "canonical" World War I authors like Robert Graves and Siegfried Sassoon in both subject matter and tone, but he writes about many of the same themes they do. As Brian Rosebury put it, "he belongs to something of a lost, or at any rate depleted, generation: the killed war poets, Owen and Rosenberg, and his fellow war-survivors, Graves and Blunden, are his closest contemporaries" (134).

Paul Fussell brilliantly analyzes the major themes of British post–World War I writing in his National Book Award–winning *The Great War and Modern Memory*. He concentrates mainly on the poets, memoirists, and novelists who wrote during and just after the war, and how their writing exhibited the new emphasis on irony that he feels is the typical literary reaction to the war.

Fussell traces the literary roots of this type of irony to Thomas Hardy's 1914 collection of poems, *Satires of Circumstance*. Many of these poems explore an "irony of situation" arising from "a collision between innocence and awareness" (Fussell, *Great War* 5). War is always ironic because "its means are so melodramatically disproportionate to its presumed ends" (*Great War* 7), and the Great War seemed particularly ironic because it contrasted so sharply with the prewar peace and innocence of early-twentieth-century England, which had not fought a major war for a century. As the poet Philip Larkin put it, "never such innocence again" (Larkin); the war was a "hideous embarrassment" (Fussell, *Great War* 8) to the certainties and decencies of society.

For someone familiar with Tolkien, reading *The Great War and Modern Memory* is a disconcerting experience. As Hugh Brogan observed, "the 1914 war as Fussell describes it is unmistakably the War of the Ring" (361). *The Lord of the Rings* is clearly outside the scope of Fussell's argument since it is not directly about the war and does not exhibit the overall ironic response Fussell was interested in; nevertheless, it feels like there is a Tolkien-sized hole running through the whole book. What Fussell describes as the "bizarre inverse quest" (*Great War* 41) of the soldiers on their way to the front resonates throughout Frodo's quest to destroy the Ring, and almost every theme in Fussell's critique appears somewhere in Tolkien's work. The inevitable question arises: Why, when so many of his contemporaries found the ironic mode the only appropriate means for remembering and communicating their war experiences and exploring these themes, did Tolkien choose the heroic?

TOLKIEN'S WAR EXPERIENCES

Several months after England declared war on Germany in 1914, Tolkien enlisted in a program that allowed him to finish his BA while taking officers' training, and when he completed his degree in 1915 he was assigned to the Lancashire Fusiliers as a second lieutenant (their motto: *Omnia Audax*, Daring Everything). He had been under some pressure from his relatives; "in those days chaps joined up, or were scorned publicly" (*Letters* 53). He was trained in signaling and appointed battalion signaling officer. Well aware of the possibility of his death in battle, he married his childhood sweetheart, Edith, shortly before he was posted to France in June 1916. Letters he wrote to Edith, and a diary he kept while on active duty, form the basis of much of the information presented by Humphrey Carpenter in his description of Tolkien's war years (*Tolkien* 276–77). A chronology of important events in his military service is provided in the appendices.

Military life was not Tolkien's ideal milieu. During training, he did not like the ragtime music many of his fellow officers enjoyed playing on their gramophones, and found the meals inedible and conditions uncomfortable (Carpenter, *Tolkien* 77). As Tolkien admitted in a 1944 letter to his son Christopher, "I was not a good officer"; he spent a good deal of time working

on his Elvish languages and histories at meals, during lectures, and even re-
portedly in dugouts while under fire (*Letters* 78). Tolkien denied this in a
1967 interview: "That's all spoof. You might scribble something on the back
of an envelope and shove it in your back pocket, but that's all. You couldn't
write" (Norman 5).

To make matters even more uncomfortable, at some time during the journey to France all of Tolkien's kit was lost—his carefully selected "camp-bed,
sleeping-bag, mattress, spare boots, washstand, everything." It all had to be
replaced by begging, borrowing, and buying (Carpenter, *Tolkien* 80)—an incident amusingly echoed in his writing many years later when Bilbo sets out
from Bag End without even a pocket-handkerchief. After three weeks at Étaples, his battalion was sent to the front, marching to the Somme in the
pouring rain at the end of June. His company was held in reserve behind the
lines at Bouzincourt, while "A" Company was sent to the trenches on July 6.
On July 14, two weeks after the commencement of the Battle of the Somme,
his company marched to the front to relieve their companions. Tolkien survived a number of engagements, finding that the "neat orderly conditions"
under which he'd trained had little in common with signaling in the field,
where telephones and Morse code buzzers were forbidden because the Germans had tapped the lines, and signalers were reduced to using lights, flags,
runners, and even carrier-pigeons (Carpenter, *Tolkien* 83). John Keegan
throws an interesting light on the futility of more up-to-date methods of communication under trench conditions:

Radio failed as a means of tactical communication on land, because of the inability to
develop a compact, portable wireless set. The British "Trench Set" of 1918 required
twelve men to carry its components, largely heavy, wet-cell batteries. . . . [U]nits were
thrown back on such traditional means as runners, dogs, flares, heliograph, carrier
pigeons, or even flags. . . . The problem of communication was never solved during
the war, and its difficulties largely determined its brutal, mechanistic character. (*Illustrated History* 48)

Signaling officers were not expected to participate in much hand-to-hand
combat, since they were taught that "the sole object of their existence is to
keep the commander in touch with the various parts of his force and to enable
his plans to be promptly and smoothly executed" (*Signalling*, 13). However,
it was not by any means a safe job. George Ashurst, in his autobiography *My
Bit*, writes of seeing a signaler ordered to call for reinforcements; as soon as
he raised his flags he was cut down by enemy fire (101). In any case, there
was no avoiding what Tolkien called the "animal horror" of the trenches
(*Letters* 72)—the dead bodies in the mud and the craters filled with water
and rats.

As Tolkien said in the introduction to the second edition of *The Lord of
the Rings*, "it seems now often forgotten that to be caught in youth by 1914

was no less hideous an experience than to be involved in 1939 and the following years. By 1918 all but one of my close friends were dead" (*Fellowship* 7).[1] On October 27, Tolkien came down with trench fever (a disease spread by lice, which caused high temperatures and aching bones and joints) and was shipped back to England on November 8. Tolkien spent the rest of the war convalescing in various infirmaries in England, becoming almost well and then succumbing to fever again, until he was finally declared fit for duty just before the war ended in November 1918. During his convalescence he wrote his first draft of "The Fall of Gondolin," and he worked on other tales during his recovery as well (Carpenter, *Tolkien* 72–79).

INFLUENCE OF THE WAR ON TOLKIEN'S WORK

C. S. Lewis wrote: "[Tolkien's] war has the very quality of the war my generation knew. It is all here: the endless, unintelligible movement, the sinister quiet of the front when 'everything is now ready,' the flying civilians, the lively, vivid friendships, the background of something like despair and the merry foreground, and such heaven-sent windfalls as a cache of tobacco 'salvaged' from a ruin" ("Dethronement" 39–40).[2]

For the most part, Tolkien did not write directly about the war, but he did speak about his wartime experiences occasionally in lectures. John S. Ryan recounts this incident: "In one of his last lectures I heard from him as Merton Professor in 1957, he deplored the fact that when his men had 'poached' a deer, while on maneuvers in Yorkshire during training, he had not been on hand to 'broach' the carcass, in the fashion described in *Sir Gawaine and the Green Knight*" (27).

Tolkien did, however, explicitly acknowledge his debt to his war experiences in several places. He once commented: "My 'Sam Gamgee' is indeed a reflexion of the English soldier, of the privates and batmen I knew in the 1914 war, and recognized as so far superior to myself" (Carpenter, *Tolkien* 81). George Ashurst's *My Bit: A Lancashire Fusilier at War, 1914–1918* is a self-portrait of a working-class soldier who served in the Other Ranks in Tolkien's regiment. He is very like Sam in his mixture of education and ignorance, his provincial prejudices combined with a "lack of any feeling of personal antipathy" (Ashurst 10) to the common soldiers who just happen to be on the other side. He shares Sam's ability to rise to the occasion when bravery is called for, but pragmatically keep his eye on long-term survival.

Another aspect of World War I that may be reflected in Tolkien's fiction is the plight of refugees and displaced populations. Discussing the crowds of townspeople forced out of Laketown by the death of Smaug in *The Hobbit*, Alex Lewis reminds us that "Tolkien must have seen first-hand . . . totally displaced refugee populations" ("Arma" 10). In *The Lord of the Rings*, Éowyn is charged with keeping the people of Edoras safe in the hidden places of Dunharrow, and the inhabitants of the Westfold take refuge in the caves behind Helm's Deep. Wagon trains of refugees leave Minas Tirith for the southern hills before the Battle of the Pelennor Fields. Displaced people from the south seek room in Bree even before the Fellowship starts its journey, and they form part of the force that later occupies the Shire. This was a theme reinforced by the experiences of World War II: the Tolkien family had refugees from London boarding with them in the summer of 1940 (*Letters* 46), and Tolkien grieves over the gloating tone of newspaper reports of refugees in one of his letters (*Letters* 111). The "Father Christmas" letters Tolkien wrote to his children during this time also bemoan the fact that so many have been displaced from their homes. Even so, this theme's deepest roots lie in World War I: in "The Fall of Gondolin," one of Tolkien's first pieces of writing after being at the Front, he spends many pages on the beleaguered flight of Tuor and his family from the ruined city (*Lost Tales II* 188–95).

In a 1960 letter, Tolkien wrote, "The Dead Marshes and the Morannon owe something to Northern France after the Battle of the Somme" (*Letters* 303). He does go on to say that they owe more to the stories of William Morris, but the dead faces floating just below the surface of the water were a standard image in Great War memoirs and fiction. One of the most telling quotes is from "On Fairy-stories," wherein Tolkien says, "A taste for fairy-stories was wakened by philology on the threshold of manhood, and quickened to full life by war" ("On Fairy-stories" 42). It shows he was already thinking in terms of expressing himself through the means of the fairy-tale; as I will argue later, this predisposed Tolkien to fit his war experiences into this framework from the start, rather than into the realistic and ironic form many other writers used.

Tolkien's writings from the time of Britain's declaration of war to the time he was shipped back to England show little or no influence of the events of the Great War. They are fantasies focusing mainly on the beauty and splendor of the Elves (at that time called Gnomes), their cities and arts, and their languages. Tolkien began writing the stories that fleshed out his linguistic world while recovering from trench fever in various hospitals in England. The two volumes of *The Book of Lost Tales* contain much of this early material. Christopher Tolkien reports that the original *The Book of Lost Tales*, of which "The Fall of Gondolin" is a part, was written in 1916–1917 (*Lost Tales I* 8). The first story in Christopher Tolkien's compilation of this early work is "The Cottage of Lost Play," written in Edith Tolkien's hand and dated February 12, 1917 (*Lost Tales I* 13). Earlier, in April 1915, while still in his undergraduate lodgings at Oxford, he wrote a poem called "You & Me/ and the Cottage of Lost Play," and material was mined from this poem for the longer story. In November 1915, while still in officers' training camp, he wrote "Kortirion among the Trees" (*Lost Tales I* 25).

Three poems that also apparently date from this period were published in *Leeds University Verse 1914–1924* and have a similar feel. "The Lonely

Isle" was written during the Channel crossing to France, and in the manuscript is subtitled "For England" (Hammond 284); it is a sad farewell to his
fairy-haunted land. "An Evening in Tavrobel" was probably written during his
convalescence in Great Haywood in 1917, but is an atmospheric piece with
no mention of war. "Princess Ni" is an earlier version of "Princess Mee,"
without the mirror-inversion of the second half of the later poem ("Princess
Mee"). All of these writings are pure escapist fantasy with more than a touch
of melancholy, and perhaps with some reference to his relationship with Edith
in the "Lost Play" materials. As Hugh Brogan described it, his work from
this period is "overwhelmingly elegiac" (357).

Tolkien's first known prose writing after his experiences on the battlefields
of northern France, "The Fall of Gondolin," expands on a mention of the city's
fall in the prose introduction to "Kortirion." It is full of extended and terrifying scenes of battle. In the original version, Melko's attack on the city and
the account of the fighting in the streets goes on for sixteen pages (*Lost Tales
II* 172–88). In *The Silmarillion*, it is reduced to just a few lines (*Silmarillion*
242). The original reads like a melding of *The Iliad* and *Le Morte d'Arthur*,
with its detailed descriptions of arms and heraldic devices and vivid, violent
portrayals of individual encounters in battle. Some elements of "The Fall of
Gondolin" echo the early phases of World War I. Gondolin stood on an island
of rock in a hidden valley, and felt secure from attack in its isolation. Britain
had learned the risks of a policy of "splendid isolation" during the Boer War,
and had taken steps to form the Triple Entente with France and Russia (Williamson 12); however, when France came under attack, divisions within the
British government delayed its commitment to come to its neighbor's defense
(Tuchman, *Guns* 91–97), just as Gondolin held itself aloof from troubles in
the wider world. Perhaps even more to the point, at the time Tolkien was
writing "The Fall of Gondolin," the United States still had not entered the
war; President Wilson's commitment to neutrality lasted until the exposure
of the Zimmerman telegram "shattered the indifference with which three-
quarters of the United States had regarded the war" (Tuchman, *Zimmerman*
184). The United States declared war on Germany on April 6, 1917, while
Tolkien was being declared fit for duty and sent for additional signaling training. Gondolin is also finally forced to take action because of treachery.

Another interesting point of comparison can be found in "the monsters
which Melko devised against Gondolin" (*Lost Tales II* 170). It is unclear
whether these monsters were living beings or machines or some combination
of the two, but what is clear is that at least one type was metallic, hollow,
and carried orcs inside to be disgorged at the scene of battle (*Lost Tales II*
176). These sound very like the tanks that first took the field at the Somme
in September 1916 (Prior and Wilson 186) while Tolkien was still on active
duty.

Tolkien's seminal essay "Beowulf: The Monsters and the Critics" was written in 1936 and still stands as one of the major tools for understanding the

poem. The hopeless bravery he observed in the trenches may have something
to do with his deep understanding and appreciation for what he calls the
northern European "theory of courage, which is the great contribution of early
Northern literature" (*Monsters* 20). He goes on to say that this is not a
"military judgment" and that this courage is not a requirement for winning
battles, and in fact may lead to defeat—"the wages of heroism is death"
(*Monsters* 27). However, there is honor in having "faith in the value of
doomed resistance" (*Monsters* 23), and in being on the right side, even if that
side is doomed to defeat. There may be more than a hint of autobiography
in his statement "Even to-day . . . you may find men not ignorant of tragic
legend and history, who have heard of heroes and indeed seen them" (*Monsters* 16). His ideas on courage without hope were here given a form that he
could later draw upon for use in *The Lord of the Rings*.

The *Hobbit*, written in 1937, introduces the Shire and the hobbits to the
map of Middle-earth. As anachronisms in Tolkien's mythical world, the hobbits allowed Tolkien to comment on the shortcomings of both the heroic age
and the idealized rural England the Shire resembled. Bilbo sets off on his
journey influenced by his Tookish adventurousness; despite his occasional wish
to be back in his nice hobbit-hole, he may also unconsciously be influenced by
the monotony of what Michael Adams called "civic claustrophobia" (73). Gandalf thinks an adventure is just what he needs to wake him up—"very amusing
for me, very good for you . . . if you ever get over it" (*Hobbit* 14). While this
is not a profound call to arms like Rupert Brooke's "Now, God be thanked
Who has matched us with His hour, / And caught our youth, and wakened
us from sleeping," it is distantly related nonetheless.

In *The Hobbit*, the northern European "theory of courage" is exemplified
by Thorin, who is defiant and proud in his defense of the Lonely Mountain,
leading to needless battle and death. It is contrasted with Bilbo's more pragmatic hobbit-courage—"as fierce as a dragon in a pinch" (*Hobbit* 26), but not
the sort of gallantry that seeks out opportunities to fight—and also with
Bard's courageous but not *ofermod*, or hubristic, leadership at the Battle of
Laketown. I will discuss World War I themes in *The Hobbit* in more depth
in the next chapter.

Tolkien's essay "On Fairy-stories" was written in 1939 on the eve of war
and crystallized his thoughts on the value of fairy-stories for adults. It seems
appropriate that this second war in his lifetime should again influence his
taste for fairy-stories, just as the first one did, and help him to achieve the
mature understanding of the form that would culminate in *The Lord of the
Rings*. His composition of *The Lord of the Rings* was halted at Bree, and
when he resumed writing, the story was darker and more focused, the stakes
were higher, and war was more imminent in both the story and the real world.
The paragraphs in "On Fairy-stories" about "Escape" are full of twentieth-
century political and war imagery—prisons and deserters, party lines and
treachery, quislings and false patriotism ("On Fairy-stories" 60–61). What

reader would not long to escape from machine guns and bombs? The companion short story "Leaf by Niggle" applies these theories in a setting where the coming war is more significant than the past one.

With "The Homecoming of Beorhtnoth Beorhthelm's Son," Tolkien again is interested in courage, but from a more experienced perspective. "The Homecoming," published in 1953 but written in 1945 or earlier, is a dramatic verse play expanding on an episode from the Anglo-Saxon poem *The Battle of Maldon.* In it two men, the young son of a bard and an old farmer, debate the courage and deeds of Beorhtnoth, whose dead body they seek at night on the battlefield where he fell. In the afterword, Tolkien discusses *ofermod,* a difficult word to translate—Tolkien defined it as the kind of over-boldness or hubristic chivalry that prompted Beorhtnoth to allow his enemies over the causeway he was supposed to guard. His actions resulted in his defeat and the death of all the men under his command, simply so the odds would be worse and the glory greater if he won. This essay discusses the continuum of courage in English literature from the heroic variety in *Beowulf* to the chivalric in "Sir Gawain." It is more skeptical about the same type of courage Tolkien praised so highly in his "Beowulf" essay, and a hint of influence from World War II may be visible in his doubtfulness. As Daniel Timmons describes it, "After living to see another horrible war in Europe, Tolkien may naturally have thought that any self-aggrandized act of a leader—in life or literature—was extremely suspect, if not condemnable" ("Mirror on Middle-earth" 75). The desire for glory can be a temptation to excess, and Tolkien sees more honor in the conduct of Beorhtnoth's men than their leader: "Their part was to endure and die, and not to question, though a recording poet may fairly comment that someone had blundered. In their situation heroism was superb. . . . It is the heroism of obedience and love not of pride or willfulness that is the most heroic and the most moving" ("Homecoming" 22). Here is the model for Sam himself, and Merry and Pippin as well.

In *The Lord of the Rings,* the Shire is used even more extensively as a contrast to the rest of Middle-earth and the horrors of war, but is itself no longer a safe haven from the troubles of the world. Like England during World War II, it was no longer isolated enough to be out of harm's way. Many types of courage are explored in this work, from the dogged determination of the hobbits to the reckless bravery of Éowyn, as well as many varieties of military leadership. The remaining chapters of this book will go into greater detail regarding this work.

A few later works touch on the theme of war very briefly and exhibit a more world-weary and perhaps more pacifist trend of thought. The poem "The Sea-Bell," also known as "Frodos Dreme" according to the preface to *The Adventures of Tom Bombadil,* was published in this form in 1962, but is revised from the early poem "Looney," published in *Oxford Magazine* in 1934 (Hammond 178). It is primarily interesting for its depiction of what might almost be described as a form of shell-shock. As Verlyn Flieger suggests, the man returning from a stay in Faerie is akin to the veteran returning from war in his inability to communicate his experiences (218). Bruce Leonard interprets this poem psychologically: "In the dream perhaps Frodo expects and fears rejection, even from the Valar. . . . The utter isolation . . . expresses the shame Frodo feels he deserves" (5).

War made its presence known in almost every work by Tolkien. Rare is the work in which there is no mention of war—*Mr. Bliss* is one of the few examples, but his writings for children were not all war-free. In *Smith of Wootton Major*, Tolkien tells how his title character was never known to forge a weapon, among all the wonderful things he made, and why (*Smith* 17). Even in *Roverandom*, written in 1925–1927 and revised for submission to his publisher in 1936, the Old Man of the Sea is reported as having been blown up by sitting on the button of a floating mine. As the editors explain, this was "[a] mine of the sort placed in waters during the First World War" (*Roverandom* 51, 101).

War even intruded into the charmingly illustrated "Father Christmas" letters Tolkien wrote for his children every year, perhaps not unexpectedly, as the children must have been concerned about the news of the world, and Tolkien was not one to "write down" to children about serious issues. The first was written in 1920, when his oldest child, John, was three years old (*Father Xmas* "Introduction"), and the last in 1943, when the youngest, Priscilla, was still a schoolgirl. Father Christmas and his household have a skirmish with the Goblins in 1932, and an all-out war in 1933 lasting several weeks (in which Father Christmas sounds much like Gandalf fighting the Goblins who capture Bilbo and the dwarves). In 1935, he writes that the Goblins are "breeding again and multiplying all over the world. Quite a nasty outbreak" (*Father Xmas* 138). This was the year Germany revoked the Treaty of Versailles and intensified its persecution of Jews, the year Italy invaded Ethiopia, the year Japanese troops swept through northern China.

However, it is the later letters that show the influence of war most clearly and distressingly: "I am so glad you did not forget to write to me again this year. The number of children who keep up with me seems to be getting smaller. I expect it is because of this horrible war, and that when it is over things will improve again, and I shall be as busy as ever. But at present so terribly many people have lost their homes, or have left them; half the world seems to be in the wrong place!"(*Father Xmas* 142). He also reports more battles with the Goblins, and his house itself is besieged: "I expect the Goblins thought that with so much war going on this was a fine chance to recapture the North" (*Father Xmas* 142). In 1942 Father Christmas apologizes that "[d]eliveries . . . are more difficult than ever this year with damaged houses and houseless people and all the dreadful events going on in your countries" (*Father Xmas* 148). The last letter, written in 1943 to Priscilla, comments that "[m]y messengers tell me that people call it 'grim' this year. I think they mean miserable: and so it is, I fear, in very many places where I was specially fond of going" (*Father Xmas* 154).

Wayne Hammond and Christina Scull point out that Tolkien's work as a visual artist and illustrator should also be considered in any survey of his work. Nothing survives of any drawings he might have made while at the Front except for one map made as part of his duties and reproduced in *The Tolkien Family Album* (Tolkien and Tolkien 40); as they say, "His experiences at the Front appear after a fashion in his writings . . . but he did not draw the horrors of warfare" (Hammond and Scull 26). Few of his drawings show any scenes of violence or conflict—except the drawings made for his annual Father Christmas letters. While he was assigned to the camp in Penkridge in Staffordshire, Tolkien and his wife, Edith, with their first child, John, and Edith's cousin Jennie Grove had lodgings in a house called "Gipsy Green," where he made a number of drawings (Hammond and Scull 26–28). There is no reference to the war in these landscapes and miniature domestic sketches except for several small self-portraits of Tolkien in uniform and on his bicycle, and an even smaller drawing of an officer in a kilt.

OTHER CRITICS ON TOLKIEN AND WORLD WAR I

Hugh Brogan is one of several critics who have noticed the applicability of Paul Fussell's critique of World War I literature to Tolkien's writing. In "Tolkien's Great War," he says the war "lay like a cloud on the consciousness of the English until it was eclipsed by the coming of an even greater conflict. It lay heaviest on the souls of those who had been combatants" (352). Was Tolkien haunted by the war as much as writers like Robert Graves were?

As Brogan indicates, Tolkien makes very few direct references to World War I in any of his published writings. But he calls attention to the passage where Tolkien describes the downfall of Sauron like a wind-blown cloud, "a huge shape of shadow, impenetrable, lightning-crowned, filling all the sky," then "a great wind took it, and it was all blown away" (*Return* 227). It is remarkably similar to a paragraph from Siegfried Sassoon's *Memoirs of a Fox-Hunting Man*: "a cloud of dark smoke expands . . . its dingy wrestling vapors take the form of a hooded giant . . . it dissolves into nothingness" (cited Brogan 353). Both writers were quite likely influenced by memories of shells bursting and smoke floating away. As Brogan asks, "if the Great War could break through so vividly at such an important moment of *The Lord of the Rings*, may it not have manifested itself elsewhere?" (354).

Brogan discusses Fussell's list of pre- and postwar vocabulary, in which flamboyant words common in prewar romances and adventure stories, like "comrade," "strife," "summons," and "foe," are contrasted with dry and unromantic postwar usages like "friend," "war," "draft-notice," and "enemy" (Fussell, *Great War* 21–22). Tolkien, the "passionate philologist" (Brogan 355), was highly sensitive to the nuances of language and was capable of varying his tone with great skill. In many places, he used the solemn, heroic, alliterative vocabulary and inverted sentence structure of *Beowulf* to great effect, but after the war and its excesses of propaganda, many other writers found this style embarrassing. Brogan quotes Hemingway's *A Farewell to Arms*: "There were many words that you could not stand to hear and finally only the names of places had dignity. . . . Abstract words such as glory, honor, courage, or hallow were obscene beside the concrete names of villages, the numbers of roads, the names of rivers, the numbers of regiments and the dates" (Hemingway 191). Brogan asks how Tolkien, sensitive as he was, "could have gone through the Great War, with all its rants and lies, and still come out committed to a 'feudal' literary style. His tenacity on this point looks like an act of deliberate defiance of modern history" (356).

While Brogan seems to have had some doubts about the merits of adhering to the values and language of Old English, I would suggest that this "deliberate defiance" was an integral part of the task of sub-creation, supporting Tolkien's theory that one of the functions of fantasy is escape—the "Escape of the Prisoner" as opposed to the "Flight of the Deserter" ("On Fairy-stories" 60), but still a deliberate distancing from the everyday and mundane. The right of a prisoner caught up in this intolerable and inexorable modern world is to attempt to escape to the "real world" outside his jail—which is no less real "because the prisoner cannot see it" ("On Fairy-stories" 60). It is the task of the storyteller to create a world in which he can believe, and in which he can feel like he lives for a while. As Ursula K. Le Guin put it, "it's our plain duty to escape, and to take as many people with us as we can" ("Escape" 196).

The vocabulary rejected by the ironists is natural to Middle-earth, and Middle-earth could not exist without it. In writing fantasy, the "inner consistency of reality," including an appropriate style and vocabulary, is necessary to evoke "Secondary Belief" ("On Fairy-stories" 47). In another essay, Le Guin argues that the "genuine Elfland accent" is essential to serious fantasy ("From Elfland" 77). When a writer is creating a new and fantastic world, he is creating "a world where no voice has ever spoken before; where the act of speech is the act of creation. The only voice that speaks there is the creator's voice. And every word counts" ("From Elfland" 85).

Tolkien of course was well aware of the need for the proper style and voice for each character, each landscape, and each event in Middle-earth. In a 1955 letter written (but not sent) to Brogan, defending his use of archaism, he quotes a speech by Théoden: " 'Nay, Gandalf!' said the King. 'You do not know your own skill in healing. It shall not be so. I myself will go to war, to fall in the front of the battle, if it must be. Thus shall I sleep better' " (*Towers* 123). Even this is a simplified, watered-down version of the truly archaic, as Tolkien proceeds to demonstrate. Then he translates it into the modern vernacular:

"Not at all my dear G. You don't know your own skill as a doctor. Things aren't going to be like that. I shall go to the war in person, even if I have to be one of the first casualties"—and then what? Théoden would certainly think, and probably say "thus shall I sleep better." But people who think like that just do not talk a modern idiom. You can have "I shall lie easier in my grave" . . . if you like. But there would be an insincerity of thought, a disunion of word and meaning. For a King who spoke in a modern style would not really think in such terms at all. (*Letters* 225–26)

In spite of his reservations about Tolkien's use of language, Brogan concludes that the quest-form allowed Tolkien to express what the Great War meant to him and to write as meaningful a commentary on the war as Graves or Sassoon did. Tolkien's work is ultimately concerned with "the debate between the old world and the new," never entirely resolved (Brogan 360); it is a bleak vision, but "not depressing because it is realistic and courageous" and it offers hope to his readers (365).

Barton Friedman also examines Tolkien's World War I experiences through Fussell's critique, and compares his work to the epic poem *In Parenthesis* by David Jones, also a veteran of the Somme. In his preface Jones says his poem deals with the period from December 1915 to July 1916; the beginning of the Somme campaign "marks a change in the character of our lives" and "things hardened into a more relentless, mechanical affair" (Jones ix). Jones participated in the earlier part of the war, distinguished by what he felt was an "attractive amateurishness, and elbow-room for idiosyncrasy," where there could be an "intimate, continuing, domestic life of small contingents of men" (ix). While Tolkien did not go to France until just before the Battle of the Somme, he may have caught a glimpse of this way of life in training camps in England. It seems to resonate in the way his various fellowships of travelers live and work together in *The Hobbit* and *The Lord of the Rings*.

In "Tolkien and David Jones," Friedman sets the scene where Sam falls in the Dead Marshes and sees dead faces in the water side-by-side with passages from Siegfried Sassoon's *Memoirs of an Infantry Officer*, Max Plowman's *A Subaltern on the Somme*, and John Masefield's *The Old Front Line*, all describing corpses in the mud of No-Man's Land. Their descriptions evoke the true horror of the trenches; the clinging mud and enemy fire prevented retrieval and burial of the dead, and trench warfare kept the living pinned in one place for weeks, too close to the corpses of their comrades for comfort. Friedman also compares the Nazgûl stooping on the tower of Cirith Ungol— "a winged shape, rending the clouds with a ghastly shriek" (*Return* 192)— with descriptions of incoming mortar rounds in Jones's *In Parenthesis* and Frederic Manning's *Her Privates We*, rushing downwards with a screaming sound (Friedman 121). Still, Tolkien's descriptions of the horrors of war lack the graphic detail seen in other writers and seem to Friedman almost "antiseptic" and perhaps too close to "celebrating the delight of war" (118).

Friedman compares the way Tolkien and Jones idealized and romanticized war, and rejected "technology unchecked by spiritual values" (120)—practically the definition of the hellish novelty of World War I in the eyes of an antimodernist like Tolkien. Jones too found the change in the way of warfare disquieting: "a rubicon has been passed between striking with a hand weapon as men used to do and loosing poison from the sky as we do ourselves. We doubt the decency of our own inventions, and are certainly in terror of their possibilities" (xiv). Friedman concludes that Tolkien and Jones both strove to apply fundamental spiritual truths to the Great War, and more or less succeeded in showing the war "as a stage in the struggle of good against evil" (133). Fussell criticized Jones for "pretending" to shame the present while actually ennobling it through reference to the past (*Great War* 147). Tolkien in his less direct approach to using his Great War memories manages to do both, honoring the courage of the common soldier while at the same time criticizing the modern trend toward anonymous and mechanized war.

Several other critics also speak to Tolkien's wartime experiences, though without reference to Fussell's theories. Verlyn Flieger in *A Question of Time* examines Tolkien's dislocation from his own time. She sees much of the tension and melancholy of Middle-earth resting in Tolkien's "nostalgic longing for a return to a lost past coupled with the knowledge that this was impossible save in the realm of the imagination" (3) and observes, "he put his Hobbits in a world that moved too fast for them, and then forced them to keep up with it" (7). She calls Tolkien "at once reactionary and avant-garde, turning [his back] on the modernism that had turned its back on the past" (17), and considers the writing of authors like Graves part of "an antiromantic reaction, a militant and narrowly defined modernity that arose after World War I" (234). For Tolkien, writing was at once an escape, an attempt to communicate the experience of the Great War, and a way of working out his vision of the interdependence of the real world and Faërie. (Flieger does mention Fussell in relation to her discussion of "The Sea-Bell" and the kinship of travelers returning from Faërie with veterans returning from war [219].)

Roger Sale, in his book *Modern Heroism*, saw *The Lord of the Rings* as very much a product of World War I. Sale characterized Tolkien's response to the war as "long delayed in taking its crucial shape" (193) and, discussing the key "quickened to full life by war" sentence in "On Fairy-stories," suggested, "it may well be that it took Tolkien a full twenty years to realize what had happened to him" (194). He went on to state:

[T]he stupidity, barbarity, squalor, and horror of the war drove a sensitive young imagination toward the conviction that he was seeing the very opposite of life as it was meant to be seen. The horrors of World War I were trite, those of the fairy tale brilliant and profound. . . . Ironically, and wonderfully . . . it was by means of his withdrawal and his imagining of a fairy tale that Tolkien could create one of the most powerful visions we have of the very world from which he was fleeing. (197)

To Sale, *The Lord of the Rings* was a powerfully modern book, a "descent into hell" (199), which in Frodo's tortured journey speaks to the modern condition and exemplifies modern heroism. In the landscape blighted by Sauron, "the old terms for the struggle of good against evil—courage, loyalty, honor, magnificence, fortitude—are mostly irrelevant" (Sale 227). To merely go on at all is heroic, and in Frodo's struggle, "valor and physical strength and the very idea of battles are not germane" (234).

Sale wrote that Tolkien found recovery in Middle-earth, not in the sense given in "On Fairy-stories" of recovering a fresh vision of what had become familiar, but simply mental recovery from "the oppressive wounds of war" (238). He saw Tolkien working out his recovery slowly, over the years: "Tolkien was writing about the pains and terrors of his twenties when he was in his fifties" (238). He felt this might have made the work more difficult to read properly as a response to the Great War. Had Tolkien written it when younger, Sale felt, "the way it rises to its greatest heights in its response to the circumstances of the modern world and the Great War should have been clear to many. By the fifties the modern age had passed and the war that did most to define it had been forgotten . . . and so *The Lord of the Rings* became a book fearfully abused" (239).

Brian Rosebury, in *Tolkien: A Critical Assessment*, described the parts of Tolkien's introduction dealing with World War I as acknowledging "the influence of wartime bereavement," and that part of the "impetus to the creation of Middle-earth and its myths was given by the experience of war" (126). He went on to say:

At a still deeper level, the mingled relief and regret of the war-survivor may have played some part in reinforcing the emotional ambivalence that is so marked a feature of Tolkien's fiction. The earlier mythical writings have . . . an insistent, almost pagan, pessimism, and a surprisingly grim level of violence, which darken, indeed come close to undermining, the affirmative theistic universe they postulate. In the later work, as if a trauma has been worked through, joy and grief are more evenly and subtly interfused. . . . It might indeed be seen in certain respects as the last work of First World War literature, published almost forty years after the war ended. (126)

Tom Shippey addressed some aspects of Tolkien's war experiences in the first edition of *The Road to Middle-earth*. He discussed the concept of defeatism, a word that did not enter the English language until 1918, and how any hint of a willingness to give up and negotiate terms with the enemy is roundly rejected by the Free Peoples of Middle-earth. As Shippey put it, "With his best friends dead in Flanders Tolkien had cause to hate that idea like poison" (*Road* 116). Even Denethor, convinced of the inevitable failure of Gondor and its allies, commits suicide and advises everyone else to do the same, rather than be a slave under a puppet government.

One of Shippey's main aims in this book was to examine Tolkien's theory

of courage, a theory based on the northern European heroic spirit and described in "The Homecoming of Beorhtnoth Beorhthelm's Son":

> "Heart shall be bolder,   harder be purpose,
> more proud the spirit   as our power lessens!
> Mind shall not falter   nor mood waver,
> though doom shall come   and dark conquer."
>
> ("Homecoming" 17)

Tolkien's characters at their best exhibit a "courage undiluted by confidence—
but at the same time untainted by rage and despair" (Shippey, *Road* 119).
They can be cheerful without hope, sad but not unhappy, and above all determined to "see it through"—an attitude common enough among firsthand
accounts of rankers in the trenches. For example, Richard Holmes, the editor
of the World War I autobiography *My Bit*, comments that for the soldier
George Ashurst, "there was an innate conviction that the allies must win; that
'sneaking away . . . like a thief in the night' was wrong; that to 'hold on
grimly, suffering heavy casualties but losing no ground' was the right way to
behave" (Ashurst 10).

Shippey concluded that, unlike many writers of his generation, Tolkien
"had not been alienated even by the Great War from the traditions in which
he had been brought up," and retained certain "fundamental decencies" that
provoked "automatic derision from much of the literary world" (*Road* 217).
The old-fashioned idea that there is merit in doing one's duty, even if one
could survive by switching sides, even if no one would ever know, was not
rendered invalid for Tolkien by an ironic response to the Great War. Shippey
proposed the horn of Rohan as a symbol of the message of *The Lord of the
Rings*—a message that would "disperse the cloud of post-war and post-faith
disillusionment, depression, [and] acquiescence, which so strangely (and twice
in his lifetime) followed on victory" (*Century* 221).

MYTHOLOGIZING THE WAR

The important question remains: Why, in the light of his war experiences,
did Tolkien choose the literary mode he did, when so many of his fellow
veteran-writers used the ironic style in their poetry and memoirs—in fact,
felt with Hemingway that the heroic style was rendered almost obscene by
the unprecedented slaughter, stupidity, and waste of the war? And why does
Tolkien emphasize that his taste for fairy-stories was "quickened to full life
by war"? It may have been because major parts of Middle-earth's mythology
and history were already forming in his mind before the war began, as background to his Elvish languages, and his experiences naturally fit themselves
into this waiting framework. Brogan states that while Tolkien's project of a
mythology for England "did not survive the Somme unaltered," it might not

have survived at all "but for the advanced stage of the linguistic inventions with which it was bound up" (357). It was an escape, pure and simple, and at the same time, it may have become a way to wrest meaning from incomprehensible experience by transforming it into something more familiar.

While Fussell is most concerned with irony, he does examine some works that incorporate mythological material, like David Jones's epic poem *In Parenthesis*, and notes Northrop Frye's conclusion that in the cycle of literary styles, the ironic mode "moves steadily towards myth, and the dim outlines of sacrificial rituals and dying gods begin to reappear in it" (Frye 42). He refutes Bernard Bergonzi's conclusion that "[t]he dominant movement in the literature of the Great War was . . . from a myth-dominated to a demythologized world" (Bergonzi 198). Fussell says, "No; almost the opposite. In one sense the movement was towards myth, towards a revival of the cultic, the mystical, the sacrificial, the prophetic, the sacramental, and the universally significant" (*Great War* 131). But Bergonzi is correct in his analysis that "[v]iolent action could be regarded as meaningful, even sacred, when it was sanctified by the traditional canons of heroic behavior; when these canons came to seem no longer acceptable, then killing or being killed in war appeared meaningless and horrible" (198). The "unchivalrous and anti-heroic" weapons of the Great War (Bergonzi 199) stripped heroic associations from battle and led to disillusionment and the ironic response on the part of many writers. However, for some writers this became instead a challenge to somehow bring meaning back to the act of war.

Fussell says of Jones's work that he showed a "desire to rescue and reinvigorate traditional pre-industrial religious and ethical connotations" (*Great War* 145) and to "[re-attach] traditional meaning to the unprecedented actualities of war" (*Great War* 146). The first goal is very like Tolkien's hope of reviving his ideal of a northern European mythology and morality; intentionally or not, Tolkien achieved the second goal as well. His chosen subject matter and use of the quest-pattern led logically to a high-romance mode and vocabulary, and therefore to a more heroic interpretation of war.

But while the Battle of the Pelennor Fields is one of the most stirring events in the trilogy, with the Rohirrim singing "for the joy of battle was on them" (*Return* 113) and great deeds being performed by the Men of Gondor, we also see the battle from the points of view of Pippin in Minas Tirith and Merry with the Riders of Rohan. Like the experience of the common soldier in the trenches of World War I, their part is far from glorious; there is tedious waiting, a sense of uselessness and futility, terror and pain and ugliness. But instead of falling back on irony as the proper response, the Hobbits illustrate Tolkien's ideal of courage, going on in spite of being without hope. Their determination "master[s] all the grief and horror . . . giving it dignity and significance" (Brogan 358). As Holmes says of Ashurst, "it was not lofty motives that kept him in the trenches," but malingering or desertion would have been "foreign to his nature" (Ashurst 10).

The creation of a world in which both heroic deeds could be done and determination without hope might be rewarded could also be, as Brogan put it, "therapy for a mind wounded in war" (358). It was a place to retreat to but not an escape, unless in the sense that Tolkien used the word "escape" in "On Fairy-stories." W.H.R. Rivers, the psychiatrist who treated Robert Graves, Wilfred Owen, and Siegfried Sassoon at the Craiglockhart officers' hospital, commented on how his patients processed the war through the dreams he recorded, "transform[ing] reality into a more bearable nightmare" (Friedman 122). Friedman notes how these dreams and nightmares repeat the romance pattern, drawing on fairy-tale images and the hero-journey sequence. As Joseph Campbell puts it, "Dream is the personalized myth, myth the depersonalized dream" (19), but while their dreams might be moving toward myth, their writing on the war was consciously realistic and ironic and still very personal. Their closeness to the war in time and their direct use of it as subject matter may have prevented these writers from mythologizing their war experiences in writing.

In contrast, Tolkien did not write *The Lord of the Rings* until many years after the war, and perhaps the memories of his war experiences had more time to become depersonalized. But he had already started thinking this way during the war; writing to his son Christopher, stationed in South Africa during World War II and thinking about becoming a writer himself, Tolkien describes his attempts to write during the Great War and how he settled on fairy-story: "So I took to 'escapism': or really transforming experience into another form and symbol with Morgoth and Orcs and the Eldalie (representing beauty and grace of life and artefact) and so on; and it has stood me in good stead in many hard years since and I still draw on the conceptions then hammered out" (*Letters* 85).

Transformed experience made "applicable" instead of "allegorical" creates forms and symbols that make a work relevant for a wide variety of readers by encouraging their own interpretations of the material. Michael Swanwick recounts one critic's theory that Samuel Beckett's play *Waiting for Godot* began as a story about two French Resistance fighters meeting their contact in the occupied countryside. If this is the true origin of the play, then by removing "all specific signifiers" that could lead the audience back to this source, Beckett "made the plight of his two heroes universal" (Swanwick 36). A work without specific allegorical referents is more universally applicable, so while there is a distinct imprint of World War I on Tolkien's trilogy, this lack of one-on-one allegorical identification makes it applicable to any upheaval and dislocation in the reader's life and at the same time increases the reader's understanding of twentieth-century history.

Because Tolkien's fantasy is escapist does not mean it is simple or one-dimensional. Escaping to a superficial stage set of a world would never satisfy a prisoner for long. Orson Scott Card, an experienced writer of compelling fantasy himself, points out the paradox implicit in the postmodern concept of writing and reading "serious" literature as a process of encoding and decoding meanings. Rather than creating a deep and resonant work, this process creates a text that is actually simple enough to be decoded by the clever-enough reader and have its one right meaning captured and pinned down. However, escapist storytelling, story told for the sake of story, requires the reader to interact with the story rather than standing aloof, and can allow a multitude of interpretations even by the same reader, rather than one "correct" reading dictated by the author. "Escapist" literature is "so complex and deep it cannot be mediated, but must be experienced" (Card 158). "[T]he story is not the text. Rather the text is the tool that the readers use to create the story in the only place where it ever truly exists—their individual memories" (Card 161).

Irony in *The Lord of the Rings* is used as a plot device or to show character—not as an underlying literary mode or philosophy. In his most recent book, Shippey discusses dramatic irony, the ironic gaps between what the characters know and what the reader knows (*Century* 110). Tolkien's failed men of power, Saruman and Denethor, sometimes speak in ironic voices, using their knowledge (which may be false, as in the case of Denethor's vision of the Corsairs of Umbar) to mock the ignorance of other characters. However, these are examples of irony in service to the plot, not irony as an attitude; as Douglas Anderson has observed, "Tolkien was not incapable of irony, but he did not write in a largely ironic tone" (139). Irony is binary and polarized, and using it as a prevailing mode would have destroyed the moral nuances of Tolkien's work.

Tolkien's rejection of the ironic mode shows that he did not allow himself to be utterly alienated by his war experiences. While he felt that "one War was enough for any man" and "either the bitterness of youth or that of middle-age is enough for a lifetime" (*Letters* 54), he still did not subscribe to the "abridgement of hope" that was the foundation of the ironists' mode (Fussell, *Great War* 3).

Tolkien is not the only author whose response to war was the fantastic mode. Tom Shippey has proposed the term "traumatized authors" for a group of twentieth-century writers who had been involved in some of the most horrific events of their times, and turned to the fantastic mode to write about their experiences. In this group he includes George Orwell, C. S. Lewis, Kurt Vonnegut, T. H. White, Joseph Heller, and William Golding, and there are other authors who might fit into this category as well (*Century* xxx). Meredith Veldman came to a similar conclusion: "The twentieth century . . . witnessed the blossoming of fantasy literature, a genre in which the ironic voice is silenced and yet the outrage of contemporary life sounds clearly" (37).

Tolkien may well have recognized that sustained irony is a sterile mode; there is no "consolation" in it. As he defined it, a proper fairy tale offers "Fantasy, Recovery, Escape, and Consolation" ("On Fairy-stories" 46), "consolation" being tied up with eucatastrophe and the happy ending forbidden in the ironic mode. If "courage without hope" was what Tolkien witnessed among the common soldiers and wanted to save out of the wreck of war, irony was not the way to express it—only fairy-tale would prove its value.

CONCLUSION

World War I was without precedent, and one of the major turning points in world history, not just because of its geopolitical consequences but also because of its status as the first "global, total, modern war" (Strachan 1). The trench experience "speaks across the century" in all its horror and futility and in the fortitude of the soldiers—it overthrew all the old certainties and became the "great emancipatory adventure-experience of the modern age . . . the representative event of our century" (Eksteins 317). Its effects on society, the arts, politics, ideology, technology, historiography, and the like are far-reaching and inescapable, even nearly a hundred years later.

Fussell describes two ways in which the writers who served in the Great War tried to sort out and communicate their memories. He gives precedence to the ironic method, concentrating on "satires of circumstance" and chronicles of official stupidity, exemplified by Robert Graves's autobiographical book *Good-bye to All That*. But he also discusses attempts to mythologize the war and relate it to heroic romance, as David Jones did in *In Parenthesis*.

Tolkien may in fact have more in common with Edmund Blunden, for whom the damage the war did to the natural world was nearly as important as the damage it did to human beings:

> I have seen a green country, useful to the race,
> Knocked silly with guns and mines, its villages vanished,
> Even the last rat and last kestrel banished—
> God bless us all, this was peculiar grace.
>
> (Blunden, "Report on Experience")

Preindustrial England was also Blunden's yardstick for measuring the soullessness of modern war, and as Fussell comments, rather than escaping into the past, he was "engaging the war by selecting from the armory of the past weapons against it which seem to have the greatest chance of withstanding time" (Fussell, *Great War* 269).[5]

Since Tolkien was a student of myths and heroic literature, it is possible that his choice of mode was based in part on his understanding of the staying power of the fairy-story—its ability to withstand time. Besides offering the artist a vast scope for sub-creation and a way to integrate the soul-satisfying four functions of fairy-stories, the mythical mode has a certain permanence about it not found in realistic depictions of contemporary events. As Shippey puts it in *Author of the Century*, "myth and applicability are timeless, allegory and legend time-constrained" (188).

In the end, because of their near-universal applicability, Tolkien's works may well outlast those of the canonical war poets and memoirists, no matter how meaningful. Tolkien's stories will always be able to speak directly to a wide audience unfamiliar with his life and times, yet will have greater significance for the reader who understands the influence of the Great War on his writing and our world. As Verlyn Flieger pointed out, "The most effective commentary on an age or an event is as often as not oblique rather than direct, and the impact is no less powerful for being rerouted" (8).

Tolkien's work and the Great War have mutual applicability—each helps us understand the other. Perhaps one reason Tolkien is so frequently voted "Author of the Century" is because he took what was a pivotal event in world history and transformed it into a comprehensible myth to help us understand how our world has changed and learn how we can still live in it with courage.

NOTES

1. Tolkien and three friends at King Edward's School had formed a club called the "Tea Club and Barrovian Society"; his fellow TCBS members G. B. Smith and Rob Gilson both died in 1916, and Christopher Wiseman, serving in the navy, survived.

2. Tolkien's close friend and fellow fantasy writer C. S. Lewis had a similar experience of the Great War. He was a student at Oxford and was commissioned as a second lieutenant in the Somerset Light Infantry. He was several years younger than Tolkien, arriving at the frontline trenches at Arras on the eve of his nineteenth birthday in 1917 (Gilchrist, "Continuing Research" 47); Tolkien was a more mature twenty-four and had arrived earlier in the war, in 1916. Like Tolkien, Lewis lost most of his close friends in the war (Gilchrist, "Lewis" 70). But unlike Tolkien, Lewis was seriously wounded when a shell exploded near him, killing his friend Sergeant Ayres ("Lewis" 64). Lewis did write some war poetry referring very specifically to his Great War experiences, most notably *Dymer*, but like Tolkien, avoided the ironic response of many of his fellow veteran-writers while still exploring many of the same themes ("Lewis" 63). Lewis was somewhat more forthcoming than Tolkien in writing about his war experiences, including a chapter titled "Guns and Good Company" in his autobiography (C. S. Lewis, *Surprised* 182–96).

3. It is possible that Tolkien might have known Blunden at Oxford; fellow Inkling Hugo Dyson once belonged to a club Blunden is known to have visited (Carpenter, *Inklings* 161), and Blunden was in competition with Lewis for the chair of poetry in 1951 (*Inklings* 229).

Chapter 3

World War I Themes in *The Hobbit* and *The Lord of the Rings*

The Front Line was behind us; but it could lay its hand on our hearts, though its bludgeoning reality diminished with every mile. It was as if we were pursued by the Arras Battle which had now become a huge and horrible idea. We might be boastful or savagely reconstructive about our experience, in accordance with our different characters. But our minds were still out of breath and our inmost thoughts in disorderly retreat from bellowing darkness and men dying out in shell-holes under the desolation of returning daylight. We were the survivors; few among us would ever tell the truth to our friends and relations in England. We were carrying something in our heads which belonged to us alone, and to those we had left behind us in the battle.

—Sassoon, *Memoirs of an Infantry Officer* 233

In this chapter, I will examine several themes that Paul Fussell found typical of British post–World War I literature in *The Great War and Modern Memory*, and show how Tolkien used them, principally in *The Hobbit* and *The Lord of the Rings*. I will look primarily at the pastoral moment, with a sidelight on gardening and flowers; ritual and romance, with some subthemes like the symbolism of the number three; and the sense of national literature. I will also more briefly discuss some additional themes that Fussell suggests: demonization of the enemy, particularly as seen in the problem of the Orcs; the underground world of the trenches; and homoeroticism and the vulnerability of the body.

THE PASTORAL MOMENT

For Fussell, war is the "ultimate anti-pastoral," destroying nature while taking place within it. He sees the English pastoral tradition as unique in several ways. One is its mixture of "highly sophisticated literary pastoralism" combined with "a unique actual ruralism" (*Great War* 231). It has its roots in both British imperialism, which encouraged in its exiles an idealized mental image of "home," and the Industrial Revolution, which transformed the rural countryside within a generation. Both of these may have influenced Tolkien, given his birth in South Africa and the industrialization of the English countryside where he grew up. Fussell further refines on this theme: "Recourse to the pastoral is an English mode of both fully gauging the calamities of the Great War and imaginatively protecting oneself against them. Pastoral reference, whether to literature or to actual rural localities and objects, is a way of invoking a code to hint by antithesis at the indescribable; at the same time, it is a comfort in itself, like rum, a deep dugout, or a wooly vest" (*Great War* 235). As an example, here is Hugh Walpole reporting on a pastoral moment shattered by war in Galicia: "The dawn was beautiful. . . . We got right into the forests which were lovely in the early morning, the sky red and gold, the birds singing. . . . The whole landscape behind us, which had been dead still, cracked into sound" (Walpole 453).

The pastoral landscape in Tolkien can include the works of Men, Elves, and Hobbits, if they are in harmony with nature. A well-tended farm is pastoral; a city like Minas Tirith can be pastoral if it has gardens and families in it. After the King is restored, "[t]he evil things will be driven out of the waste-lands. Indeed the waste in time will be waste no longer, and there will be people and fields where once there was wilderness" (*Return* 272). Even a dwarf-cave can be in harmony with nature; Gimli's rhapsody on what the Dwarves would do to open up the beauties of the Glittering Caves of Aglarond (*Towers* 152–53), full of lush and organic imagery, stands in stark contrast to descriptions of the more industrial Mines of Moria, where the Dwarves delved too deep. Douglas A. Burger said that "the Shire shares with the traditional pastoral an emphasis on the simplicity of life and freedom from the ambiguities and complications of advanced civilization" (150). In keeping with Tolkien's abhorrence of the Age of Machines, the Shire is still a place where the simplest of machines—nothing "more complicated than a forge-bellows, a water-mill, or a hand-loom" (*Fellowship* 10)—are in service to their makers rather than vice versa. Tolkien's pastoralism, then, is "a complex interplay between wilderness and cultivation, and between nature and civilization" (Drout and Wynne 115), rather than a simplistic or purely "green" environmentalism.

The enemy forces in *The Hobbit* and *The Lord of the Rings* are deeply antipastoral. The Desolation of Smaug, once "green and fair" (*Hobbit* 216), is now bleak and barren. Even in the light satirical story "Farmer Giles of

Ham," the giant is described as "the ruin of roads and the desolation of gardens" who did in five minutes "more damage than the royal fox-hunt could have done in five days" (*Farmer Giles* 11–12). In the same tale, the dragon Chrysophylax leaves behind a ruin of "broken trees, burned hedges and blackened grass, and a nasty uncanny silence" (*Farmer Giles* 40). Brian Rosebury describes how the effects of World War I influenced Tolkien's war-ravaged landscapes:

> The ineradicable memory of a land pulverised by "total war" is evident (though combined with images suggestive of industrial pollution, and fully absorbed into the wider imaginative geography) in the most hauntingly repellent landscapes of his work—less, perhaps, in the desert plains of Mordor than in the Dead Marshes, with their preserved corpses, half-real, half-hallucinatory, staring out of deep water; and the "obscene graveyard" before the Gates of Mordor. (Rosebury 126)

The enemy's orcs were bred to be the opposite of the Elves, and "it seems their delight to slash and beat down growing things that are not even in their way" (*Towers* 22). Saruman "has a mind of metal and wheels" and a special enmity for trees—"there are wastes of stump and bramble where once there were singing groves" (*Towers* 76–77). Sauron does not just destroy nature but uses and perverts it. When he dwelt in Mirkwood, the forest was an unwholesome place inhabited by spiders. Morgul Vale is a parody of the pastoral: "Wide flats lay on either bank, shadowy meads filled with pale white flowers. Luminous these were too, beautiful and yet horrible of shape, like the demented forms in an uneasy dream; and they gave forth a faint sickening charnel-smell; an odour of rottenness filled the air" (*Towers* 313). Mount Doom, under his dominion, makes a noise like "a rumour and a trouble as of great engines throbbing and labouring" (*Return* 222). As Roger Sale points out, "The landscape through which Frodo must move is Sauron's most powerful weapon, a valley of the shadow of death" (234).

Tolkien uses a comparison to the pastoral ideal to show both the depth of Frodo's torment and what he has lost by carrying the Ring. When he first begins to understand about his quest, he says, "I feel that as long as the Shire lies behind, safe and comfortable, I shall find wandering more bearable; I shall know that somewhere there is a firm foothold, even if my feet cannot stand there again" (*Fellowship* 71). His last summer in the Shire is reminiscent of the glorious summer of 1914 in England, the calm before the storm. But by the end, Frodo says, "I tried to remember the Brandywine, and Woody End, and The Water running through the mill at Hobbiton. But I can't see them now" (*Return* 195). "No taste of food, no feel of water, no sound of wind, no memory of tree or grass or flower, no image of moon or star are left to me" (*Return* 215).

Fussell also feels that the English pastoral is distinguished by the "special kind of sense [the English make] out of the classical tag *Et in arcadia ego*

. . . they take it to mean (correctly) 'Even in Arcadia I, Death, hold sway' "
(Fussell, *Great War* 245–46). The Old Forest is a prime example of this.
The Withywindle valley is "the center from which all the queerness comes"
(*Fellowship* 124), where Old Man Willow is filled with "pride and rooted
wisdom, and with malice" (*Fellowship* 141). Lórien is a nearly perfect Arcadia, but "those who bring some evil with them" (*Fellowship* 353) find their
doom there. Another illustration of this theme occurs in Ithilien, when Sam,
looking for a place to rest, stumbles on the remains of an orc campsite, a
"place of dreadful feast and slaughter" that he conceals from his companions;
he was "reminded suddenly of their ever-present peril" (*Towers* 259). Siegfried Sassoon in *Memoirs of an Infantry Officer* describes leaving training
camp one evening for his "favorite sanctuary, a wood of hazels and beeches.
The evening air smelt of wet mold and wet leaves; the trees were misty-
green." Yet even here, he cannot escape the echo in his mind of the lecturer
on the use of the bayonet, telling him, "Stick him between the eyes, in the
throat, in the chest. . . . [W]hen he coughs, go and look for another" (*Memoirs of an Infantry Officer* 16).

Yet balancing this theme is its opposite: finding a pastoral oasis in the midst
of destruction. Like many Great War memoirs, the action of much of *The
Lord of the Rings*, and particularly *The Fellowship of the Ring*, consists of
"bucolic interludes . . . sandwiched between bouts of violence and terror"
(Fussell, *Great War* 236). These moments of pastoral peace indicate the
norm by which the surrounding horrors should be judged. Rivendell and Lórien are obvious pastoral oases, but it is the smaller moments that are more
reminiscent of life in the trenches; as C. S. Lewis called them, "heaven-sent
windfalls" ("Dethronement" 40). For example, Merry and Pippin create a
small private pastoral oasis after escaping from the orcs by pausing for a bite
of *lembas*: "The taste brought back to them the memory of fair faces, and
laughter, and wholesome food in quiet days now far away. For a while they
ate thoughtfully, sitting in the dark, heedless of the cries and sounds of battle
nearby" (*Towers* 61).

The pastoral oasis in *The Hobbit* is less clearly defined by contrast with its
surroundings, because except for the final battle, the action of the book does
not take place in a landscape dominated by war. Here the "pastoral moment"
usually does not occur immediately after a moment of great stress. After the
party escapes the trolls, there is still a long march before they reach Rivendell,
and between the battle with the wargs and goblins and the stay in Beorn's
house, the party spends the night with the Eagles, which Bilbo at least does
not find entirely restful. The transition from danger to a place of refuge is
more gradual.

The pastoral refuge contains in it a "clarifying or restorative force" (Fussell,
Great War 239). In the short story "Leaf by Niggle," the first stage of Niggle's
purgatory is set in a dim railway station and a hospital where "the windows
all looked inwards" ("Leaf" 97), and it is when he moves on to the next stage

—a pastoral life, building a house and garden in the forest with Parish—that he understands clearly what his task is and is able to go on to the mountains. Rivendell restores and heals the hobbits and Strider after their flight from Weathertop, and the Council of Elrond clarifies their mission; as Tolkien comments in a 1951 letter, Rivendell is "not a scene of *action* but of *reflection*" (*Letters* 153). Their stay in Lórien helps the Company recover from the death of Gandalf in a place "where the days bring healing not decay" (*Towers* 106), but is clarifying in a more dangerous way when Galadriel tests the survivors and reveals confusing visions to Frodo and Sam. Ithilien, on the edge of war, restores the spirits of Sam and Frodo: "the hobbits breathed deep, and suddenly Sam laughed, for heart's ease not for jest" (*Towers* 259). And here again they have their mission clarified by advice from Faramir. Later, as they rest in the mountains of Mordor, Sam experiences a pastoral moment as he sees a star through the clouds: "The beauty of it smote his heart, as he looked up out of the forsaken land, and hope returned to him. For like a shaft, clear and cold, the thought pierced him that in the end the Shadow was only a small and passing thing; there was light and high beauty for ever beyond its reach" (*Return* 199). Almost the same mood is evoked in a soldier's letter home quoted by Fussell: "Presently a misty moon came up, and a nightingale began to sing. . . . It was strange to stand there and listen, for the song seemed to come all the more sweetly and clearly in the quiet intervals between the bursts of firing. There was something infinitely sweet and sad about it, as if the countryside were singing gently to itself, in the midst of all our noise and confusion and muddy work" (quoted Fussell, *Great War* 161).

Leaving or losing the pastoral oasis creates a sense of melancholy. As the Company departed from Lórien, it seemed as if the land was "slipping backward, like a bright ship masted with enchanted trees, sailing on to forgotten shores, while they sat helpless upon the margin of the grey and leafless world" (*Fellowship* 393). The Elves sing melancholy songs anticipating the day when they shall have to leave Middle-earth. Fussell quotes a review of Edmund Blunden's *Undertones of War*, which says of the author that "the sight of a rich and fruitful land, much like his own, laid waste was an additional torment" (quoted *Great War* 259). Tolkien describes many places blighted by the Enemy as once having been fair and green (the Wizard's Vale comes to mind), making his crimes against nature all the darker.

The "inverted, sardonic pastoral" (*Great War* 166) is a way of using natural imagery in an ironic sense to depict the horrors of war. Blunden's poem "Rural Economy" is a prime example of this, with its country scenes of plowing and planting juxtaposed with the "iron seeds" of bullets and grenades and its "roaring harvest home" of dead and dying soldiers ("Rural Economy"). Tolkien does use natural imagery extensively in his major set-piece battle scenes at Helm's Deep, the Battle of the Pelennor Fields, and at the Black Gate, although he does not seem to exhibit any particular sense of irony in doing so. His use of this imagery may actually give the reader more of a sense that this kind of battle, unmechanized, hand-to-hand, is almost a normal part of nature or at least a natural occurrence. At Helm's Deep the walls are like "sea-delved cliffs," the orcs "as thick as marching ants," the area before the gate "boiling and crawling" with orcs, or tossing like a "great field of dark corn" (*Towers* 137, passim). In the Battle of the Pelennor Fields, the charge of the Rohirrim "roared like a breaker foaming to the shore," and "the drawing of the scimitars of the Southrons was like a glitter of stars" (*Return* 112–14). Before the gates of Mordor there are "teeming broods of evil things," Nazgûl "hovering like vultures," the Mouth of Sauron playing "these mice" cruelly, and the time-honored cliché "sea of enemies" (*Return* 163–67). Even the description of Gandalf's fireworks at Bilbo's party marries warlike and natural imagery: "there was a forest of silver spears that sprang up suddenly into the air with a yell like an embattled army, and came down again into the Water with a hiss like a hundred hot snakes" (*Fellowship* 36).

In addition to the fact that Tolkien avoids the ironic sense of the inverted pastoral, there are two more interesting points about his use of this technique in *The Lord of the Rings*. First, at the end of the Battle of Helm's Deep and in the description of the attack on Isengard by the Ents, the nature metaphors become real as the trees attack. When Tolkien writes about the orcs fearing "the waiting shadow of the trees" (*Towers* 147), or describes the ents "tossing up huge slabs of stone into the air like leaves" (*Towers* 173), it is no longer a metaphor or device but a simple report of events. Nature personified rebels against the antipastoral enemy. Second and more interesting, in the description of the Scouring of the Shire, Tolkien uses no nature imagery to lend any glamour or poetry to the proceedings. Unlike the other battles, it is described in a very straightforward manner verging on the Hemingwayesque; there is nothing to distract from the fact that a nasty, bloody battle is taking place in the once-safe Shire. Arrows do not whine or sing; the ruffians are simply shot. And when Merry slays the leader, he doesn't fall like a rock or a tree, he merely dies (*Return* 295). I will have more to say about this battle in later chapters.

The importance of gardens and gardening to the British blossoms into a particular subspecies of pastoral literature. They have long been passionate gardeners, and British soldiers during World War I maintained their interest even in the field. A visitor to one battalion behind the lines, where each company had set up an elaborate flower bed, called them "gardeners camouflaged as soldiers" (Fussell, *Great War* 234). According to Fussell's count, fully half the poems in the edition of *The Oxford Book of English Verse* available during the Great War are about flowers, and a third about roses in particular (*Great War* 231). Winston Churchill once told Siegfried Sassoon, "War is the normal occupation of man. War—and gardening" (quoted Fussell, *Great War* 234).

Tolkien himself was an avid gardener, and Sam in particular reflects his interests. Sam's vision of himself as The Hero of the Age, when he puts on the Ring on the border of Mordor, turning the desert plain of Gorgoroth into "a garden of flowers and trees" (*Return* 177), is a reductio ad absurdum of the British urge to domesticate nature in a garden plot. Though he realized the "one small garden of a free gardener was all his need and due" (*Return* 177), he does have the opportunity to bring the Shire back to life with the earth from Galadriel's box. Legolas sounds very English for an Elf when he observes, on entering Minas Tirith for the first time, "They need more gardens. . . . The houses are dead, and there is too little that grows here and is glad" (*Return* 148).

Crimson roses, associated in England with sacrificial love, soldiers' wounds, and loyalty, and symbolizing England itself, are a "conspicuous feature of the British military cemeteries in France" (Fussell, *Great War* 245). As the official website of the Commonwealth War Graves Commission reports, "The concept was to create a sentimental association between the gardens of home and the foreign fields where the soldiers lie, and the Commission continues this tradition today by planting species native to its member countries in cemeteries wherever possible. The overall aim . . . is to give the effect of a garden rather than the common concept of a cemetery" (*Horticulture*, 1).[1] The memorial to the hobbits who died in the Battle of Bywater of course has a garden around it, although the particular flowers in it are not listed (*Return* 295). While roses are mentioned only a few times in *The Lord of the Rings* (there are rose-brambles in Ithilien, and Ioreth compares the fragrance of *athelas* to the roses of Imloth Melui in the Houses of Healing), Middle-earth's unique flowers and gardens in general are frequently described. Tolkien also tries to describe local wild plants that match the climate and season through which his characters are traveling; he is more successful in the area of the Shire than with the Mediterranean climate of North Ithilien (Schulp 131–33). The name of Sam's love, Rose Cotton, is particularly appropriate, as Hugh Brogan points out—in one image he thinks of her and the Shire (standing in for England) at the same time, conflating ideas of home, peace, and domestic harmony (362). However, poppies, the quintessential flowers of the Great War, are nowhere mentioned in *The Lord of the Rings*.

The pastoral is also a reminder that "ecstasy [is] still an active motif in the universe" (Fussell, *Great War* 242), that the Shadow really is small and passing in Nature's scheme of things. When Sam, Frodo, and Gollum come to the crossroads at sunset, they see that the orcs have defaced the statue of the king, setting a rock in place of the king's head: "Frodo saw the old king's head: it was lying rolled away by the roadside. 'Look, Sam!' he cried. . . . 'The king has got a crown again!' . . . A trailing plant with flowers like small white stars had bound itself across the brows as if in reverence for the fallen king, and in the crevices of his stony hair yellow stonecrop gleamed. 'They cannot conquer forever!' " (*Towers* 311). There is a strange echo of this scene in a line from David Jones's *In Parenthesis*, where the Queen of the Wood decorates the dead with wildflowers: "Emil has a curious crown, it's made of golden saxifrage" (185). Cecil Lewis describes a similar moment: "Yet (Oh, the catch at the heart!), among the devastated cottages, the tumbled, twisted trees . . . the poppies were growing! . . . undaunted by the desolation, heedless of human fury and stupidity, Flanders poppies, basking in the sun" (quoted Fussell, *Great War* 254).

Pastoral ecstasy segues into the ecstatic relief of the arrival of Rohan at the Battle of the Pelennor Fields. The Lord of the Nazgûl confronts Gandalf at the gates of Minas Tirith, and a pastoral image breaks his spell: "And in that very moment, away behind in some courtyard of the City, a cock crowed. Shrill and clear he crowed, recking nothing of wizardry or war, welcoming only the morning that in the sky far above the shadows of death was coming with the dawn. And as if in answer there came from far away another note. Horns, horns, horns. . . . Great horns of the North wildly blowing" (*Return* 103). Contrast this with a similar moment in the trenches, reported by "Saki" and acerbic with irony: "In the chill misty hour of gloom that precedes a rainy dawn, where nothing seemed alive except a few weary water-logged sentries and many scuttling rats, the lark would suddenly dash skyward and pour forth a song of ecstatic jubilation that sounded horribly forced and insincere" (Munro 471).

The final and most important pastoral oasis, of which the rest are but dim reflections, is home: "[T]here was yellow light, and fire within; and the evening meal was ready, and he was expected. And Rose drew him in, and set him in his chair, and put little Elanor upon his lap" (*Return* 311).

"MYTH, RITUAL, AND ROMANCE"

The intensity of war both reduces life to its essentials and creates a desire to understand and control experiences by fitting them into a structure that gives meaning to chaos. For the soldier in the field, ritual is a charm for maintaining an aura of normalcy amid surrounding turmoil. For example, Frodo's ritual of continuing to celebrate Bilbo's birthday (*Fellowship* 51) provides him with a sense of continuity and connection. The rituals of courtly love offer Gimli a behavior pattern into which he can properly channel and enact his feelings for Galadriel. These rituals give him a legitimate way to respond to the "love and understanding" he sees "in the heart of an enemy" (*Fellowship* 137).

Superstition, amulets, and rituals were a part of many soldiers' ways of dealing with the war through magical thinking. Robert Graves, for example, held the superstition that if he remained a virgin he would survive the war (Fussell, *Great War* 124). In the nightmare landscapes of World War I, where traditional individual military acts were rendered meaningless by mortar-shell bombardment and poison gas, how many soldiers fantasized that there might be one thing, one seemingly insignificant but magical task, that could bring the bloody machinery of war to a grinding halt and restore life to the pastoral norm? A soldier's magical thinking becomes Frodo's quest.

Ritual helps define mutual roles, as when Frodo ritually takes responsibility for Gollum, formally swearing to Faramir to take the creature under his protection. "Sam sighed audibly; and not at the courtesies, of which, as any hobbit would, he thoroughly approved. Indeed in the Shire such a matter would have required a great many more words and bows" (*Towers* 299–300). Ritual is also a way to center and channel healing powers, as Aragorn does when he sings over the Morgul-blade that wounded Frodo (*Fellowship* 210). And ritual provides a template for responding to overwhelming events, as when Sam ritually passes through the stages of mourning and composes Frodo's body after the attack by Shelob (*Return* 340).

The way the hobbits joke about serious emotions has elements of ritual, as they do it to protect themselves from despair and to show "a decent solicitude" for the feelings of the person they are talking with (Fussell, *Great War* 182). After their capture by the orcs, Merry greets Pippin with, "So you've come on this little expedition, too? Where do we get bed and breakfast?" (*Towers* 52). Aragorn, knowing their ways through long acquaintanceship, teases Merry about his tobacco after healing him from the Black Breath (*Return* 146). These comic exchanges are reminders of the celebrated phlegmatic British restraint in the trenches, the "stoical reticence" and "formulaic understatement" that could lead a young officer to describe life in the trenches as "darned unpleasant," or the unrelenting rain as "a certain dampness" (Fussell, *Great War* 181). Legolas and Gimli demonstrate this trick of being "entirely unflappable" in their slightly macabre competition at the Battle of Helm's Deep. Bilbo sets the tone in *The Hobbit* when he describes the Battle of Five Armies as "very uncomfortable, not to say distressing" (*Hobbit* 297). Soldiers used formulaic phrases and stock jokes in their letters home—"hope this finds you as it leaves me," "in the pink," "keep smiling," "keep the home fires burning" (Fussell, *Great War* 182)—to reassure their families and friends. George MacDonald Fraser writes of the value of this kind of ritual reassurance: "Whatever sorrow was felt, there was no point in talking or brooding about it, much less in making, for form's sake, a parade of it. Better and healthier to forget it, and look to tomorrow. The celebrated British stiff upper lip, the resolve to conceal emotion which is not only embarrassing and useless, but harmful, is just plain common sense" (89). Undoubtedly, this is exactly how a hobbit would see it.

The number three, already significant in folklore and myth, gained additional resonance for soldiers in the Great War because of its association with the trench system (front, support, and reserve trenches) and the rhythm of life associated with it (a period in battle, in support, and in rest). Living under this "tripartite" system, as Fussell pointed out, led to a tendency to see everything as divisible by three (*Great War* 125). Counting off by threes to form work parties added its own "portentous implications" (*Great War* 127):

Which party would be sent forward into danger, and which two would stay behind in relative safety?

Tolkien uses the number three quite often in *The Hobbit* and *The Lord of the Rings*. For example, in *The Hobbit*, Gandalf speaks to the trolls three times (*Hobbit* 50), and the dwarves make three attempts to join the feasting woodland elves (*Hobbit* 163). In *The Lord of the Rings*, three of the hobbits have dreams in Tom Bombadil's house (Sam, however, sleeps like a log) (*Fellowship* 138–39). At the feast the night before the Council of Elrond, there are three carefully balanced and formulaic descriptions of Gandalf, Glorfindel, and Elrond (*Fellowship* 239). Saruman makes three attempts to seduce Théoden with his voice during the parley at Isengard (*Towers* 184). The list could go on. However, it is unlikely that the significance of the number three among the soldiers of the Great War did anything other than intensify the importance it already had to a student of folk- and fairy-tale. Still, some influence of this "tripartite" way of life may be found in the rhythm of action and relief in *The Hobbit* as compared to *The Lord of the Rings*. As I noted earlier, the action in *The Hobbit* does not usually go straight from activity to rest but includes a less adventurous or "support" interlude between the two.

"Romance" can be considered as a sort of meta-ritual, blending individual rituals into the pattern of the quest. Soldiers of a literary bent saw their lives taking on the quest-pattern; as Fussell points out, "The experiences of a man going up the line to his destiny cannot help seeming to him like those of a hero of medieval romance if his imagination has been steeped in actual literary romances or their equivalent" (*Great War* 135). Fussell lists the three stages of the quest as described by Northrop Frye (the journey, the struggle, and the exaltation of the hero) and comments that "it is impossible not to be struck by the similarity between this conventional 'romance' pattern and the standard experience re-enacted and formalized in memoirs of the war" (*Great War* 130). The writers who came closest to mythologizing their experiences, like David Jones in *In Parenthesis*, used the quest-romance to structure their stories, as Tolkien did in *The Hobbit* and *The Lord of the Rings*. The quest-structure and the hero's journeys of Bilbo and Frodo have been thoroughly examined elsewhere and clearly follow the pattern of separation, initiation, and return as defined by Joseph Campbell in *The Hero with a Thousand Faces* (30).[2]

Tied in with romance is the concept of chivalry. Some historians of World War I feel that chivalric ideals did far more harm than good; Michael Adams in *The Great Adventure*, for example, claimed that "[c]hivalry veneered the naked use of force" (71), and felt that "[w]hat developed was a frightful combination: the presence of advanced military technology alongside a warrior code that willed combat as a high male endeavor and refined the butcher instinct by associating it with the aura of the search for the grail" (72). Peter Parker in his *The Old Lie* said that "[c]hivalry, patriotism and self-sacrifice draped the less acceptable facts of warfare" (112–13); chivalry provided excellent recruiting slogans, monument inscriptions, and phrases for comforting the bereaved, but did not have much applicability in the trenches. Siegfried Sassoon accuses women of believing "[t]hat chivalry redeems the war's disgrace" ("Glory of Women"). But Fussell acknowledges the usefulness of chivalric romance literature to the individual soldier, who was able to use this framework to help him understand and cope with his memories (*Great War* 135–37), and Adams also admits that "while chivalry was a disaster militarily, it worked psychologically for the military. Through chivalry, soldiers could avoid confronting disturbing elements in their own makeup and the work they did" (70). In Tolkien's Middle-earth, there is a clear dividing line; the unmechanized forces of the West, particularly in Rohan and Gondor, are chivalric, and the antipastoral Enemy is not. But the chivalric ideal of war as a "high male endeavour" is questioned by Faramir, for one, who sees war as a means but not an end in itself, and thus finds another way to confront the "disturbing elements" of being a warrior.

The journey, or separation, stage of the quest is often characterized by rituals of meeting and parting, and by ritual interactions with strangers. When the nine companions prepare to leave Rivendell, the charge laid on Frodo, the parting gifts and advice, and the sounding of Boromir's horn are traditional signs of the beginning of a formal quest (*Fellowship* 288–94). Similar rituals take place in Lórien. *The Two Towers* is particularly rich in such interactions, as the companions pursue their several paths, beginning with the farewell to Boromir (*Towers* 19) and continuing with interactions with the Rohirrim, the Ents, and Faramir's company.

A failure to follow the script in these interactions, as when Gollum turns his back on the farewells between Faramir and Frodo (*Towers* 304), is a "refusal of the call" (J. Campbell 59); the character refuses the opportunity to take the hero's journey and cuts himself off from his community. The preliminaries to the Battle of the Five Armies in *The Hobbit* are conducted in a series of ritual exchanges that define each side's position, and it is when Thorin breaks the ritual sequence by shooting at the herald that battle becomes inevitable (*Hobbit* 277). Although Elrond laid no oath on the Ringbearer's companions, it is understood that they are to protect Frodo, and when Boromir breaks this unspoken promise and tries to take the Ring, he turns fatally aside from his hero-journey (*Fellowship* 414–16; *Towers* 16).

A hero who accomplishes the journey and the struggle is marked by a change that sets him apart from the community to which he returns. Frodo's inverse quest is similar to the experiences of the men in David Jones's *In Parenthesis* in that "the experience of the Soldier is taken . . . as representative of essential human experience" (Fussell, *Great War* 145). We all carry our burdens through enchanted and dangerous territories to No Man's Land and the undiscovered country beyond. Like a soldier, Frodo is called upon to offer himself up for sacrifice; the "Christ-soldier analogy," where the soldier "becomes a type of the crucified Christ" (Fussell, *Great War* 119), is explicit in the way Frodo understood he had to give everything up so that others may have it. Sam and Merry and Pippin settle back into the Shire seeming little changed, although Sam initially doesn't know how to explain his experiences to Rose in less than "a week's answer" (*Return* 288); however, Frodo, "wounded with knife, and sting, and tooth, and a long burden" (*Return* 268), can never be healed in Middle-earth.

Some of those who have been through an experience like the Great War, through such "inexpressible terror long and inexplicably endured" (Fussell, *Great War* 115), may feel like initiates in one of the ancient mystery religions; they cannot make their experiences comprehensible to those who have not shared them, whether it is taboo to discuss them or not. As Aragorn says in refusing to discuss his experiences in Moria, "the memory is very evil" (*Fellowship* 310). Fussell speculates that the problem may not lie so much in the inadequacy of language—the English language does after all contain such words as "blood, terror, agony" and worse—but in the fact that such truthful descriptions violate standards of gentility and optimism, and "no one is very interested in the bad news [soldiers] have to report. What listener wants to be torn and shaken when he doesn't have to be?" (*Great War* 169–70). Siegfried Sassoon wrote, "The man who had really endured the war at its worst was everlastingly differentiated from everyone except his fellow soldiers" (*Memoirs of an Infantry Officer* 280). K. James Gilchrist, in his analysis of the Great War's effect on C. S. Lewis, says: "Anyone studying war's effect on individuals understands that silence is no accurate measure of the impact of such experience. Overwhelming evidence, written, oral, and anecdotal, illustrates that innumerable veterans, radically traumatized in war, refuse to discuss their experiences, even peripherally, with even those closest to them—and if at all, only with other veterans" ("Lewis" 63).

Interestingly, Verlyn Flieger compares this inability to communicate on the part of Great War veterans to that of travelers returning from Faërie, although for them that which cannot be described is beautiful, not horrible (219). In his essay "On Fairy-stories," Tolkien says one of the qualities of Faërie is that it is indescribable ("On Fairy-stories" 10); Fussell comments on the "inadequacy of language itself to convey the facts about trench warfare" (*Great War* 170). Flieger goes on to say:

In the way that extremes can sometimes meet, War and Faërie have a certain resemblance to one another. Both are set beyond the reach of ordinary human experience. Both are equally indifferent to the needs of ordinary humanity. Both can change those who return. . . . Perhaps worst of all, both war and Faërie can change out of all recognition the wanderer's perception of the world to which he returns, so that never again can it be what it once was. (224)

THE SENSE OF NATIONAL LITERATURE

Fussell points out that the typical British soldier of World War I was surprisingly well versed in his literary heritage. Popular education and self-improvement had wide appeal at this time, and led to a feeling that literature was "near the center of normal experience" and accessible to all, not just to intellectuals (*Great War* 157–58). Letters written by Other Ranks show an unexpectedly broad range of literary allusion, not only demonstrating their familiarity with literature but also presupposing the same familiarity on the part of their correspondents at home. The efficiency of the postal service to the Front meant that a steady supply of books was available to the troops; *The Oxford Book of English Verse* was especially popular.[3]

At its simplest level, literature was a consolation and a reassurance. Many soldiers drew great comfort from comparing themselves to Christian in *The Pilgrim's Progress*. In the same way, many characters in *The Hobbit* and *The Lord of the Rings* have a thorough grounding in the songs and legends of Middle-earth, and can draw consolation from past events with which they feel connected. Bilbo feels comforted when he discovers his sword was forged in Gondolin "for the goblin-wars of which so many songs had been sung" (*Hobbit* 80). The dwarves use their songs to stiffen their resolve under siege. In "Farmer Giles of Ham," Giles "had a queer feeling of pride and encouragement when he learned that his sword was actually Tailbiter," a sword famous in dragon-slaying lore in the Middle Kingdom (*Farmer Giles* 35). When Gandalf tells Frodo the history of the Ring, he speaks of the alliance of Men and Elves at the end of the Second Age, and says, "This is a chapter of history which it might be good to recall; for there was sorrow then too, and gathering dark, but great valour, and great deeds that were not wholly vain" (*Fellowship* 61). Frodo's laughter at Sam's performance of *The Oliphaunt* "released him from hesitation" (*Towers* 255), and the besieged inhabitants of Minas Tirith took comfort in singing "amid the gloom some staves of the Lay of Nimrodel, or other songs of the Vale on Anduin out of vanished years" (*Return* 98).

Sam in particular is sensitive to the consolations of literature, cheering Frodo with his imaginings of how their tale might sound when their adventure is over (*Towers* 322), and in the Tower of Cirith Ungol, when things seem darkest: "[M]oved by what thought in his heart he could not tell, Sam began to sing. . . . He murmured old childish tunes out of the Shire, and snatches of Mr. Bilbo's rhymes that came to his mind like fleeting glimpses of the country of his home. And then suddenly new strength rose in him" (*Return* 184–85).

Familiarity with literature also helped the soldiers interpret their experiences, by finding "an analog in a well-known literary text" (Fussell, *Great War* 137), or by placing their experiences "in the tradition" so they can be understood (*Great War* 146). Again it is Sam, "crazy about stories of the old days" (*Fellowship* 32), and Tolkien's closest representation of the common but well-read soldier, who expresses this best:

"The brave things in the old tales and songs, Mr. Frodo: adventures, as I used to call them. I used to think that they were things the wonderful folk of the stories went out and looked for . . . because they were exciting and life was a bit dull. . . . But that's not the way of it with the tales that really mattered, or the ones that stay in the mind. Folk seem to have been just landed in them, usually. . . . But I expect they had lots of chances, like us, of turning back, only they didn't. And if they had, we shouldn't know, because they'd have been forgotten. We hear about those as just went on. . . . I wonder what sort of a tale we've fallen into?" (*Towers* 320–21)

Throughout *The Lord of the Rings*, characters comment that they feel like they are "inside a song" (*Fellowship* 365), or that they are taking part in an adventure with roots deep in the past. This feeling is underscored by the immense age of races like the Elves and the Ents, who actually lived through the old stories and to whom Men are but "a passing tale" (*Towers* 155); in fact, when Pippin tells Treebeard about Gandalf's death, he says, "The story seems to be going on, but I am afraid Gandalf has fallen out of it" (*Towers* 69). The imagery of "being in a song" is a logical development from Tolkien's underlying mythology, where originally the Valar sang the world into being. Participants in the Great War often had a sense that they were acting in a play—wearing costumes, delivering their lines, making grand entrances and final exits. This parallels Tolkien's metaphor of feeling like being inside a song or tale. Fussell comments that, in retrospect, because of the odd ironies and overall theatricality of the war, "sometimes it is really hard to shake off the conviction that this war has been written by someone" (*Great War* 241). Fraser says the same thing in his memoir of the Burma campaign during World War II: "War is like that, full of clichés, and of many incidents and speeches that you couldn't get away with in fiction" (17).

Aragorn, Sam, and the older Bilbo are all unusually conscious of their place in history and connections to the past and future through story. As Bilbo asks in Rivendell, "Don't adventures ever have an end? I suppose not. Someone else always has to carry on the story" (*Fellowship* 244). He wonders if he will live long enough to hear about Frodo's part in the story, and Gandalf reminds him, "If you had really started this affair, you might be expected to finish it. But you know well enough now that *starting* is too great a claim for any, and that only a small part is played in great deeds by any hero" (*Fellowship* 283).

Aragorn is always mindful of the weight of history behind him and the hopes riding on his success. Even Sam, who has little pretense about the importance of his part in history, knows that he is involved in a never-ending story. When Sam talks about the tale of Beren and Lúthien and realizes that the light in Galadriel's phial can be traced back to the Silmaril, he says, " 'Why, to think of it, we're in the same tale still! It's going on. Don't the great tales ever end?' 'No, they never end as tales. . . . But the people in them come, and go when their part's ended' " (*Towers* 321). And the last thing Sam says to Frodo on the slopes of Mount Doom before the Eagles come is: " 'What a tale we have been in, Mr. Frodo, haven't we? . . . I wish I could hear it told! Do you think they'll say: *Now comes the story of Nine-fingered Frodo and the Ring of Doom?* . . . I wish I could hear it! And I wonder how it will go on after our part' " (*Return* 228–29). Interestingly, Tolkien uses this same "in a story" imagery in a letter to his son Christopher in South Africa with the R.A.F.: "[I]n real life things are [not] as clear cut as in a story. . . . [A]ll stories feel like that when you are *in* them. You are inside a very great story!" (*Letters* 78).

The chapter "The Field of Cormallen" (*Return* 226–35) ties together all three of these themes. The history of the Ring-bearer's mission is placed in the national literature and turned into myth; the heroes are honored with great ceremony, which becomes part of an annual "national" ritual through the changed date of the New Year; and the whole is placed in an idyllic pastoral setting emphasizing healing, rebirth, and contrast to war. This is the idealized celebration of the returning warrior. In contrast, the Scouring of the Shire and the lack of respect for Frodo that so troubles Sam is reality seen through the "disillusionment of the returned veteran" (Shippey, *Century* 156). But as Frodo knows so well, it is the part of some heroes to give things up "so that others may keep them" (*Return* 309).

DEMONIZATION OF THE ENEMY: "FINGERS OF THE HAND OF MORGOTH"

One of the most vexing problems in considering the theology of Middle-earth is the question of the orcs. Do they have souls? If so, are they so far past redemption that it cannot even be considered an option for them? There is no indication in *The Lord of the Rings* that they are redeemable; none of the orcs are reported throwing down their arms and suing for mercy after Sauron's fall. But how could an unredeemable soul fit into Tolkien's theology?

Tom Shippey's chapter in *Tolkien and His Literary Resonances* contains an excellent examination of this question. A close study of the six conversations between orcs reported in *The Lord of the Rings* reveals that they "recognize the idea of goodness, appreciate humor, value loyalty, trust, group cohesion, and the ideal of a higher cause than themselves, and condemn failings from these ideals in others." As Shippey goes on to ask, "if they know what is right, how is it that they persist in wrong?" ("Orcs" 186). This vexed question, applicable to humanity itself, is one that concerned the other Inklings as well. Shippey sees a possible explanation in a comparison to C. S. Lewis's space trilogy, where some characters "have got into their state as willing conspirators with evil through initial weakness or necessity, reinforced by fear, and made to seem palatable or even admirable by the steady, dulling use of a rhetoric of smartness and shrewdness" ("Orcs" 187).

One of the roots of the depiction of the orcs could lie in common attitudes toward the enemy in World War I. There was a widespread exaggeration of the differences between "us" and "them," which Fussell calls "gross dichotomizing": " 'We' are all here on this side; 'the enemy' is over there. 'We' are individuals with names and personal identities; 'he' is a mere collective entity.

We are visible; he is invisible. We are normal; he is grotesque. Our appurtenances are normal; his, bizarre. He is not as good as we are" (*Great War* 75). An eyewitness to the march of the German army through Brussels in August 1914 reported that they had "lost the human quality," that they were "not men marching, but a force of nature like a tidal wave, an avalanche, or a river flooding its banks." It was "uncanny, inhuman"; their march had the "pertinacity of a steam-roller" (Davis 445–48).

Like the enemy in World War I, the orcs are described in terms of "animal figuration" (Fussell, *Great War* 77); they are creatures with fangs and have arms that hang to the ground, with clawlike hands; their tongues loll out and they lick the blood off their knives, and most cannot stand the daylight. Some eat man's-flesh, because they are the "fighting Uruk-Hai" and the servants of Saruman (*Towers* 49); this is reminiscent of the rumors of German "corpse-rendering plants" turning human cadavers into tallow for candles and lubricants (Fussell, *Great War* 116). The trolls at the Black Gate were especially to be feared because "these fell creatures would bite the throats of those that they threw down" (*Return* 169). The orcs use saw-edged knives, like the saw-edged bayonets the Germans were rumored to use because they caused nastier wounds (Fussell, *Great War* 117). They swarm like ants, and "wander witless and purposeless" when the will of Sauron is withdrawn from them (*Return* 227).

Tolkien may have used stereotypes, rumors, and propaganda about "the Hun" in his depiction of the orcs, but these did not reflect his own attitude toward the German people as individuals. In a letter to his son Michael, serving in World War II, he describes the Germans as enemies with the virtues of obedience, patriotism, bravery, and industry, led by a madman misusing and perverting the "northern spirit" he felt was so noble (*Letters* 55–56). During his own time as a soldier, he recalled speaking with a captured German officer and offering him water (Carpenter, *Tolkien* 84). Still, he did refuse a German publisher the right to issue a translation of *The Hobbit* because he was asked for a certificate of his Aryan origin (*Letters* 37).

Whatever other traits they may have had, depicting the orcs in conversation with a recognizably human (though crude) sense of humor, and with comprehensible motivations and attitudes, made them less alien and less easy to dismiss as soulless automatons. And the human troops on the side of Sauron were, like the Germans under Hitler, not entirely to blame that a madman led them. When Sam sees the Southron soldier fall in Ithilien, his reaction shares something of the spirit of the dedication to David Jones's *In Parentheses*: "to the enemy front-fighters who shared our pains against whom we found ourselves by misadventure" (Jones xvii). The human soldiers who surrender when Saruman and Sauron are defeated are treated by their captors as fellow human beings, not as soulless creatures.

As Shippey points out, the problem of the orcs continued to concern Tolkien throughout his life until he set down his "final view" of the question in the notes and essays collected in *Morgoth's Ring* by Christopher Tolkien. In the earliest notes, probably written in 1955 or 1959, Tolkien tried to work the "known facts" about orcs into his system. Orcs appear to have independent wills because they can criticize or rebel against Melkor or Sauron, so therefore they must be corruptions of something preexisting, since Melkor cannot create life. But the question remained: Could the orcs be "amended and 'saved'?" (*Morgoth's Ring* 409). In this set of notes he thought it unlikely that orcs could be corrupted Elves, and finally concluded that orcs were "beasts of humanized shape (to mock Men and Elves) deliberately perverted/ converted into a more close resemblance to Men. Their 'talking' was really reeling off 'records' set in them by Melkor. Even their rebellious critical words—he knew about them" (*Morgoth's Ring* 410). He speculated that "the wills of Orcs and Balrogs etc. are part of Melkor's power 'dispersed,' " and "[t]hey had little or no will when not actually 'attended to' by the mind of Sauron" (*Morgoth's Ring* 413).

However, in a later undated essay, somewhat more polished, he stated, "it is probable that these Orks [*sic*] had a mixed origin. Most of them plainly (and biologically) were corruptions of Elves (and probably later also of Men)." He went on to say that their leaders may in some cases have been corrupted minor spirits or Maiar (*Morgoth's Ring* 414).

The last essay on the origin of the orcs was probably written in 1959–1960. This more finished essay contradicts Tolkien's earlier writings on the topic in several places. He said that if Melkor had attempted to make creatures of his own, they would have been mere puppets and "would have acted only while the attention of his will was upon them." However, "Orcs were not of this kind." They were indeed corrupted, but it was "the corruption of independent wills. . . . They were capable of acting on their own, doing evil deeds unbidden for their own sport; or if Morgoth and his agents were far away, they might neglect his commands" (*Morgoth's Ring* 417–48). He pointed out that they continued to live, breed, and speak among themselves even after Morgoth was overthrown, and therefore had to have independent wills. In a letter to W. H. Auden in 1965, Tolkien said he was not sure if his "notion of orcs is heretical or not," but confirmed that "the orcs are not evil in origin" (*Letters* 355).

Did they have souls? Tolkien said that the Wise taught that "the Orcs were not 'made' by Melkor and therefore were not in their origin evil. They might have become irredeemable (at least by Elves and Men), but they remained within the Law. That is . . . [while] they must be fought with the utmost severity, they must not be dealt with in their own terms of cruelty and treachery. . . . If any Orcs surrendered and asked for mercy, they must be granted it, even at a cost" (*Morgoth's Ring* 419). In a note, Tolkien added, "Few Orcs ever did so in the Elder Days, and at no time would any Orc treat with any Elf." When Morgoth was defeated, the surviving orcs were leaderless and "almost witless." However, Sauron "achieved even greater control over his

Orcs than Morgoth had done" (*Morgoth's Ring* 419). In the interim, orcs had had enough independence of will to set up "petty realms of their own," but Sauron had such control that "they would sacrifice themselves without hesitation at his command" (*Morgoth's Ring* 420).

Tolkien's last fragmentary notes on the orcs, written in 1969, clarify the question of free will and control by "the State" in the form of Sauron:

Those orks [*sic*] who dwelt long under the immediate attention of his will . . . would act as herds, obeying instantly, as if with one will, his commands even if ordered to sacrifice their lives in his service. . . . [T]he greater part of the orks, though under his orders and the dark shadow of their fear of him, were only intermittently objects of his immediate thought and concern, and while that was removed they relapsed into independence and became conscious of their hatred of him and his tyranny. Then they might neglect his orders, or engage in [text ends]. (*Morgoth's Ring* 421–22)

What does this reflect about attitudes toward the Germans in World War I? Paul Fussell quotes one description of the world on the other side of the trenches as "peopled by men whose way of thinking was totally and absolutely distinct from our own" (*Great War* 77). Hate-spreading editorialists speculated whether or not the enemy was even human. The orcs are as alien and inhuman as the worst helmeted Huns depicted in the press for the purpose of stirring up civilian feelings against the enemy. Still, the orcs as depicted in *The Lord of the Rings* remain a conundrum only partially solved by the material in *Morgoth's Ring*. And as Hal Colebatch has intriguingly pointed out, "A book about orcs from the inside would have been a different kind of book" (94).

UNDERGROUND: "THE TROGLODYTE WORLD"

The enduring image of World War I warfare is the trench system that stretched across Europe from the North Sea shore of Belgium to the border of Switzerland at Beurnevisin. The front line was over 1,300 miles long, and with support and communication trenches added, along with their equivalents on both sides of the line, the total might have added up to nearly 25,000 miles (Fussell, *Great War* 37). Scars from these trenches can still be seen in northern France; the air smells rusty on damp mornings, and farmers occasionally plow up anonymous remains in the fields on the Somme (Keegan, *First World War* 4). Fussell points out that given the influence of the romantic poets and painters on the British aesthetic sense, and particularly the influence of Ruskin's *Modern Painters*, with its celebration of the natural world and the open sky, it is no wonder that the juxtaposition of unspoiled nature with the scars man left upon the land was such a prevalent theme in postwar literature (*Great War* 52–53).

In the flat landscape of Flanders, sunrises and sunsets, the rare moments of beauty detached from the battlefield, made a particular impression on those who wrote after the war. Siegfried Sassoon said once that "the sky was one of the redeeming features of the War" (*Memoirs of an Infantry Officer* 45). At these times, the men were able to look over the edges of the trenches and see more than just a narrow strip of sky. But the strategic advantage of attack at these times transformed the "Georgian literary symbolism of vague high hopes into a daily routine of quiet terror" (Fussell, *Great War* 60). Morning and evening "stand-to" were "moments of heightened ritual anxiety" (*Great War* 52), repeated every day at sunrise and sunset to watch for enemy movements and possible attack.

The breathless moment when the Rohirrim pause at the ruined north gate of the outwall of Minas Tirith exemplifies this feeling: Merry at first "neither saw any hope of morning, nor felt any wind, changed or unchanged"; King Théoden sat on his horse motionless, and "[t]ime seemed poised in uncertainty." Then the wind changes, the sun rises, and they see from afar the lightning flash of the fight between Gandalf and the Witch-king at the city gates. The king blows a blast on his horn and springs away, and the spell of morning stand-to is broken (*Return* 111–12). Frodo and Sam's night-journey with Gollum follows the inverted trench schedule of anxious rest during the day and cautious activity during the hours of darkness: " 'Day is near,' [Gollum] whispered, as if Day was something that might overhear him and spring on him" (*Towers* 228). At Helm's Deep, Aragorn steps out above the gates after battle has raged all night, and as he looks out to see the dawn, the orcs mine the gateway below him. Yet even as the archway falls, the Huorns appear and Erkenbrand and his troops arrive (*Towers* 145–57).

There are several places where Tolkien uses an underground motif that might have been influenced by his trench experiences. The hobbits, especially the wealthy and the poor, live in holes in the ground—not "nasty, dirty, wet" holes (*Hobbit* 11) like the actual British trenches in the field, but comfortable dugouts, more like the exhibition trench built in Kensington Gardens. This was "clean, dry, and well-furnished," the ideal trench designed to make the civilians feel their sons were not too badly off after all (Fussell, *Great War* 43). In fact the Baggins hobbit-hole is very like the German trenches captured by Tolkien's battalion. They were "deep, clean, [and] elaborate" and had "real kitchens, and wallpaper and overstuffed furniture. . . . Their occupants proposed to stay where they were" (Fussell, *Great War* 44–45). "Except that when we reached them," as Tolkien reported, "they faced the wrong way about" (Norman 4). The goblin-caves under the Misty Mountains possess more of the ambiance of the actual British trenches—"wet, cold, smelly, and thoroughly squalid" (Fussell, *Great War* 43). Shelob's nightmare tunnels are also evocative, with their "still, stagnant, heavy" air, their foul reek and "sense of lurking malice" (*Towers* 326–28).

As troops neared the front line, they entered a sloping communication trench, similar to the trench leading to the underground entrance to the Old

Forest; gradually the light narrowed to a strip of sky above. There was a sense of disorientation and claustrophobia in entering the trenches: "One saw two things only: the walls of an unlocalized, undifferentiated earth and the sky above" (Fussell, *Great War* 51).

Underground episodes abound in Tolkien's writings, and their symbolism has been examined in articles such as James Obertino's "Moria and Hades: Underworld Journeys in Tolkien and Virgil." Obertino speculates that for Tolkien, like many other Great War survivors, the trench experience set up an association with other underground spaces that "offered shelter yet para-doxically induced . . . horrifying fantasies about being buried alive" (157).

In mystery religions, going underground is often one of the stages of an initiation rite, a device that disorients the participant and separates him from his everyday life. It is speculated that a phase of the Eleusinian Mysteries included "dramatic representations" of the underworld, if not an actual un-derground rite (Beach), and the rites of Mithras, popular with Roman sol-diers, generally took place in "a small rectangular subterranean chamber . . . with a vaulted ceiling" (Ulansey). As a student of folk stories, Tolkien was surely aware of the mythological significance of underground adventures when he wrote about the goblin battle in the passages under the Misty Mountains and the terrifying uncertainty of entering Smaug's caverns in *The Hobbit*, or the disorienting tunnels of the mines of Moria, the ghosts crowding the Paths of the Dead, and the stench of Shelob's Lair in *The Lord of the Rings*. But the importance of this motif for Tolkien, and the vocabulary of images avail-able to him for describing it, may well have been augmented by his under-ground experiences in the Great War.

HOMOEROTICISM AND VULNERABILITY

Fussell defines the term "homoerotic" in the atmosphere of the Great War as implying a "sublimated (i.e., 'chaste') form of temporary homosexuality," akin to the " 'idealistic,' passionate but non-physical 'crushes' which most of the officers had experienced at public school" (*Great War* 272). What in-spired these wartime crushes was not just the attractiveness and proximity of their object, but the heartbreaking sense of his innocence and vulnerability. Handsome young soldiers were attractive in part because they were doomed. Generally this "protective affection" went from superior to subordinate, but sometimes the lower ranks had hero-worshipping crushes on their officers as well (Fussell, *Great War* 274). Faramir describes this latter type of "crush" in his analysis of Éowyn's attraction to Aragorn: "as a great captain may to a young soldier he seemed to you admirable" (*Return* 242).

David M. Craig alleges in his article "Queer Lodgings" that "the boundaries between male friendship and homosexuality were somewhat fluid" during World War I; not all of these homoerotic relationships were chaste, although Fussell is of the opinion that actual sexual relations were quite rare on the

Front. Craig argues that C. S. Lewis's "rigid separation between male friendship and homosexual feeling," as defined in *The Four Loves*, is unrealistic, but also quotes Tolkien's claim that he had never heard of homosexuality by the age of nineteen, in spite of his many close male friendships (Carpenter, *Tolkien* 45). Indeed Tolkien did quite rigidly and consciously separate his life of the mind with his male companions from domestic life with his wife, as shown by his letter on marriage to his son Michael (*Letters* 48–52). What Tolkien valued most in his masculine friendships was intellectual stimulation, although there was also a shared appreciation of nonsexual physical pleasures like food, drink, a good pipe, and a walk in the country. Tanya Wood called it "homosociality" and said "his intellectual and social needs were largely fulfilled by men" (T. C. Wood 102).

Without this background in mind, it can be easy to fall into the trap of reading too much into the descriptions of physical relationships between the male characters in *The Lord of the Rings*.[4] It can be difficult for us, as readers influenced by our surrounding culture, to read how Sam "tried to comfort Frodo with his arms and body" (*Return* 217), or witness Pippin cradling Merry's head in his lap and holding his hands after finding him wandering dazed through Minas Tirith (*Return* 135), without the intrusion of sexual imagery not intended by the author.

Yet these descriptions are perfectly within the tradition of sentimental and homoerotic Great War poetry. The wartime *Pietà* of a dead or wounded soldier in his companion's arms was a common theme, and meditations on the beauties of a lost companion even more so, as in poems like Wilfred Owen's "Disabled" or "*Dulce et Decorum Est.*" The lament for Boromir that begins *The Two Towers* draws on this tradition (and far earlier traditions as well, of course): Aragorn sings of "his head so proud, his face so fair," and he is described as Boromir the Tall, Boromir the Fair, and Boromir the Bold (*Towers* 19–20). Sam cradles the wounded Frodo in his arms in Cirith Ungol, feeling he could sit there "in endless happiness" if only he had time (*Return* 186), in a kind of reversed *Pietà*, with the beloved companion brought back from the brink of death.

There are many examples of visual works based on *The Lord of the Rings* that are very explicit soldierly *Pietàs* of this type. In the Peter Jackson movie *The Fellowship of the Ring*, for example, Aragorn and Boromir are in extensive physical contact and clasp each other's shoulders or forearms as Boromir dies, instead of Aragorn simply kneeling beside him as he does in the book (*Towers* 16; *The Lord of the Rings: The Fellowship of the Ring*, scene 38). The Michael Whelan painting of Sam and Frodo on the slopes of Mount Doom after the destruction of the Ring (Whelan) refers openly to Michelangelo's Vatican *Pietà* and lesser-known Palestrina *Pietà* in the Galleria dell'Accademia in Florence (*Representations*). In the *1980 J.R.R. Tolkien Calendar*, where the Whelan picture appeared, there is also a much clumsier painting of the death of Boromir, which copies one of Michelangelo's last

Pietàs, this one in the Florence Cathedral Museum (Brothers Gentile; Hartt and Finn 68). Other collections of Tolkien-inspired art include similar pictures.

Craig's observation that Frodo and Sam's relationship "is a story of love in the face of adversity" is a valuable one. While there is obviously a great deal of affection on both sides of the Sam-Frodo relationship, we see Sam's love for his master more than Frodo's love for his servant. But as Roger Sale has suggested, Frodo's love manifests itself more subtly, as "weary generosity" (235) and "lovely courtesy" (236). Sam is more open emotionally, and it is part of Frodo's nature to want to spare those he loves pain by hiding his thoughts and feelings—witness his attempts to move to Crickhollow secretly, leave the Fellowship at Parth Galen, and conceal his illness and his plan to go over the sea at the end. It is an unselfconsciously physical relationship because the culture of the Shire permits this kind of closeness, and also because of its purpose. W. H. Auden describes the master-servant relationship in literature in his essay "Balaam and His Ass": "The relationship between Master and Servant is not given by nature or fate but comes into being through an act of conscious volition. Nor is it erotic; an erotic relationship . . . comes into being in order to satisfy needs which are, in part, given by nature; the needs which are satisfied by a master-servant relationship are purely social and historical" (Auden, "Balaam" 107).

It may have begun as a contractual relationship where both parties agreed mutually on the terms and could renegotiate if necessary, but Sam also accompanied Frodo for some of the same reasons Auden feels Sancho Panza followed Don Quixote: "love of his master, and that equally unrealistic of motives, love of adventure for its own sake" ("Balaam" 137). As Sam says, "Me go and see Elves and all! Hooray!" (*Fellowship* 73). And as Auden points out in his analysis of the relationship between Phineas Fogg and his servant Passepartout in *Around the World in Eighty Days*, the contractual relationship is transcended when one party risks his life for the other; self-sacrifice "cannot be a clause in any contract" ("Balaam" 143) and raises the relationship to that of equals. Sam and Frodo risk their lives for each other too many times to stay on an unequal footing.

Describing an officer's feelings at watching his soldiers bathing naked became, as Fussell puts it, "a set-piece in almost every memory of the war. . . . [T]his conventional vignette of soldiers bathing under the eye of their young officer recurs not because soldiers bathe but because there's hardly a better way of projecting the awful vulnerability of mere naked flesh" (*Great War* 299). The leadership roles taken by Bilbo and Frodo are influenced by a sense of responsibility resulting from seeing the vulnerability of those they led, and Tolkien uses the device of bathing or nakedness to illustrate this process in several places.

In *The Hobbit*, the eagles carry the party to a rocky island called the Carrock, and Gandalf tells Bilbo and the dwarves he will be leaving them. After they fail to convince him to stay, they take off their clothes to bathe in the river and dry themselves in the sun (*Hobbit* 124–25). While Tolkien does not emphasize their nakedness in any way, it is interesting to note that after this scene Gandalf begins mentoring Bilbo quite obviously, explaining his strategy for approaching Beorn and advising him about the path ahead, and it is in Mirkwood that Bilbo begins to take on a leadership role, beginning with rescuing the dwarves from the spiders.

There are more examples in *The Lord of the Rings*. Before bathing in Crickhollow with Pippin and Sam, Frodo has a moment of dread about breaking the news that he will be leaving them as soon as possible. Their innocent exuberance makes it all the more difficult. He has been agonizing over telling his friends he must leave them and the Shire, and had decided long ago that he had to go alone and couldn't take his friends into deadly peril. When he does give in to their plans to accompany him, they call him "Captain Frodo" (*Fellowship* 115–16). Frodo is forced to take a leadership role in the episode on the Barrow-downs, awakening to find his friends threatened by the Barrow-wight. He takes responsibility for rescuing them, and afterward Tom tells them to "run naked on the grass" while he collects their ponies. Interestingly, Tom says, "You've found yourselves again, out of the deep water. Clothes are but little loss, if you escape from drowning" (*Fellowship* 155). As a metaphor for their danger in the Barrow, it is one well chosen to reinforce the hobbits' vulnerability. And when Merry is found on the road in Bree after encountering the Black Breath of the Nazgûl, he says "I thought I had fallen into deep water" (*Fellowship* 186).

These examples may stretch the analogy a bit, but two others are more significant. When Frodo and Sam are taken to the hidden caverns of Henneth Annûn, one of Faramir's guards discovers Gollum diving for fish in the pool below. Frodo sees his awful vulnerability—Gollum is "wretched and hungry, and unaware of his danger" (*Towers* 295). He listens to Gollum muttering with "pity and disgust" and wishes he could be "rid of the miserable voice forever" (*Towers* 297). But he realizes Gollum has a claim on him—the master has a responsibility toward the servant. He feels miserable about tricking him, and tries to reassure him that he will not be harmed. He promises to take Gollum under his protection, in terms much like those used by Théoden and Denethor when they swear Merry and Pippin respectively into their services. Similarly, when Sam finally finds Frodo in the tower of Cirith Ungol, he is lying naked and unconscious on a pile of filthy rags, whipped and beaten and in despair over the supposed loss of the Ring and end of the quest (*Return* 186). Frodo's brief madness when Sam offers to help carry the Ring and his obvious physical weakness make it clear to Sam that he will now have to be the stronger of the two, planning the rest of their journey, husbanding their food, directing and leading Frodo, and even carrying him when needed. From this point on Sam is the physical leader of their quest, taking on the responsibility of making sure Frodo will be able to complete his mission. It is Frodo's naked helplessness here, and earlier the piteous defenselessness of his supposed corpse, that prompt Sam to take a leadership role.

CONCLUSION

Tolkien was concerned with many of the same themes that interested other writers who were veterans of the Great War. The rhythm of the war flows through his writings, and with the ending of the Third Age, there is the same sense of a changed world, where one could only look back with longing nostalgia to a time that could never be recaptured. His own interpretation of these themes, symbols, and motifs, however, was influenced by his religious views and his interest in fantasy, which add another layer of meaning and a sense of timelessness to his writing.

NOTES

1. The commission maintains over 450 hectares of gardens around the world, and the website goes into some detail about the types of plants chosen for different climates and how the headstones are integrated into the plantings.

2. Anne Petty's *One Ring to Bind Them All*, for example, uses the work of Campbell, Vladimir Propp, and Claude Lévi-Strauss to analyze the plot of *The Lord of the Rings*.

3. Troops in the field during World War I had an incredible hunger for books. Four agencies were providing books and magazines to British troops in training and abroad almost from the beginning of the war: the British Red Cross and Order of St. John Library; the Camps Library; the YMCA; and the British Prisoners of War Book Scheme (Young 12). These served as models for the American Library Association's War Library Services program, which by the end of the war had distributed more than 10 million books on U.S. bases and abroad (Young xi). The ALA's central library in France became the core of the American Library in Paris, established in 1920 and still in existence today (*The American Library in Paris*).

4. In fact, the work lends itself particularly well to the form of fan fiction known as "slash," which posits homosexual relations between characters who have no such actual relationship in the source material. For examples, see "Least Expected: A Tolkien Slash Archive" at www.femgeeks.net/tolkien; Victoria Bitter's page at http://hosted.insanity-inc.org/vb/index.html; or the amusing "The Secret Diaries" at http://diaries.diagon.org. Be aware that these sites contain adult material.

Chapter 4

World War II: "The Young Perish and the Old Linger, Withering"

War [is] a time of human plague when, as the historian Herodotus said,
fathers bury sons, rather than sons fathers.

—Hanson, *Autumn* 64

J.R.R. Tolkien wrote much of *The Lord of the Rings* during World War II,
but denied that his work had any allegorical relationship to the war. In the
foreword to the second edition, he asserted: "The crucial chapter . . . was
written long before the foreshadow of 1939 had yet become a threat of inevitable disaster, and from that point the story would have developed along
essentially the same lines, if that disaster had been averted. . . . [L]ittle or
nothing in it was modified by the war that began in 1939 or its sequels. The
real war does not resemble the legendary war in its process or its conclusion"
(*Fellowship* 6–7).

However, there are themes throughout the work that reflect his perspective
as a parent of two combatants and as a veteran of an earlier war, and there
are plot elements that reveal the attention he paid to world events as he
wrote. As he admits later in the foreword, "an author cannot remain wholly
unaffected by his experience" (*Fellowship* 7), and he said early in its writing
that "[t]he darkness of the present days has had some effect on it" (*Letters*
41). There is no denying that the second global war in his lifetime was taking
place in the world outside his Middle-earth, and that Tolkien was deeply affected by it. It is obvious from his letters during this time that he paid a great
deal of attention to the military and political issues of the day and discussed
events with his correspondents, including both major news like D-Day (*Letters*

84) and the bombing of Hiroshima and Nagasaki (*Letters* 116), and less dramatic occasions like summit meetings and elections.

While I feel that thematically and stylistically *The Lord of the Rings* is in many ways more clearly a product of his World War I experiences, the World War II elements are worth studying for the additional light they shed on Tolkien's attitudes toward war in general, and modern warfare in particular. As Meredith Veldman has pointed out, "World War II did not shape Tolkien's myth; rather, his myth shaped his experience of the war" (88). The roots of Tolkien's thoughts on war lie in the Great War, just as the roots of World War II do; as John Keegan points out, "no explanation of the causes of the Second World War can stand without reference to those roots" (*First World War* 3), and the same applies to Tolkien's philosophy on war. This chapter will examine some of the World War II themes and motifs in *The Lord of the Rings* and Tolkien's *Letters*, and compare them to the prewar *Hobbit*.

TOLKIEN AS A POST-WORLD WAR II WRITER

Some of the earliest critics of *The Lord of the Rings* saw the work as an allegory of World War II, so much so that Tolkien felt it necessary to deny any such intent in the foreword to the second edition. *The Lord of the Rings* was, after all, begun in 1936, while the "awful rumour" of war was building; parts of it were sent in serial form to his son Christopher, serving in the Royal Air Force in South Africa; and it was finished in 1949, several years after the end of the war. It is understandable that these critics viewed the Ring as an allegory for the Bomb. As Brian Rosebury puts it: "[R]eaders living in the 1950s, in a world reconstructing itself after the Second World War, might be forgiven for missing the emotional depth of a work whose origins lie, far below its surface, in private and public events of a much earlier date; or for misconstruing the work as an allegorical commentary (unaccountably inflated in scale) on the recent events which for them were formative: the war against Hitler, the encroaching 'shadow of the Bomb' " (134). Veldman agrees that "[t]he desire to decipher the code and to reduce Tolkien's work to an elaborate puzzle obscured the intentions of Tolkien's work from many readers" (106). Verlyn Flieger points out, "To subject it to such a reading is to ignore chronology and to reduce a rich and densely textured narrative to a political tract" (7). Tolkien's work on Middle-earth actually began years earlier, during World War I.

In fact, in May 1944, well before Hiroshima, Tolkien was already writing to his son that the Allies were "attempting to conquer Sauron with the Ring," referring not to the Bomb but to allied tactics and air power (*Letters* 78). And in a long letter to Rayner Unwin in 1955, Tolkien explicitly states that although Book Four was sent with his letters to Christopher in South Africa, and the remaining two books were drafted in 1944–1948, "[t]hat of course does not mean that the main idea of the story was a war-product" (*Letters*

216). In Tolkien's opinion, the germ of the story—the matter of the Ring—is visible from Book One, Chapter Two, which Tolkien first drafted sometime in 1937.

A few recent critical works examine this position more plausibly, focusing less on one-to-one correlations between Tolkien's work and real-world events, and more on the broader picture. John A. Ellison, in his 1989 article " 'The Legendary War and the Real One': *The Lord of the Rings* and the Climate of Its Times," argues that the early success of the book was due to a readership "who had had the Second World War as a central part of their experience" and therefore "saw embodied the truth of their own experience" (20). However, this is a logical fallacy, arguing from results back to causes. In truth, what Tolkien's readers brought to the books had nothing to do with what he put in them; that his readers saw their own unique individual experiences mirrored in the books supports Tolkien's own argument that allegory resides in the purposed dominion of the author and applicability in the freedom of the reader (*Fellowship* 7). To quote Flieger again, "[a] story need not be about a particular war in order to show its effects. . . . The most effective commentary on an age or an event is as often as not oblique rather than direct" (8).

Ellison's most interesting passage, on the "odd but diverting impression of amateurishness pervading much of *The Fellowship of the Ring*" (18), which he compares to the "Phony War" stage of World War II before Churchill became prime minister in 1940, could as easily apply to the early stages of Britain's involvement in World War I. Barliman Butterbur tells the hobbits in Bree, "you want looking after and no mistake" (*Fellowship* 211), and Gandalf tells Frodo in Rivendell that he is lucky to be alive, after "all the absurd things" he did after leaving home (*Fellowship* 231). The younger hobbits especially have no idea of the scope of events they are soon to be involved in, finding the whole thing, as Paul Fussell says of the British in 1914, "strenuous but entertaining" (*Great War* 25). In Moria, Gandalf has to chastise Pippin for dropping a pebble down a well: "Fool of a Took! . . . This is a serious journey, not a hobbit walking-party" (*Fellowship* 327). It was only after the start of the Battle of the Somme that "the innocent army fully attained the knowledge of good and evil" (Fussell, *Great War* 29); it could be argued that it is only after Gandalf falls in Moria that Merry and Pippin begin to understand the stakes, and only after their capture by orcs that they are compelled to a mature understanding of their own personal danger. But this is true of almost any war, not just the two world wars; the early stages are usually marked by tentativeness and blundering, and Ellison's arguments do more to show the applicability of Tolkien's work to armed conflict in general than to any particular war.

Tom Shippey clearly stated that he felt Tolkien belonged to a post–World War II group of writers in his 1993 article "Tolkien as a Post-War Writer," but in his recent book *J.R.R. Tolkien: Author of the Century*, he modifies this view somewhat and gives almost equal time to World War I influences. In the original article Shippey considered *The Lord of the Rings* as part of a group of post–World War II nonrealistic works including *The Lord of the Flies* (William Golding), *Nineteen Eighty-Four* (George Orwell), *Animal Farm* (also by Orwell), *That Hideous Strength* (Tolkien's close friend C. S. Lewis), and *The Once and Future King* (T. H. White). He felt that all of these works were similar because they dealt with the question of evil and were marked by their authors' war experiences. They stand apart from the mainstream of post–World War II literature because the authors chose the fantastic mode to communicate their themes. He particularly notes that these books "were all effectively or as regards their major impact post–World War II by publication date" ("Post-War" 85). He also sees their writing as in part a reaction to between-the-wars literature, dominated as it was by cynicism and a type of pacifism that believed more in the rejection of all forms of violence than in the active pursuit of peace.

Shippey expands on this theme in *J.R.R. Tolkien: Author of the Century*, and calls the writers of these and a few selected other works "traumatized authors": they are all writers who have lived through war or similarly traumatic events, and have reacted by writing in the fantastic mode about questions of human evil. In the book he adds *Slaughterhouse-Five* by Kurt Vonnegut (present at the bombing of Dresden) and the short story "The Ones Who Walk Away from Omelas" by Ursula K. Le Guin (intimately familiar through her father's work with the last survivor of the genocide of the Yahi Indians of California) to his original list (*Century* xxx).[1]

Shippey raised the question in his article: Which war influenced Tolkien the most? Chronologically, all of these works were published between 1945 and 1958. All of the authors in the original article lived through both world wars, though only Tolkien and Lewis served in the first one; T. H. White was the only one never in active service during a war. White may come closest to Tolkien's medievalism in style and subject matter. However, his dark pessimism about *homo ferox* and his emphasis on the centrality of sex and "the human urge to murder" (*Century* 159) to the whole matter of Britain in the later parts of the story may mark *The Once and Future King* as more influenced by World War II (as well, of course, as by the original source material). As useful as it is to consider Tolkien among Shippey's traumatized authors, the other authors in this group seem much more clearly influenced by World War II, or later wars, in terms of both their conclusions about the evil inherent in man and their literary style. Shippey summed up their conclusions on evil: Orwell could find no coherent explanation, Lewis tried to revive a religious explanation, White thought the problem genetic, and Golding had elements of the other three mixed together ("Post-War" 88). In some of his recent criticism, Shippey has been exploring the notion that Tolkien thought of evil as an addiction, with its effects manifested in the way the One Ring and the nine rings "for mortal men" turn their wearers into wraiths, and the idea is a compelling one (see "Tolkien as a Post-War Writer" 89; *J.R.R. Tolkien: Author of the Century* chap. 3; and "Orcs, Wraiths, Wights" in *Tolkien and His Literary Resonances*).

In *Author of the Century*, Shippey discusses Tolkien's own dissection of the allegorical reading of *The Lord of the Rings*. Tolkien's point in rejecting this reading was that a true allegory should have a one-to-one correspondence with its subject, and this is emphatically not the case with *The Lord of the Rings* and World War II. Nevertheless, the "[h]ints of correspondence between our history and the history of Middle-earth are in fact fairly frequent," as Shippey demonstrates (*Century* 164). There is an echo of Neville Chamberlain's "peace in our time" speech in Frodo saying, "I wish it need not have happened in my time" (*Fellowship* 60), and Gandalf emphasizes several times that the whole concept of appeasement must be rejected. The fortification of the Rammas Echor, the outwall of Minas Tirith, is a reminder of the futility of the Maginot Line, which gave France a false sense of security against German invasion. Sauron's offer to the armies assembled at the Gates of Mordor is "in effect the creation of a demilitarized zone, with what one can only call Vichy status, which will pay war-reparations, and be governed by what one can again only call a Quisling" (Shippey, *Century* 166). Charles Nelson also directs our attention to another parallel in his recent article on the seven deadly sins in Middle-earth: "Saruman's long disquisition on the exercise of power refers to the old order and formal alliance that must be swept away along with sneering asides about the fading races. . . . His argument . . . echoes Hitler's justifications for World War II" (86).

The situation in the Shire under Sharkey, despite Tolkien's denials, does have a great deal in common with the situation in England under the Socialist government of 1945–1950—the "gatherers" and the "sharers," plenty of production for export and not much for distribution at home, the rhetoric of "fair distribution" masking corruption and profit making. As Shippey suggests, "the overall picture was one all too familiar to post-war Britons . . . poor food, ration-books, endemic shortages, and a rash of 'prefabs' and jerry-built 'council houses.' " But as he is quick to point out, creating a "mere allegory" for the postwar situation would be a "petty and transient conclusion for a work of such scope" (*Century* 168).

Alex Lewis illustrates another echo of the World War II era in *The Lord of the Rings*. During the war, many Londoners were evacuated to Oxford, which had been declared a "safe city" and therefore exempt from bombing (although its close neighbors Coventry and Exeter were attacked). Only one enemy plane is known to have flown over Oxford, and its mission was to photograph the Cowley automotive works. This temporary influx of refugees came on top of a 26 percent rate of increase of population from 1921 to 1931, and was followed by a 23 percent growth rate from 1931 to 1950. Lewis points out the similarity of the situation to that when the Southron refugees started to appear in Bree at the time of Frodo's first visit: "If room isn't found for them, they'll find it for themselves. They've a right to live, same as other folk" (*Fellowship* 168). The Oxford character was being diluted; "[t]he Sam Gamgees of Oxfordshire were becoming a rarity" (A. Lewis, "Lost Heart" 35–36). However, immigration, overcrowding, and the loss of local characteristics were not unique to Tolkien's Oxford by any means.

If there is one piece of published writing by Tolkien that seems to exhibit a strong World War II influence, it is the short story "Leaf by Niggle." The work was originally written just before the war began and read aloud to the Inklings in early 1940, and as Sebastian Knowles writes in *A Purgatorial Flame*, it "is thus a product of the pre-war twilight, the purgatorial period after Munich and before the fall of France" (135). Tolkien was stalled in his writing of *The Lord of the Rings*. He had been unwell, and the state of the world was depressing: "the war had arisen to darken all horizons" (cited Knowles 136). As Knowles argues, "That Niggle's purgatory is a response to war has gone unnoticed in Inklings criticism mainly because critics are looking for the war in the wrong place. The most common snare is to perceive *The Lord of the Rings* as an allegory of war" (136). In a short stand-alone work unconnected with his Middle-earth sub-creation, Tolkien had the freedom to examine some World War II issues more directly, particularly the implications of socialism and the place of art in a society of scarcity.

Verlyn Flieger also points to references to World War II in the unfinished book *The Lost Road*, written before the start of World War II and full of the sense of a time "balanced uneasily on the wreckage of the past, about to tip into an ominous future" (63–64), and in the later book *The Notion Club Papers*, set in what might be termed an "alternate history" Oxford, after a "Six Year's War" in which "an atomic explosion has created a black hole in the United States" (129). Tolkien did not ignore world events and was capable of using parallels to them in Middle-earth where applicable, but the fact that a one-to-one correspondence does not exist shows that he was not creating an allegory but rather allowing the reader to find instances of applicability, both to Tolkien's time and to his own.

CHARACTERISTICS OF WORLD WAR II LITERATURE

Apart from the chronology of its antecedents and the author's own statements about the war's lack of influence on the plot of his story, there are other reasons why *The Lord of the Rings* does not fit in with mainstream post–World War II writing. There is little if any evidence of any distinctively and clearly World War II influence on its themes or style.

Paul Fussell discusses the typical themes and characteristics of World War II literature in *Wartime: Understanding and Behavior in the Second World War*. One recurring theme is the distrust of authority, traceable to three main causes: the prevalence of "blunders, accidents, and errors" (*Wartime*

26) by both military and civilian leaders; the use of propaganda and rumors by both sides in psychological warfare and on their own troops (*Wartime* 35–48); and the "ideological vacuum" (*Wartime* 129) resulting both from a lack of a clear meaning and purpose for fighting, and from the "demoralizing . . . repetition of the Great War within a generation" (*Wartime* 132). The fact that civilians at home were under direct and sustained attack made the British troops surer of their purpose than the Americans; however, common soldiers from both countries frequently said the reason for fighting World War II was simply "to get home" (*Wartime* 141). There was no romanticism to the beginning of World War II—no Rupert Brooke writing in all sincerity, "Now, God be thanked Who has matched us with His hour" (Brooke). Fussell quotes Robert E. Sherwood's remark that this was the first war "in which general disillusionment preceded the firing of the first shot" (quoted *Wartime* 132).

Tolkien rejects disillusionment as antithetical to his theory of courage, where the highest good is to go on without hope and the gravest sin is defeatism. There is notably little mistrust of authority among the allies in *The Lord of the Rings*, and this may be because blind obedience to orders is not expected by leaders like Aragorn, Faramir, and Théoden. Among the Riders of Rohan, in particular, warriors "surrender less of their independence to their superiors than we do" (Shippey, *Century* 96). Authority rightly held and fairly used is respected, not resented; there is no question that Aragorn, by virtue of his ancestry, experience, and demonstrated ability, is competent to lead. Saruman's authority as the duly appointed head of the White Council is not mistrusted, despite his odd behavior, until Gandalf reveals his treachery at the Council of Elrond. This is typical World War I behavior; as the introduction to George Ashurst's autobiography *My Bit* points out, "[a]uthority was accepted instinctively, even when those wielding it were disliked" (Ashurst 9). There is some evidence of resented authority on the enemy's side, however; for example, some of the orcs express a desire to go someplace where there are "no big bosses" after the war (*Towers* 347). But on the side of the allies, even when a leader makes a questionable decision or rule, their followers may argue the decision but do not distrust the authority to make it.

There are few "blunders, accidents, and errors" on the part of the Free Peoples. Perhaps the only examples are some of Denethor's decisions, such as his insistence on pointlessly fortifying the Pelennor Wall (*Return* 21, 89–90), which merely serves to slow down the Rohirrim when they have to fight through the enemy forces who have taken it. Enemy leaders are more feared than respected by their troops, and some of the orcs do express doubts about their leadership abilities. Uglúk of Isengard and Grishnákh of Barad-dûr revile each other's leaders in their march across Rohan with the captured Merry and Pippin (*Towers* 49, 55). In the tunnel under Cirith Ungol Sam overhears Gorbag saying, "But they can make mistakes, even the Top Ones can" (*Towers* 346); "ay, even the Biggest, can make mistakes" (*Towers* 347). And when

Sam and Frodo are hiding from the pair of orcs seeking them in the jagged peaks of the Morgai, both the tracker and the soldier express doubts about their leaders' knowledge and abilities (*Return* 202).

However, there are some blunders, born of mercy, that in the end wind up benefiting the allies. In *The Hobbit*, Bilbo lets Gollum live. "What a pity that Bilbo did not stab that vile creature, when he had a chance!" cries Frodo, and Gandalf answers him "Pity? It was Pity that stayed his hand. . . . My heart tells me that he has some part to play yet" (*Fellowship* 68–69). The Elves of Mirkwood allow Gollum to climb the trees to feel the wind at their tops, hoping for his cure—"we had not the heart to keep him ever in dungeons under the earth" (*Fellowship* 268). Gollum escapes them, but in the end his treachery is essential to the eucatastrophe on Mount Doom.

There are a number of examples of the enemy side employing psychological warfare tactics. Sauron feeds false information to Denethor (*Return* 132, 154), and his lieutenant shows the mithril mail and elven cloak to the allies at the Gates of Mordor (*Return* 165). Sauron uses the debilitating psychological effects of terror by catapulting the heads of fallen defenders into Minas Tirith and having the Nazgûl fly low over the city. The enemy leaders also use these tactics on their own people: Saruman lies to his allies the Dunlendings about how the men of Rohan would treat them if they were defeated (*Towers* 150), and the orc captains Shagrat and Gorbag are well aware that their leaders have placed spies among their own troops (*Towers* 346).

However, the allied leaders do not use any tactics like this on their own soldiers; there is too much mutual respect between the leader and the led. The closest approach to this might be in some of Denethor's manipulations of Faramir, but this is part of his personal psychological war against his surviving son, and not a matter of Denethor's policy toward his troops in general—and in any case, Denethor was already under Sauron's influence at this point.

There is also no ideological vacuum on the side of the allies—almost all know the reason why they are fighting, and understand the stakes. Beregond, who calls himself "a plain man of arms," has a long conversation with Pippin in Gondor where he shows himself to be exceedingly well informed about the causes and consequences of the war (*Return* 37–39). There would have been little need of a series of *Why We Fight* movies among the Free Peoples (Fussell, *Wartime* 138), although there are some soldiers in the march to the Black Gate who "walked like men in a hideous dream come true, and they understood not this war nor why fate should lead them to such a pass" (*Return* 162). Aragorn sends these men to free Cair Andros, as a task better suited to their understanding. If there is any vast ideological vacuum in Middle-earth, it is on the part of some of the human allies of Mordor, forced to fight in a war they do not have a real stake in, far from their own lands, and who, in the aftermath of Sauron's destruction, "cast their weapons down and sued for mercy" (*Return* 227). The enemy leaders of Middle-earth personify the failings the enlisted men saw in their own leaders during World War II, but the allies represent an idealized relationship between the leaders and the led.

Another characteristically World War II theme is the conflict between the individual and the officially sanctioned uniformity and anonymity of the soldier. In contrast to the poetry of the Great War, poems of World War II do not typically name or describe individuals; they speak of "The Ball Turret Gunner" (Randall Jarrell, cited Fussell, *Wartime* 67) or the nameless pilot and observer of "When a Beau Goes In" (Gavin Ewart, cited *Wartime* 140). The war was intolerant of "individualistic performances" (*Wartime* 74); this was the war in which GI Joe became the generic term for the American soldier. Jean Cocteau called it "the conspiracy of the plural against the singular" (cited *Wartime* 69). "[I]n the Second World War you're one of sixteen million. You might as well be an inert item of Government Issue, like a mess kit or tool, entrenching" (*Wartime* 70).

But in Middle-earth, even common soldiers among the allies are not anonymous; consider the lists of the dead of Rohan, for example (*Return* 124–25), or of the Hobbits killed in the Scouring of the Shire. Aragorn is mindful of individual variation in capabilities and bravery when he provides some troops with the option of retaking Cair Andros instead of going to the Gates of Mordor (*Return* 162). Individual performance is highly important and can turn the tide of a battle, the prime examples being Bard shooting down Smaug, and Merry and Éowyn conquering the Witch-king. We even witness individuality among the enemy's troops, in Sam's brief meditation on the dead Southron in Ithilien (*Towers* 269), and in the portrayal of some of the orcs of Isengard and Minas Morgul. But in general, we see Saruman and Sauron treating their troops as faceless interchangeable parts; think of the seething masses hoisting ladders at Helm's Deep or wielding the battering ram Grond at the gates of Minas Tirith.

Typically, the English-language literature of World War II was also far more hetero-erotic than that of the Great War. This was no longer an exclusively male world, with an officer class drawn from the even more exclusively male world of the British public school system. World War II literature is far more concerned with heterosexual sex than with homoerotic friendship, and there is an unfortunate corresponding coarsening of language and response (Fussell, *Wartime* 148) and an increasing use of obscenity (*Wartime* 92). This was also a more secular war (*Wartime* 51), in spite of the chaplain corps and the pocket-sized New Testaments. Fussell notes that by the time of the Second World War, *The Pilgrim's Progress*, familiar to both the highly educated officer class and the Other Ranks in World War I, "is almost never invoked, let alone read" (*Wartime* 232).

The emphasis is on male friendship rather than romantic male-female relationships throughout *The Lord of the Rings*; although romance is not entirely neglected, it is the friendships, particularly that of Sam and Frodo, that are at the center of the story. And it would be difficult to find a coarsening of response or casual use of obscenity anywhere in the work, particularly on the part of the allies. Even the orcs seem rather restrained and entirely PG-13 in their language. There is no overt sexual obscenity in any of the evil Tolkien depicts. The closest thing we see to this is a bare hint at Wormtongue's lust for Éowyn (*Towers* 124), a hint greatly expanded on in Peter Jackson's movie. It is possible to read Shelob's attack on Frodo and Sam as "female sexuality run rampant . . . a grim perversion of the sex-act" (Craig 13), an "attempted female rape of Sam . . . almost embarrassingly explicit" (Otty 177), or "a violent sexual struggle between man and woman" (Partridge 190); however, because of the way Tolkien handles this sequence, it actually takes a conscious effort to detach this scene from its surroundings and read it this way. Whatever various critical schools may make of authorial intent, it is extremely unlikely Tolkien had any conscious desire to have it interpreted in this manner at all.

The Lord of the Rings is most emphatically not a secular work, and its underlying themes are deeply religious. Enough has been written on this elsewhere, and particularly in Tolkien's own letters, that I will only mention that the lack of any overt religious practice (aside from the Standing Silence observed by the men of Gondor before meals) can make it seem thoroughly secular if read shallowly, and therefore more typical of World War II than World War I. But it takes very little effort to read below this surface, and a reader who misses this the first time is not likely to pass over it again.

TOLKIEN'S PERSONAL LIFE AS INFLUENCE

Tolkien's perspective as a veteran, as a "traumatized author" in Shippey's phrase, gave him an outlook on World War II not shared by most of the young men and women then enlisting. A veteran's point of view may be seen in *The Hobbit*, in Bilbo's comment after the Battle of Five Armies: "Victory after all I suppose! . . . Well, it seems a very gloomy business" (*Hobbit* 299). However, the outbreak of a second global war in his lifetime added another dimension to his writing of *The Lord of the Rings*. We can see some of his insights on the retrospective futility of World War I in a speech by Elrond, who remembers the last great battle with Sauron and the years between the wars: "Sauron was diminished, but not destroyed. His Ring was lost but not unmade. The Dark Tower was broken, but its foundations were not removed" (*Fellowship* 257). In Frodo's plaintive yearning "I wish it need not have happened in my time" (*Fellowship* 60) is an echo of Tolkien's own feeling of darkening horizons.

However, there is an aspect of *The Lord of the Rings* that sets it apart from Tolkien's prewar writing and shows the influence of World War II in a somewhat unexpected way. During this war, Tolkien was not just a veteran and an active participant in homeland defense efforts, but also the parent of two combatants. Michael became an antiaircraft gunner and saw active duty

defending aerodromes in Britain and France. Christopher joined the Royal
Air Force and was sent to South Africa to train as a fighter pilot. Tolkien's
eldest son John, though not in the armed forces, was training for the priest-
hood in Rome and had to be evacuated from Italy shortly before the war
broke out (Carpenter, *Tolkien* 193; Tolkien and Tolkien 70–71; a chronology
of the Tolkien family's involvement in World War II is given in the appendices).

All this gave Tolkien an additional perspective on war to explore in his
writing. It is not World War II itself, but the new and personal experience
of being an anxious parent of grown children in active military service that
gives his writing on war an added poignancy. Losing a parent was sadly familiar to the orphaned Tolkien, but the possibility of losing a child was something frighteningly new and different. In fact, in one letter to Christopher he
very pointedly comments that too many of the leaders of the war are childless
and view the war from a safe "vantage point [in their] large motor-cars"
(*Letters* 89). George MacDonald Fraser, writing about his family's experiences at home during World War II, comments, "whatever anxieties the soldier may experience in the field can be nothing to the torment of those at
home. I don't know how parents and wives stand it" (73).

In Tolkien's letters to Christopher in South Africa, what could have been
more natural than to think back on his own war experiences? Tolkien even
admits a nostalgic desire to revisit the trenches and roads of northern France,
the scene of his World War I service (*Letters* 111). In his letter of April 18,
1944 (*Letters* 71–73), Tolkien compares Christopher's situation in the Royal
Air Force to his own in the trenches of World War I, and comments on the
prevalence of stupidity in wartime. He hopes that the experience will prove
useful for Christopher in the future, as his did. "May you, too, escape—
strengthened," he writes (*Letters* 77). All of his letters to Christopher and
Michael are full of a tender concern for their physical and spiritual safety and
a longing to be able to share their danger.

How does this theme work out in Tolkien's fiction? In the pre–World War
II *Hobbit*, there are no actual parent/child pairs. The closest relatives are
Thorin and his nephews, Fili and Kili. Gandalf may be parentlike, but he is
never worried about Bilbo in the same way he is concerned for Frodo's safety
in *The Lord of the Rings*. There was no global war going on, and the thought
of his own children ever serving in the military was probably not uppermost
in Tolkien's mind. The Shire is a peaceful country, and war is part of the
distant past—"Swords in these parts are mostly blunt, and axes are used for
trees, and shields as cradles or dish-covers" (*Hobbit* 30). Children never seem
to die before their parents. However, there are many parent/child pairs in
The Lord of the Rings, and Tolkien explores a variety of parental reactions
to the risks their children run in war. Consciously or not, Tolkien may have
been examining all the ramifications of his possible reactions to what could
happen to Michael and Christopher, and what might have happened to Pris-

cilla if she could have served in combat, or to John if he hadn't left Rome in time.

Fittingly, the first parent/child pair we encounter is Bilbo Baggins and his adopted heir Frodo. He is troubled to learn of the danger he put Frodo in by giving him the Ring: "I am sorry: sorry you have come in for this burden: sorry about everything" (*Fellowship* 244). Gandalf says of Bilbo that he "would never have passed on to you anything that he thought would be a danger" (*Fellowship* 56). Bilbo tries to take on the quest himself during the Council of Elrond (*Fellowship* 283), and gives Frodo his sword Sting and his mithril coat to keep him safe. When Frodo later learns that his mail coat is worth the price of the Shire, he "felt no doubt that Bilbo knew quite well" what a "kingly gift" this was (*Fellowship* 330). In Bilbo, we see a parent figure with a deep concern for his child, willing to take the danger of his task on himself if only it were possible. It is similar to the feelings Tolkien expresses in his letters to Christopher and Michael: "If only I could do something active!" (*Letters* 55).

Among the hobbits, we also have a few glimpses of the relationship between Hamfast Gamgee and his youngest son, Sam. He is a bit puzzled by Sam's appetite for Bilbo's tales and interest in the wider world: "Mr. Bilbo has learned him his letters—meaning no harm, mark you, and I hope no harm will come of it" (*Fellowship* 32). In the Emyn Muil, when Sam chastises himself for forgetting the rope in his pack, he recalls his gaffer, calling him "nowt but a ninnyhammer" (*Towers* 214). But Sam thinks of his father's teasing with fondness at the Black Gate: " 'My word, but the Gaffer would have a thing or two to say, if he saw me now! . . . But now I don't suppose I'll ever see the old fellow again. He'll miss his chance of *I told 'ee so, Sam*: more's the pity. He could go on telling me as long as he'd got breath, if only I could see his old face again' " (*Towers* 245).

Upon their return to the Shire, the elder Gamgee asks Frodo if "my Sam's behaved hisself and given satisfaction," and though he seems pleased, he still "don't hold with wearing ironmongery, whether it wears well or no" (*Return* 293–94). Sam is a "representative hobbit" (*Letters* 329), and this appears to be a typical hobbit father/son relationship, given their tendency to use light words and "say less than they mean," even when "a jest is out of place" (*Return* 146). While Hamfast Gamgee is mystified by his son's desire to go out into the wider world, he is supportive. And there is a great depth of feeling here; Sam's vision of his father in Galadriel's mirror is a powerful temptation to abandon his quest.

Parents in wartime worry about their other children as well as their sons or daughters on the front line. One of the most tragic parent/child pairs in *The Lord of the Rings* is Elrond Half-Elven and his daughter Arwen. As Tolkien said of him in Appendix A, "For Elrond . . . all chances of the War of the Ring were fraught with sorrow" (*Return* 315). Even if the war were won and his sons Elladan and Elrohir survived unscathed, victory for the Free

Peoples would mean the end of the Third Age and of the power of the three elven rings, and the departure of the Elves from Middle-earth. Worst of all it would mean separation forever from his only daughter Arwen, her soul's fate tied to Aragorn's by their marriage: "Bitter was their parting that should endure beyond the ends of the world" (*Return* 256).

Little is said about King Théoden's relationship with his son Théodred, although when Gandalf and his companions come to Edoras five days after Théodred's death, the king is bowed with grief: "The young perish and the old linger, withering" (*Towers* 121). He had long before adopted his sister Théodwyn's children when they were orphaned (*Return* 351) and, after Gandalf's healing, transfers his trust to his heir Éomer. He also acts as a father to Merry "for a little while" (*Return* 51). While he regards Éomer as equal to his other captains in maturity and courage and never urges him to caution, he tries to prevent both Éowyn and Merry from following him to battle. He does not want his warriors to be burdened by worrying about women and children in combat, although shieldmaidens are not unknown among the Rohirrim, and very young men participated in the defense of Helm's Deep. Merry of course is not a child and is ashamed to think of staying behind (*Return* 75), and Éowyn bitterly resents the traditional role in which she is imprisoned. In spite of his age, Théoden tries to shelter his dependents by going into battle himself, but both are inspired by love and loyalty to follow in spite of his orders, and are the last to stand by him when the Nazgûl attacks. This father wants to protect the children he sees as weaker than himself, in spite of their desires and his own advanced age, but admits the right and duty of his grown sons to risk themselves honorably in battle.

The parent/child relationship most deeply explored and most difficult is that between Denethor and his sons Boromir and Faramir. There are more references to this family in Tolkien's *Letters*, and especially to Denethor and Faramir, than to any other parent/child pair. Denethor is bitterly jealous of any influence over his sons except his own, wanting to keep control of them. Although he loves both sons, he also has a marked preference for one of them, and it was this preference that sent Boromir on the fatal journey that ended at Parth Galen. Denethor knew of Boromir's ambitious nature and how he chafed at being heir to a steward and not a king, but still he "loved him greatly: too much perhaps; and the more so because they were unlike" (*Return* 25). Gandalf has to warn him to "be not unjust in your grief" (*Return* 27) when he cries out that Faramir should have gone on the journey instead; he has to learn that the responsibility is his, and eventually understand that he mixed this cup of bitterness himself (*Return* 86). As Shippey has pointed out, Denethor and Théoden see Faramir and Éomer as "doubtful replacements" for their dead sons (*Century* 51).

Denethor exemplifies the frustration of a parent who loses control over his children as they grow up. He accuses Faramir unjustly of disloyalty: "[Mithrandir] has long had your heart in his keeping" (*Return* 85). Yet he cannot admit that Boromir might have turned from him if he had taken the Ring: "[Boromir] would not have squandered what fortune gave. He would have brought me a mighty gift. . . . I who was his father say that he would have brought it to me" (*Return* 86). Faramir, as Tolkien wrote in a letter, was "daunted" by his father's personality and rank, and was "accustomed to giving way and not giving his own opinions air" (*Letters* 323).

Survivor guilt drives both Denethor and Faramir; it leads Denethor to expect Faramir to do the work of two, and Faramir to follow his orders in spite of his better judgment. Denethor tries to displace his guilt by blaming Faramir. But when Faramir is wounded and lies near death, he is broken by remorse: "I sent my son forth, unthanked, unblessed, out into needless peril" (*Return* 97). Still his pride keeps him from bending, and he declares that if he cannot have all things as he desires them, with a son who does not listen to wizards to follow him as steward, then he will have nothing.

Denethor embodies the horrible dilemma of the parent who loses one child to war—how can he face the guilt of having allowed him to go into danger, even if he really had no choice in the matter, and how can he comfort his surviving children, who are also grieving? A basic definition of survivor guilt states that "bereaved parents often withdraw to extremes," and "survivor guilt may interfere with grieving and is often at the kernel of unresolved grief and depression" (Valent 557). In Denethor's case his inability to resolve these problems, coupled with despair over what he sees as Sauron's inevitable victory, leads to madness and suicide.

There are a few other examples of parent/child pairs affected by war in *The Lord of the Rings*. Bergil, the ten-year-old son of the soldier Beregond, is one of the few children allowed to stay in Minas Tirith after the evacuation of the civilians. Beregond says he is one of the "young lads that will not depart, and may find some task to do" (*Return* 36). When Bergil meets Pippin, he is afraid he will be sent away to join the aged, women, and children who have been evacuated from Minas Tirith (*Return* 42). The boys are somewhat protected—they are "no longer allowed to pass the Gate without an elder" (*Return* 43)—but they are employed to run errands for the Healers. Bergil takes Pippin's message about Merry to Gandalf, and brings the *athelas* to the Houses of Healing for Aragorn and witnesses the healing of Faramir. Also, the Ents seem to stand in a parental relationship to some of the more Ent-like trees (although they characterize themselves as tree-herds), and their destruction of Saruman's fortifications is a parents' dream of vengeance. Treebeard in particular treats Merry and Pippin like his own Entings while they are with him, pouring them Ent-draughts and asking them where they would like to stand to sleep (*Towers* 81).

But what about mother/child pairs? Mothers also agonize over their children in wartime. Yet there is little in *The Lord of the Rings* about mother/son relationships except a brief mention of Gilraen, mother of Aragorn, in the "Tale of Aragorn and Arwen" in Appendix A. She dies eleven years before the main events of the book, saying, "Now that it draws near I cannot face the darkness of our time that gathers upon Middle-earth" (*Return* 342). The only other mother/son pair mentioned is Lobelia and Lotho "Pimple" Sackville-Baggins; she is crushed when she learns that Lotho was murdered by Wormtongue, and gives Bag End back to Frodo (*Return* 301).

There are a few sweethearts on the home front, though. Rose Cotton is deeply concerned about Sam's safety, but in typical hobbit fashion she uses light words to greet him when he returns home: "You haven't hurried, have you?" (*Return* 287). She was unhappy that Sam had left the Shire, but as he hadn't spoken she had to keep it hidden (*Return* 304). Arwen waits in Rivendell for Aragorn and sends him the battle standard she makes for him. Éowyn, in love with Aragorn as well, rejects the woman-waiting-at-home role entirely: "All your words are but to say: you are a woman, and your part is in the house. But when the men have died in battle and honour, you have leave to be burned in the house, for the men will need it no more" (*Return* 58). The only other women we see whose lives are closely affected by the war are the women left in the Houses of Healing in Minas Tirith; Ioreth worries about orcs breaking through the defenses and disturbing her patients (*Return* 137).

Tolkien did not neglect mothers and lovers of soldiers in wartime entirely, but was evidently far more comfortable writing about the relationships between fathers and sons, a relationship with which he was more personally familiar. Priscilla was too young to have a sweetheart in uniform during World War II, since she was only ten when war broke out, and his own mother died in 1904, long before her sons served in World War I. Tolkien could have cast his memory back to Edith's experiences while he was a soldier for material, and it is possible that some of her unhappiness with life as a pregnant war bride is reflected in Éowyn. He ought to have been intimately familiar with Edith's fears for Christopher and Michael during World War II, and it is somewhat surprising they are not reflected in his work. But Humphrey Carpenter cites a passage from C. S. Lewis's *The Four Loves* to characterize what he felt were Tolkien's attitudes toward women: "What were the women doing meanwhile? How should I know? I am a man and never spied on the mysteries of the Bona Dea" (cited Carpenter, *Tolkien* 153). This is an unfortunate weakness in Tolkien's writings about war; while Éowyn is a fully drawn character whom the reader can appreciate and sympathize with, the other women affected by war are too sketchily drawn for their fears and motivations to be completely understandable.

CONCLUSION

Tolkien cannot really be considered a typical writer of either postwar period—he lacks the ironic response of the post–World War I writer and the disillusionment and secularity of the post–World War II writer. He moved beyond irony and disillusionment to mythologize his war experiences and create a more universally applicable story.

While the themes with which he was most consistently engaged are those of World War I, he did not ignore World War II, and there are a number of events from the latter with Middle-earth parallels. The fact that Tolkien was living through the second global war in his lifetime, after the futility of "The War to End All Wars," is echoed in the melancholy of the long-lived Elves, who have "through ages of the world . . . fought the long defeat" (*Fellowship* 372). One of the most interesting influences of World War II on *The Lord of the Rings*, however, was Tolkien's newly added perspective on war as the parent of two sons in the armed forces. In keeping with the northern European "theory of courage," the sympathetic fathers in *The Lord of the Rings* reject despair, but they still cannot help wishing they could protect their children from the risks of war.

NOTE

1. I think a few other writers could be added as well: for example, Mervyn Peake, who wrote much of the first volume of the *Gormenghast* trilogy during his service in World War II while recovering from a nervous breakdown, and Anthony Burgess, who served in the Royal Army Medical Corps in World War II and wrote *A Clockwork Orange*. There are few more chilling depictions of human evil in literature than Peake's Steerpike and especially Burgess's Alex.

Chapter 5

Military Leaders and Leadership

I was brought up in the Classics, and first discovered the sensation of
literary pleasure in Homer.

—J.R.R. Tolkien, *Letters* 172

This is War. This is what Homer wrote about.

—C. S. Lewis, *Surprised* 196

THE MORALITY OF PERSONAL LEADERSHIP

Because Tolkien had been an officer in wartime, he was able to invest his
depictions of military leadership in Middle-earth with the authenticity of personal experience. His literary criticism and letters show that he thought long
and deeply about heroism and leadership as depicted in the Greek and Roman
classics and in the northern European literature that became his specialty. As
George Clark points out, "His fantasy fiction rewrites heroic literature and
the hero; so do his critical studies" (40). In his criticism, particularly of *Beowulf* and in the afterword to "The Homecoming of Beorhtnoth Beorhthelm's
Son," Tolkien considered how such early literary conceptions of heroism and
leadership could be reconciled with Christianity, as well as with his real-life
experiences and observations of war. In his fiction, he depicted different leadership styles, and offered his own judgments about their moral worth.

One of the clearest conclusions we can draw from Tolkien's fictional examples of military leadership is that he felt the proper place for a leader was
in the forefront of his troops, sharing their danger in battle and setting an
example of courage and character for them to follow. As John Keegan suggests in *The Mask of Command*, "[I]n front—always, sometimes, never? is

. . . the question which must lie at the heart of any commander's examination of conscience" (*Mask* 328). In the way Tolkien clearly divided his war leaders into frontline warriors and "château generals," and in his depiction of King Théoden reborn and leading his cavalry into battle, we can see Tolkien's preferred answer to this question. Modern, technology-reliant methods of war make it increasingly difficult for a leader to do a good job of managing the flow of information and directing the action without being at some distance from his frontline troops. It follows logically that Tolkien's preference for on-the-spot leadership is closely tied to his distaste for the modern "war of the machines" and his preference for ancient models of heroism and methods of warfare.

Leadership in the forefront of battle is a moral duty for generals and other leaders in Middle-earth. Leaders who are at the head of their own troops in battle are legitimized by the risks they share with their men, as seen in the examples of Aragorn, Éomer, Théoden, and Faramir, and even Sam, Merry, and Pippin at the Battle of Bywater. Matthew B. Ridgway asked which leader is most likely to be followed:

Is it the one who has failed to share the rough going with his troops, who is rarely seen in the zone of aimed fire, and who expects much and gives little? Or is it the one whose every thought is for the welfare of his men, consistent with the accomplishment of his mission; who does not ask them to do what he has not already done and stands ready to do again when necessary; who with his men has shared short rations, the physical discomforts and rigors of campaign, and will be found at the crises of action where the issues are to be decided? (7)

It is not just the risk to himself that a commander must be willing to face in the field. He must also have sufficient faith in his purpose and firmness of will to ask others to face death with him—to take on the dreadful burden of feeling responsible in his soul for what happens to them, yet still push forward to his goal. Consider General George B. McClellan during the American Civil War—he was "so solicitous" of his troops that he "refused to risk their lives in battle, an apparently ironic fault which soldiers are quicker to perceive as such than members of less dangerous professions" (Stokesbury 147). A leader has to inspire his followers "to risk their lives for some greater end," and more important, he has to "have himself the courage to demand that they do so. It is of course in this particular that military leadership differs from other kinds" (Stokesbury 152).

In *The Lord of the Rings*, all leaders who direct from behind the lines are either on the side of the enemy or under his influence. Sauron broods in Barad-dûr and sends the Witch-king out to direct his battles; Angmar in turn rules them with fear, "driving his slaves in madness on before" (*Return* 92). Saruman empties Orthanc of his troops, watching his "splendid army" (*Towers* 173) march out, but remains behind himself in what he thinks is a safe stronghold. The Steward of Gondor, in the high tower of Minas Tirith, strives with Sauron in the *palantír* and believes he sees the course of battle clearly, all the time falling under the enemy's influence of despair. Denethor offers pragmatic justifications for leading from behind, comparing himself to Sauron: "He uses others as his weapons. So do all great lords, if they are wise. . . . Or why should I sit here in my tower and think, and watch, and wait, spending even my sons?" (*Return* 92). Denethor may be on the side of the allies against Sauron, but his adoption of the enemy's method of leadership leads to fatal misjudgments. Even Lotho "Pimple" Sackville-Baggins holes up in Bag End, leaving the running of his little socialist empire to his ruffians until he is made their prisoner, and Sharkey (who also stays in Bag End and is never seen in public) takes over. And in *The Hobbit*, the Mayor of Laketown cravenly flees the stricken city in his "great gilded boat" (*Hobbit* 261) and leaves its defense to others.

Leading from behind is morally suspect in Middle-earth and tactically flawed as well, for a lack of firsthand knowledge of conditions in the field leads to blunders like leaving the ents out of one's calculations or not noticing two weary hobbits crawling across Mordor. Such a leader rules by fear rather than example. If the actions of Sauron and Saruman inspire anyone, it is only those who see easy profit in dominating the weak and powerless. Under the influence of Wormtongue, Théoden is persuaded of the folly of trying to lead his own men in battle and sits bent with age on his throne; the purpose of his healing by Gandalf is a spiritual redemption that will make him fit to command again. Gandalf tries to heal Denethor's spirit as well; when the Steward of Gondor threatens self-immolation in the tombs, Gandalf reminds him: "Your part is to go out to the battle of your City, where maybe death awaits you. This you know in your heart" (*Return* 129). But Denethor is too deep in prideful despair to listen.

Can a leader hold power legitimately in wartime if he is unwilling to lead his troops in battle? As Keegan puts it, "Those who are led ask 'Where is our leader? Is he to be seen? What does he say to us? Does he share our risks?' " (*Mask* 314). Keegan points out that in a theocratic society, a ruler is under no obligation to prove himself fit to command, since his authority is direct from the gods and therefore not to be questioned. However, leaders in secular societies can offer no such "moral exemption." They have a fine line to walk—"They must therefore either go in person or else find the means of delegating the obligation without thereby invalidating their right to exercise authority outside the battlefield and in times of peace" (*Mask* 312).

In spite of Middle-earth's underlying theology and Tolkien's own religious preferences, the societies encountered in *The Lord of the Rings* are strictly secular. Sauron's enslavement of orcs and men may verge on the theocratic, however, since he is a Maia and therefore an angelic power. In fact in Tolkien's letters, he mentions that during his time among the Númenóreans, Sauron wanted to be worshipped as a "God-King" (*Letters* 243), but there is no indication of this in the Third Age. Otherwise, even the High Elven societies of Lórien and Rivendell have no priestly class or divinely anointed rulers. Aragorn may have the advantage of his Númenórean ancestry in advancing his right to the throne, but this in itself is not strong enough to support his claim—he must also prove his worth through word and deed. The wizards or Istari could have claimed to rule through theocratically supported right, since they were sent to Middle-earth by the Valar after the end of the Second Age (*Return* 365), and in fact Saruman is hubristic enough to try to play the "high and ancient order" card with the uncooperative Gandalf (*Towers* 186). However, in the contrasting characters of Gandalf and Saruman we see that even a claim at this level must be legitimized by moral action and earned authority.

But does Tolkien really prefer the ancient models when it comes to leadership and heroism? His criticisms of Beowulf and Beorhtnoth show that he did not fully accept their values, and in some ways his war leaders and their leadership styles are anachronistic and far more modern than their settings. For example, compared with his sources in the heroic literature of the ancient and medieval worlds and with his earlier writings, like "The Fall of Gondolin," Tolkien devotes little time in *The Lord of the Rings* to describing the arms and armor of his war leaders. For the most part, leaders are distinguished only by carrying a banner or having it carried near them by a standard-bearer. As Keegan points out, those who lead "in the precise sense of the word," that is, in front of their troops, "needed to be seen and to be recognized instantaneously" (*Mask* 61). Those leaders who maintained an "unostentatious appearance" on the battlefield, like Wellington or Grant, had a managerial rather than heroic leadership style and generally stayed farther back from the front line of battle. Leaders like Alexander the Great, however, made sure they could be seen by their troops and by the enemy at all times by wearing conspicuous armor or riding a distinctive horse. Even in the early days of World War I, British officers in the field wore uniforms with an extravagant silhouette consisting of "melodramatically cut riding breeches [and] flare-skirted tunics with Sam Browne belts" (Fussell, *Great War* 50). However, they soon discovered that their jodhpurs and flashy trim make them easy targets for enemy sharpshooters. By 1915, a newly commissioned officer would be advised that in the field he would adopt "practically the same kit and equipment as a private soldier . . . to render himself as little conspicuous as possible, and thus avoid being 'sniped' by the enemy" (Wyndham 6–7); for example, rank would be indicated by shoulder tabs instead of more visible sleeve bands. Modern field uniforms now generally follow this pattern of camouflage and subtle (to a civilian) rank distinctions.

What then do we make of Aragorn? At the Battle of the Pelennor Fields he is distinguished only by the Star of Elendil on his brow and by the sword Andúril, but Elladan and Elrohir also wear similar gemmed circlets and might easily be mistaken for him, having the same dark hair and grey eyes. At Helm's Deep, too, there is nothing to distinguish him from others but his sword, and at the Black Gate he wears only the "piece of elvish glass," the eagle brooch given to him by Galadriel (*Return* 165). Tolkien here depicts a king who wants to maintain solidarity with his followers by living and dressing like one of them. As his actions after the victory at Minas Tirith demonstrate, Aragorn's policy was always to refuse to claim more than he felt was his due. This is a far more modern attitude than one might expect in his place and time, a world that Tolkien implied was pre-Christian (*Letters* 237, 287), but it demonstrates his humility or "lowliness," one of the "king-becoming graces" Shakespeare listed in *Macbeth* (IV:iii). Faramir too dresses exactly as his men do in the woods of Ithilien, and though he has a silver goblet, it is plain and he drinks the same wine as his troops. The Riders of Rohan, however, are as traditional in the dress of their leaders as they are in other matters: King Théoden bears a golden shield, Erkenbrand has a red one, and Éomer wears a horsetail on the crest of his helmet that makes him visible from far off. The Rohirrim are described as less advanced than the men of Gondor, and these visual divisions between the leaders and the led stand in contrast to the behavior of the men who will lead Gondor into the Fourth Age.

The archetypal example of the value placed on personal and highly visible battlefront leadership in the Western world is the career of Alexander the Great. Tolkien was well aware that this kind of leadership requires the "Alexander-touch," but he felt that taking it too far "orientalized" Alexander: "The poor boob fancied (or liked people to fancy) he was the son of Dionysus, and died of drink" (*Letters* 64). In his analysis of the Beorhtnoth incident from *The Battle of Maldon*, Tolkien shows his distrust of the kind of charismatic, overreaching leadership that allows a man drunk with dreams of glory and fame to lead his men to probable slaughter. As Clark points out, what Tolkien rejected about Beorhtnoth was his "decision that promised to enhance his personal glory rather than subordinating the quest for honor to [his] duty of defending the land against the Vikings" (50–51). For Tolkien, heroism had to be about something more than the quest for fame and glory; it needed to be about the fulfillment of a worthwhile duty through morally acceptable means.

What kinds of leadership did Tolkien witness and experience as a soldier during World War I? Unfortunately, there is no evidence in his published letters of his assessments of his commanding officers, so we must rely on the analysis of historians for a general picture. But given Tolkien's emphatic identification of "leading from behind" with the enemies of all that is good in Middle-earth, it is likely that he was well aware of the problems caused by the relatively recent pattern of generals establishing their command posts many miles behind the front lines. And as a signaling officer, he was sure to have been all too familiar with the difficulties of getting accurate and timely information to and from headquarters even with the most modern equipment available.

John Keegan offers this cogent analysis of the strategic factors that led to this innovation:

The trend of weapon development had for several centuries been acting to drive commanders away from the forward edge of the battlefield, but they had nevertheless resisted it. What occurred at the end of the nineteenth century was a sudden acceptance by the generals of all advanced armies that the trend could no longer be gainsaid and that they must abandon the post of honour to their followers. (*Mask* 331)

Fifty years later, their descendants—French and German indiscriminately—were not to think of quitting their headquarters at any time. . . . It was from those secluded places that the great slaughter of the trenches would be directed, totally out of sight and, unless for a trick of the mind, also out of sound of all the headquarters responsible for it. (*Mask* 333)

At first glance, locating headquarters well out of the danger zone seems a sensible precaution and a reasonable "compromise between prudence and exposure" (Keegan, *Mask* 332). It was an "understandable reaction" to the development of long-range weapons. However, "its effect on the relationship between leaders and led was so deadening that even the most arrogantly insensitive of generals should have taken steps to ameliorate it" (Keegan, *Mask* 331). In any case, the French command settled in "château comfort" at Chantilly, the Germans at the resort town of Spa in Belgium, and the British in the walled town of Montreuil.

But psychologically this was an unfortunate step. Mystification can be an important ingredient in the charisma of a commander, and a sense of distance, very carefully calculated, can lend him an aura of untouchable prestige and power. But this same distance also prevents him from sharing his soldiers' danger and thus legitimizing his right to command. Keegan strongly criticized the "château generals," pointing out that every commander needs to be able to

convey an impression of himself to his troops through words, to explain what he wants of them, to allay their fears, to arouse their hopes, and to bind their ambitions to his own. It is a mark of the depths to which the art of command fell in the era of château generalship that this need was served barely, if at all, by any of the generals of the First World War. Their armies were, by an ironic twist of social and constitutional development, the most literate and politically conscious mass forces ever to have taken the field. By an equally ironic twist, the Staff College culture which informed their leadership had, by a bogus scientism, so sanctified the importance of purely theoretical principles of warmaking, and consequently so depreciated the importance of human emotion, that the common soldiers were not thought worth the expenditure of their commanders' breath. (Keegan, *Mask* 319)

Sauron and Saruman would never have seen any reason to address their troops personally; after all, they were only expendable orcs and enslaved men

(Saruman's speeches to his army in Peter Jackson's *The Two Towers* were inserted by the scriptwriters). Denethor and Théoden—before his redemption—are depicted speaking only with their commanders and never directly to their troops.

There were other ways of creating and maintaining distance as well, and the rigid class structure of Great Britain at the time did nothing to help matters. Officers were drawn from the upper classes and were given special privileges, like the services of batmen to look after their physical needs and reserved railway carriages for returning from leave in England. Distance was thought essential for discipline. Robert Graves recounts an incident where a soldier called a corporal by his first name; the soldier was given field punishment and the corporal reduced in rank for permitting such familiarity (Graves 179). Graves even reports that officers and men resorted to different houses of prostitution, the Blue Lamps and Red Lamps respectively, and speculates as to whether the Blue Lamp women "had to show any particular qualifications for their higher social ranking" (180). A book written for young British men preparing to join the army hastens to assure the reader that although "[a] striking feature of sport in the British Army is the intermingling between officers and men," fortunately this mixing of the ranks, "far from being subversive of discipline, tends to bring the ranks closer together" ("The Major" 51).

The highest levels of command gave an impression of lack of concern for the common soldier. W. A. Senior recounts General Douglas Haig's reaction to the carnage of the first day of the Battle of the Somme, in which 58,000 British soldiers died: "such losses would not be 'sufficient to justify any anxiety as to our ability to continue the offensive.'" Senior continues, "It does not require a long leap from Haig's statement to the Witch King of Angmar, Lord of the Nazgûl, driving his own troops to slaughter before the walls of Minas Tirith and trampling them as he approached" (175). Haig also reported to the War Cabinet his satisfaction with conducting a war of attrition: "The casualties the Germans would sustain, he said, would 'amply compensate' for those of the British" (Babington 75). General Sir William Robertson tried to justify the loss of 95,000 at Loos by saying it had provided "useful experience in the handling of new troops" (Babington 62). This is blackest irony without any need for editorial comment.

During World War I, the "simulated absolute monarchy of château generalship" (Keegan, *Mask* 334) was one of the contributing factors that provoked uprisings among all the armies that suffered from it. While at the start of the war, most European armies treated the soldier "as an object rather than an agent," by the end of 1916, commanders began to realize that "[m]odern mass armies . . . were found to be teeming with assertive individuals who resisted the prescribed roles for which they had been cast" (Englander 93). Grievances about "pay and allowances, clothing and comforts, shelter, warmth, and rest . . . leave and family income support" (Englander

201) were all exacerbated by the gulf between the leaders and the led. Parts
of the French army revolted in May 1917, the Belgians in the summer of
1917, the Russians in October 1917, the Italians in November 1917, the
Germans in September 1918, and even the British in September 1917 and
March 1918 (Keegan, *Mask* 334; Englander 196–97).

At the root of all these spiritual crises lay a psychological revolt by the fighting soldiers
against the demands of unshared risk. . . . [O]rders had emanated from an unseen
source that demanded heroism of ordinary men while itself displaying heroism in no
whit whatsoever. Far from it: the château generals had led the lives of country gen-
tlemen, riding well-groomed horses between well-appointed offices and residences,
keeping regular hours and eating regular meals, sleeping between clean sheets every
night. . . . Meanwhile those under their discipline, junior officers and soldiers alike,
had circulated between draughty billets and dangerous trenches, clad in verminous
clothes and fed on hard rations, burying their friends in field corners. . . . The impli-
cation of such disparities can be suppressed in the short term. . . .

   Yet . . . hierarchy and discipline cannot suppress the implications of risk disparities
forever. (Keegan, *Mask* 335)

   Unlike Tolkien, and in spite of his criticism of the château generals, Keegan
sees "sometimes" as the correct answer to the question of when to lead from
the front. Alexander's rashness put his mission and his whole army at risk
every time he took the field. On the other hand, Hitler and his staff unwisely
adopted the strategy of the château generals and chose never to lead from
the front, putting their faith in the "artificial vision" granted by the telegraph
and telephone. But their reliance on intelligence at a remove from the actual
situation led to fatal errors in their analyses of battlefield situations. Other
World War II leaders took the château generals' failures as a cautionary
lesson and made at least token visits to the front; Keegan states that "[t]he
history of the emotional life of armies ever since has been one of a retreat
from this disjunction" (*Mask* 336). Keegan sees the bitterly antiwar literature
of the late 1920s as a product of this policy of "remote control." Younger
officers who had suffered at the front line determined that "their style of
command would be different," and in fact during World War II, "[g]eneralship
once again became conspicuous. . . . The result was a sharp rise in fatalities
among the higher ranks, but also a renewed confidence in their leaders among
ordinary soldiers and a return of something like heroic status to the most
bold and successful of them" (*Nature* 68).
   Keegan argues that "[t]he 'sometimes' generals . . . achieved a notably
more consistent record of success than the 'always' or 'nevers' " (*Mask* 328).
Two other generals Keegan examined in his book, Wellington and Grant, as
well as other legendary leaders like Julius Caesar, used a pragmatic mixture
of leadership styles:

Sometimes a commander's proper place will be in his headquarters and at his map table, where calm and seclusion accord him the opportunity to reflect on the information that intelligence brings him, to ponder possibilities and to order a range of responses in his mind. Other times, when crisis presents itself, his place is at the front where he can see for himself, make direct and immediate judgments, watch them taking effect and reconsider his options as events change under his hand. (*Mask* 328)

But Tolkien does not show any of his war leaders taking this middle path. For them, the choice is "always" or "never," or perhaps "when I was young and reckless, but not now in my age and despair"—but never "sometimes." For Tolkien, a leader must be legitimized by his position in the front lines on the battlefield.

LEADERS IN *THE HOBBIT* AND *THE LORD OF THE RINGS*

Who acts as a leader at what point in *The Hobbit* and *The Lord of the Rings*, and what does this tell us about Tolkien's attitudes toward military leadership? What does leadership style reveal about character in Middle-earth? One conclusion we can reach is that for Tolkien's characters, experiencing the responsibility of personal on-the-spot leadership is an essential part of the maturation process, even if the character in question prefers to evade a leadership role. I will look at several characters who take a strong leadership position or for whom leadership is an important test of personal growth.

Bilbo

The Hobbit is in many ways a story about the "journey to maturity," as William H. Green has pointed out. Like Frodo, Bilbo first appears to us as a young adult of independent means and no responsibilities; his wealth does not come, so far as we can see, from running a farm, owning a business, renting property, or any other venture that would require his attention, but is simply inherited. Gandalf shakes him out of this pleasant rut and sends him on an adventure—"Very amusing for me, very good for you" (*Hobbit* 14)— that ends with Bilbo as a mature adult, capable of fully independent thought and action.

In *The Hobbit*, when Gandalf is on hand, he leads the company, and when he is not, Thorin is the leader. However, as the story progresses, Bilbo takes on an increasing responsibility for leadership, and at several points he is "the real leader in their adventure" (*Hobbit* 233). The fragments of Tolkien's notes published as "The Quest for Erebor" in *Unfinished Tales* show that Gandalf knew Bilbo as a child and was impressed by his eagerness for the old tales and his questions about Tookish relatives who had disappeared on adventures (*Unfinished* 331–32). When Thorin asked Gandalf for advice on

reclaiming his kingdom, the wizard remembered the young hobbit and suggested him as a companion. But he was as dismayed as the dwarves to find a
"little fellow bobbing on the mat" (*Hobbit* 26), gone "rather greedy and fat,"
whose "old desires had dwindled down to a sort of private dream" (*Unfinished*
323). The troll episode, early in the story, shows a Bilbo not yet ready to be
a leader. He allows the dwarves to send him up to the trolls' fire against his
better judgment, and blunders his way through his conversation with Bert,
Tom, and William, to the point where the trolls capture the whole party.
Gandalf had always had high hopes for Bilbo and thought him capable of great
things, but this was too soon to give Bilbo a chance to prove himself—the
hobbit lacked experience.

However, his solo exploits under the Misty Mountains change Bilbo. Alone
in the dark after being separated from the dwarves, with only himself to rely
on, Bilbo's inner courage awakens, and he discovers that a stout Gondolin
blade does wonders for his self-confidence. Finding out the secret of the Ring
gives him the ability to escape Gollum and the goblins. After acquiring the
Ring, Bilbo is a changed hobbit; as Gandalf observes, "Mr. Baggins has more
about him than you guess" (*Hobbit* 105). As I suggested in Chapter 3, Gandalf
begins mentoring Bilbo as they approach Beorn's house, explaining his strategy for approaching Beorn and advising Bilbo about the path ahead.

In Mirkwood, Bilbo begins to step into a leadership role, filling the "vacuum
of leadership" caused by Gandalf's absence (Green 82). When he rescues the
dwarves from the spiders, they gain a great deal of respect for him, "for they
saw that he had some wits, as well as luck and a magic ring—and all three
are very useful possessions" (*Hobbit* 177). This episode is the closest Bilbo
gets to military leadership, and he shows a fine command of strategy in rallying and deploying his followers and drawing the spiders off with a series of
feigned attacks. He is absolutely in the forefront of battle—the dwarves,
weakened by venom, are hardly able to help him at all.

The adventure of the Elvenking's halls marks the peak of Bilbo's responsibilities as a leader. He engineers the clever escape of the dwarves from their
prison, and brings them safe (if a bit waterlogged) to Laketown. Here, however, Thorin takes charge of the group again, and manages all the plans for
approaching the Lonely Mountain. Now Bilbo begins to act more independently, interacting with Smaug alone and stealing a cup from the dragon's
hoard, then picking the Arkenstone out of the treasure-heap and hiding it
from the dwarves. He begins to have serious doubts about Thorin's leadership
when the dwarf starts fortifying the mountain against the Men of Laketown
and the Elves, but rather than attempt to bring the other dwarves around to
his point of view or challenge Thorin's leadership, he makes a clandestine
effort to stop the coming battle. As Green points out, "Bilbo's maturation is
complete only when he becomes . . . a whistle-blower, so devoted to Thorin
and Company that he is willing to be hated by them" (90).

Bilbo has discovered himself capable of leadership, but does not really want to be a leader. Nor does he want to be a follower. During the Battle of Five Armies, he quite independently chooses to make his invisible stand near the Elves for both practical and sentimental reasons. He is content in the end to be "only quite a little fellow in a wide world after all" (*Hobbit* 317). Leadership in a crisis has matured Bilbo, but he finds that it is not his calling in life. His disobedience to his leader's orders in pursuit of a higher good, however, is an interesting point to consider, and I will discuss obedience and disobedience later in this chapter.

Frodo

Until the hobbits' meeting with Aragorn at the Prancing Pony in Bree, much of the focus of *The Lord of the Rings* is on Frodo's development as a leader. Frodo is a very unwilling leader; throughout the story, he alternates between reluctantly accepting a leadership role thrust upon him and rejecting or trying to escape it, until his very last act of trying to slip away to the Grey Havens unnoticed. In Frodo's case, the traditional leadership role is not the one he should be fulfilling, and he is right to push it away because his task is best accomplished on a completely different basis. In fact, the Ring itself makes leadership a temptation and a trap for the Ring-bearer.

Early in the book, after Bilbo leaves for Rivendell, Frodo takes his uncle's place in society and finds "that being his own master and *the* Mr. Baggins of Bag End was rather pleasant" (*Fellowship* 45). His social position as a wealthy young bachelor-about-town entitles him to be perceived as a leader in the community without exerting any effort. He does not even have live-in servants to be responsible for at the beginning—only part-time gardeners.

However, upon learning the history of the Ring from Gandalf, Frodo discovers that "Mr. Baggins of Bag End," while a person of no importance in the wide world, is in fact far too prominent. The name of Baggins is known to the Enemy. "I am a danger, a danger to all that live near me," he realizes (*Fellowship* 71). Gandalf assigns Sam to Frodo as his companion, thus inaugurating a pattern of followers being more or less forced on Frodo, usually much against his desire.

Frodo is afraid to endanger his friends, and would rather bear his risks alone. In this way he is the opposite of Beorhtnoth, whose "desire for honor conflicted with [his] duty to [his] followers" (Clark 50); Frodo is often constrained from freedom of action by his desire to protect the safety of his companions. From the beginning, Frodo sees this as a solo quest and not one in which he would be acting as a leader—"The thought that he would so soon have to part with his young friends weighed on his heart" (*Fellowship* 77). But he falls into the leadership of the party traveling to Crickhollow, directing Sam's actions and deciding where and when the group will stop for rest and food. Still, he is a rather tentative leader, apologizing for wanting to get off the road the first time they meet the Black Rider (*Fellowship* 83), and tacitly surrendering leadership to Gildor when they meet the Elves. Gildor is another person who urges companions on Frodo: "[D]o not go alone. Take such friends as are trusty and willing" (*Fellowship* 94). But Frodo still doubts his right to be a leader: " 'It is one thing to take my young friends walking over the Shire with me, until we are hungry and weary, and food and bed are sweet. To take them into exile, where hunger and weariness may have no cure, is quite another—even if they are willing to come. The inheritance is mine alone. I don't think I ought even to take Sam' " (*Fellowship* 95–96). He tries to dissuade Sam from following, but as George Clark has pointed out (46), Sam practically swears a heroic oath when he tells the elves "I am going with him, if he climbs to the Moon; and if any of those Black Riders try to stop him, they'll have Sam Gamgee to reckon with." "If you don't come back, sir, then I shan't, that's certain," he tells Frodo (*Fellowship* 96).

At Crickhollow Frodo once more contemplates going on alone—"he wondered again how he was going to break the news to them that he must leave them so soon, indeed at once" (*Fellowship* 114). But his friends have every intention of going with him, even though Frodo says he could not allow it. Sam quotes Gandalf's words to him: "He had some sense, mind you; and when you said *go alone*, he said *no! take someone as you can trust*" (*Fellowship* 115). As a determined Merry puts it, "we are coming with you; or following you like hounds" (*Fellowship* 116), and Sam clinches the argument by quoting Gildor's advice as well: "Gildor said you should take them as was willing, and you can't deny it" (*Fellowship* 116).

In the Old Forest, Frodo allows Merry to guide and direct them, and wonders "if he had been right to make the others come into this abominable wood" (*Fellowship* 122). Merry is not the hyper-competent Aragorn, however, and their detour nearly ends in disaster as they are caught by Old Man Willow. Frodo is forced to take charge again, trying out plans to get the tree to release Merry and Pippin, and then running to look for help. And as with the meeting with the Elves, Frodo is all too willing to accept Tom Bombadil and his hospitality without question, even to the point of allowing him to handle the Ring. He is happy to have an excuse to escape from the responsibility of leadership when it rains: "Frodo was glad in his heart, and blessed the kindly weather, because it delayed them from departing" (*Fellowship* 140).

On the Barrow-downs, Frodo experiences a major leadership crisis. The hobbits fall asleep after their noon meal and awake to find they are lost in the fog at sunset. Frodo tries to lead them to the road, but they are caught by the Barrow-wight and laid out as sacrifices in his tomb. Although his courage has been awakened by the situation, Frodo's first thought is of flight, both from the Barrow-wight and from responsibility for his friends:

At first Frodo felt as if he had indeed been turned into stone by the incantation. Then a wild thought of escape came to him. He wondered if he put on the Ring, whether the Barrow-wight would miss him, and he might find some way out. He thought of himself running free over the grass, grieving for Merry, and Sam, and Pippin, but free and alive himself. Gandalf would admit there had been nothing he could do.

But the courage that had been awakened in him was now too strong: he could not leave his friends so easily. . . . Suddenly resolve hardened in him. (*Fellowship* 152–53)

"That was touch and go," as Gandalf says later; "perhaps the most dangerous moment of all" (*Fellowship* 231). In his enigmatic way, Gandalf was surely referring to more than just the physical danger of the moment. And after resisting this temptation, Frodo is a more responsible leader, though still not very competent. He cautions the other hobbits about using his name before they enter Bree, but while talking to Strider in the inn, loses track of Pippin and nearly causes a disaster when the Ring slips onto his finger. But at least he shows some caution in dealing with Strider, and does not entirely trust him until Gandalf's letter is corroborated by Strider's verses. "Even if I wanted another companion, I should not agree to any such thing, until I knew a good deal more about you, and your business," he says, and Strider approves of his newfound carefulness (*Fellowship* 175). Butterbur puts his finger on the fatal irresponsibility of Frodo's leadership: "Well, you do want looking after and no mistake: your party might be on holiday!" (*Fellowship* 181).

As they begin their journey to Weathertop, Strider defers to Frodo as the real leader of the group and serves as their guide. At one point, Frodo asks, "What do you advise us to do?" (*Fellowship* 196), speaking as the head of the expedition, and Strider asks for his help in interpreting the sign left by Gandalf on Weathertop. But Frodo still sees himself as alone rather than as a member of a group; when they spot the Ringwraiths from the hilltop, he says, "If *I* move, *I* shall be seen and hunted! If *I* stay, *I* shall draw them to *me*!" (*Fellowship* 202, emphasis added). Although it is true that the Riders would follow only Frodo if the party split up, Strider has to remind him that he is not alone.

Frodo is forced by his wound to surrender all leadership to Aragorn and it is all he can do to survive the trip to Rivendell. After the Council of Elrond, he is again assigned companions. Leadership is not entrusted to any one person, but tacitly assumed by Gandalf. But when a decision must be made about entering Moria, Frodo is given the last and deciding voice in the (never resolved) debate. After Gandalf's fall, Aragorn leads the companions to Lórien and then on down the Anduin River.

At Parth Galen the choice about the Company's direction can be put off no longer, and Aragorn defers to Frodo to make the decision. Here Frodo again rejects a leadership role, but with better reason than before—he has seen the evil the Ring can work on his companions. "I will do now what I must," he says; "I will go alone. Some I cannot trust, and those I can trust are too dear to me" (*Fellowship* 417–18). But he reckons without Sam's desire to follow him voluntarily, whether he wants a companion or not. Leadership is again thrust upon Frodo.

Interestingly, once Gollum is added to their group, Frodo appears to grow as a leader. The challenge of having to control a follower whom he cannot trust and does not like requires him to use a firmer hand and all the strategies he has learned from observing Gandalf and Aragorn. He finds that in some ways it is easier to manage a follower who is not also a friend. But could this be the Ring tempting him with the power to control others? Being stern and commanding, and having one's enemy do one's bidding, is a tempting drug. But when Faramir shows Frodo that Gollum has discovered the hidden pool of Henneth Annûn and asks if he should be killed, Frodo remembers that Gandalf thought Gollum was somehow important to his quest and comes to the realization that Gollum had a claim on him now. "The servant has a claim on the master for service, even service in fear" (*Towers* 296). He hates himself for tricking Gollum, but realizes that there is no escaping his moral responsibility for the creature, and defends him to Sam all the way through Shelob's lair.

Sam takes over the duty of the quest temporarily when he believes Frodo is dead, but when Frodo reclaims the Ring after Sam rescues him from the orcs, he also reclaims the leadership of their mission. In his unreasoning panic to get the Ring back from Sam, he accuses his friend of thievery, and is aghast at seeing the influence of the Ring on his behavior: "It is the horrible power of the Ring. I wish it had never, never been found" (*Return* 188). However, as Frodo grows progressively weaker, Sam has to take on the responsibility of seeing the quest through to the end. Frodo gives his sword to Sam, saying, "I do not think it will be my part to strike a blow again" (*Return* 204). Eventually he is forced to tell Sam quite explicitly, "Lead me! As long as you've got any hope left. Mine is gone" (*Return* 206).

One of the Ring's properties is enhancement of the will and power to dominate others; it was, after all, designed to bring all the other Rings to it and rule them. Boromir in his temptation says the Ring would give him the power of Command, and Sam has visions of "armies flocking to his call" (*Return* 177). Shippey sees the power of the Ring as an addiction, and in fact the need to dominate others can be an uncontrollable obsession. Power-mad leaders are an unfortunate truth in both military and civilian life. Could the Ring have been drawing companions and followers to Frodo, and trying to either force or tempt him to control them for its own purposes—or to find someone more malleable who could take the Ring from Frodo? Frodo may have been wiser than even he knew all along in rejecting his followers and companions. Roger Sale sees the central power of the Ring, and the heart of Sauron's evil, to be "binding"—"to be bound is to have that part of oneself that is unique destroyed" (209); "the Ring . . . embodies the final possessiveness, the ultimate power to bind things apart from ourselves to ourselves" (217). Sale points out that "[i]n his instinctive wish to save and tame Sméagol rather than destroy him, Frodo creates his heroism" (225)—but there is a knife's edge of difference between "taming" and "possessing," and Frodo is in grave danger of surrendering to the Ring while the temptation to "tame" Gollum exists. Frodo's physical weakness saves him, for a while: "As long as Frodo is thus openly dependant, the urge to possessiveness can be quelled by . . . his recognition of the blessed and cursed otherness of his servant and his wretched guide" (Sale 235).

Crawling up the face of Mount Doom within reach of their goal, Sam and Frodo are attacked by Gollum. Frodo explicitly uses the Ring to cow Gollum to his will and threaten him with death; the voice that curses Gollum comes out of the "wheel of fire" at Frodo's breast (*Return* 221). He has already fallen to the temptation, the unbearable pressure, to dominate others with the Ring; claiming it as his own at the Cracks of Doom is the final formality. With that declaration, he (and the Ring through him) attempts to take control of all Middle-earth. The addiction to domination has claimed him, but is abruptly withdrawn from him when the Ring is destroyed.

After this, Frodo rejects leadership roles altogether. Sam guides him away from the Sammath Naur, where he would have given up all hope of life: "If you wish to go, I'll come," Frodo says (*Return* 228). On their return to the Shire, Frodo is angered by the changes he sees, and speaks his mind almost as much as Sam, Merry, and Pippin do. However, he becomes withdrawn and silent when he begins to realize that it might take violence to save his home, and refuses to draw a sword or fight. Merry tells him, "You won't rescue Lotho, or the Shire, just by looking shocked and sad, my dear Frodo," but he still holds back and leaves leadership of the campaign to Merry and Pippin (*Return* 285). However, it may not just be a distaste for violence that is influencing Frodo; perhaps he remembers what it was like to dominate and rule others, if only in that brief instant of claiming the Ring, and still feels the temptation. Frodo temporarily holds the office of deputy mayor while Will Whitfoot recovers from his imprisonment, but does very little (reducing the number of Shirriffs fits the pattern of rejecting leadership), resigns within six months, and then withdraws from public life altogether. When he leaves for the Grey Havens, he invites only Sam to go with him; and when he sets sail, he is at last free of any temptation or responsibility for leading others.

Aragorn

In ancient Rome, young men of good family and political ambition followed the *cursus honorum*, a sequence of military and public offices designed to give them progressive experience in leadership and in handling power. Keegan points out: "War is indeed an extension of politics and, if it is to be fought in a manner that serves political ends, soldiers must understand how the two interact. The Romans, masters in the exercise of power, had grasped the necessity and designed a training *cursus* which made its products adepts of both worlds" (*Mask* 5). Before we meet Aragorn at the Prancing Pony in Bree, he has already been through an extensive "course of honor" of his own.

At the age of two Aragorn is taken to Rivendell as Elrond's foster-son and his true name concealed (*Return* 370). As Estel, he travels and does "great deeds" with Elrond's sons (*Return* 338), and at the age of twenty his heritage is revealed to him. After meeting and falling in love with Arwen, he goes out into the wild and "labour[s] in the cause against Sauron" (*Return* 340) for twenty-nine years. In the fifth year of his wanderings he meets Gandalf, then his "great journeys and errantries" begin (*Return* 371).

During this period he serves both King Thengel of Rohan and King Ecthelion II of Gondor under the name Thorongil, becoming a "great captain" and adviser to Ecthelion (*Return* 335). Keegan affirms the necessity of actual battlefield experience in determining a leader's mettle: "[M]ountain skirmishing and siege warfare cannot substitute tutorially for the test of leadership in pitched battle. It is in the open field, when armies clash face to face in the grip of those terrible unities of time, place, and action, that a man's real powers of anticipation, flexibility, quick-thinking, patience, spatial perception, thrift and prodigality with resources, physical courage and moral strength are tried to the extreme" (*Mask* 77). He advances in rank and reward in Gondor, to the point where the young Denethor grows jealous of his influence (*Return* 336). After winning a great sea battle for Gondor, Aragorn then goes alone into the East and South (*Return* 341). At the age of forty-nine, after meeting and serving under some of the great rulers of his time, he returns to Lórien and plights his troth to Arwen. Her father then charges Aragorn to complete his course by becoming King of reunited Gondor and Arnor before she can marry him (*Return* 342). At the time we meet Aragorn, thirty-eight years later, he has been mostly living in the wild, hunting Gollum on and off, but has now reached the crisis point where he must prepare to openly declare himself and lead men into battle with the aim of claiming his throne.

During the journey from Bree to Weathertop, Aragorn defers to Frodo as the leader of the group, but when Frodo is wounded, he takes charge of getting them to Rivendell. After the Council of Elrond, Gandalf leads the Company at first, but Aragorn is his closest adviser, and it is he who chooses the course over Redhorn Gate that ends in disaster. When Gandalf falls to the Balrog, Aragorn immediately takes command: "Come! I will lead you now!" (*Fellowship* 345). He guides the Company out of Moria and down to Lórien, and has to assert his leadership when they are blindfolded: "If I am still to lead this Company, you must do as I bid" (*Fellowship* 362).

Like Frodo in Bombadil's house, Aragorn is glad that traveling along the river allows him to put off his decision about the Company's future path, and stays on the Anduin until the last possible moment at Rauros Falls. During the orc attack at Parth Galen, Aragorn expresses private doubts about his decisions—"Alas! An ill fate is on me this day, and all that I do goes amiss" (*Towers* 15). He has to make a choice about whether to follow the orcs and their captives, or Frodo and Sam: "Let me think! . . . And may I now make a right choice, and change the evil fate of this unhappy day! . . . My heart speaks clearly at last: the fate of the Bearer is in my hands no longer. The Company has played its part" (*Towers* 21).

One of the more unfortunate changes to the original story in the script of the Peter Jackson movie of *The Fellowship of the Ring* is a sequence where Aragorn expresses doubts to Arwen about his ability to be king, before the Council of Elrond meets; he fears his past and is afraid the "weakness" of Isildur is in his blood (*The Lord of the Rings: The Fellowship of the Ring*, scene 21). The extended DVD version makes these self-doubts even more explicit, producing a dramatic change in Aragorn's character. In the book the closest Aragorn ever comes to expressing any such doubt in Rivendell is to say, "I am but the heir of Isildur, not Isildur himself" (*Fellowship* 261). His meaning is that he fears he may not be as powerful as Isildur; but when Arwen echoes these words in the movie, she implies instead that he fears he is tainted by Isildur's inability to give up the Ring.

Aragorn leads Legolas and Gimli to Rohan in pursuit of the orcs, and fights by the side of Éomer under Théoden's command at Helm's Deep. It is shortly after the Dúnedain meet them on the road back to Edoras that he looks into the *palantír* and formally reveals himself to Sauron as the heir to the throne of Gondor. He wrenches the Stone to his own will, and what he sees convinces him that he must leave the troops of Rohan and strike off in a different direction with his Dúnedain. From that time on, he acts as an independent commander, leading them through the Paths of the Dead, to the Battle of Harlond, and up the Anduin to relieve the siege of Minas Tirith.

After the Battle of the Pelennor Fields, Aragorn refuses to enter the City as king unbidden: "I will not enter in, nor make any claim, until it be seen whether we or Mordor shall prevail" (*Return* 137). He proposes that Gandalf lead them all until the war is over, and at Gandalf's suggestion he leads the assault on the Black Gate. Aragorn announces himself as the King of Gondor when they reach the Morannon, but Gandalf negotiates with the Mouth of Sauron as spokesperson for the West.

Aragorn enters the City and takes up his kingship with all due ceremony. His first act is to sit in judgment in the Hall of Kings, pardoning and making peace with Sauron's allies, dispensing praise and rewards for valor, and granting mercy and a new task to Beregond for his disobedience to Denethor. As a new leader, he must consolidate his power base and make sure everyone is as satisfied as possible with his or her part in his kingdom. Little else is said of his reign in the appendices, but he does ensure the independence of the Shire by forbidding Men to enter it and making the Took, Thain, and mayor his counsellors (*Return* 377).

In Aragorn, has Tolkien described his ideal of a perfected Alexander the Great, free from the Macedonian king's hubris, bloodthirstiness, and taste for the theatrical? As Victor Davis Hanson says, "The ancient world produced no man more personally courageous, militarily brilliant, and abjectly murderous than Alexander" (*Carnage* 90). In fact, Aragorn does share several of Alexander's leadership qualities, and there are parallels between the historical situation and Middle-earth events as well.

Like Persia, Mordor was "a despotic power bent on robbing [their enemies] of liberty and reducing them to subject status," and like Alexander, Aragorn was "his civilization's champion" (Keegan, *Mask* 23). However, the two leaders had vastly differing ultimate goals. Aragorn was reclaiming and defending an ancient kingdom, and Tolkien does not report that he attempted to expand his kingdom beyond its previous bounds (as some of the earlier Gondorian kings did). Alexander was creating an entirely new empire out of the squabbling Greek city-states, and for all his talk of spreading Hellenism, he was unquestionably out for conquest and rule of the world as well. In an earlier era, spreading civilization through invasion and colonization may not have seemed a contradiction in terms, but the first half of the twentieth century rendered all of the old assumptions suspect. W. W. Tarn ended his hagiographic biography of Alexander by praising him for preaching the brotherhood of man and citizenship in one state, and downplayed the possibility that "[p]erhaps he gave no thought to the slave world" (147). But in a postscript to the 1948 edition, he writes, "I have left the latter part of this paragraph substantially as written in 1926. Since then we have seen new and monstrous births, and are still moving in a world not realised; and I do not know how to rewrite it" (148). Napoleon claimed his military descent from Alexander, but so too did Hitler.

Still, there is no disputing Alexander's success as a leader for the brief span of his reign, and no telling now what it might have come to if he had had a chance to consolidate his conquests under a stable and bureaucratic government. Aragorn shared a preference for consensual leadership with Alexander; both constantly sought the advice and agreement of their companions. Aragorn's armies are also similar to Alexander's in some ways: they were "neither a tribal war band nor a royal regular army, nor were they conscripts or mercenaries. . . . They were . . . a sort of nation-in-arms . . . following their king as much out of comradeship as obligation" (Keegan, *Mask* 44). As such, they consented to follow their leader freely. Like Alexander, Aragorn granted indulgences from time to time; Alexander cancelled debts and let married men go home in the off-season, and Aragorn allowed soldiers too shaken by proximity to Mordor to take another objective instead. They were both also personally concerned with their wounded troops. Alexander is reported "visiting each [and] examining their wounds" (Keegan, *Mask* 46), and Aragorn was involved with healing them personally. Also like Alexander, he made sure the dead were buried with all proper ceremony and reverence after battles as a "first, sacred duty" (quoted *Mask* 46).

With what type of men did Aragorn choose to surround himself? The associates of a commander facilitate communication between the leader and his troops, and their quality determines the stability of his command. Keegan analyzes several commanders:

Grant and Wellington both succeeded . . . in creating a bond of kinship between themselves and their followers by surrounding themselves with men who posed no threat to their primacy yet were of sufficient soldierly quality to command the army's respect. Alexander, on the other hand, was fated to be surrounded by men who, while their soldierly qualities were not in doubt, so powerfully shared his ethic of heroic individuality that he could never truly rest at ease with them. Hitler went to the other extreme: his intimate circle was selected by the test of sycophancy, which made for perfect domestic ease at headquarters but denied him any bond of understanding with the fighting men at the front. (*Mask* 318)

Boromir, thrust upon Aragorn by circumstance and not by choice, is sometimes a challenge to his authority during their journey because his private agenda conflicts with the goal of the Company, and because of his own personal desire for renown as a heroic leader. His father Denethor presents an insurmountable problem—his ambition prevents his acceptance of Aragorn's claim, and if he had lived, he would have disputed Aragorn's right to the throne. But the younger men Aragorn picks as his associates and advisers are not his "competitors in heroism," as Alexander's Diadochi could sometimes be (Keegan, *Mask* 318). Éomer, Faramir, and Imrahil were confident in their own positions and had no wish to upstage Aragorn—Éomer and Imrahil because they had kingdoms of their own, and Faramir because of the nature of his own attitude toward war.

In Aragorn, Tolkien presents an ideal king, proven worthy by his long *cursus honorum* and by his battlefield experience; an able and responsible leader, without hubris or the overmastering desire for conquest and power. Aragorn claims the throne he knows is his by right of birth, but he has no quarrel with being required to prove himself worthy of it.

Merry and Pippin

Merry and Pippin also follow a course of honor, not as demanding as Aragorn's but befitting their eventual roles as de facto stewards of the Shire. Both are only sons and likely heirs of the most prominent families in the Shire (*Return* 381–82), and during their adventures they move into positions of increasingly official responsibility.

Originally, they join Frodo's somewhat casually organized flight from the Shire, and then are more formally made part of the Fellowship by Elrond. During their ordeal as prisoners of the orcs, Pippin takes the initiative in leaving a clue for Aragorn, cutting his bonds, and manipulating Grishnákh into carrying them away from the encampment. He manages the details of getting free, fed, and under cover of the trees. Once they enter Fangorn

Forest, however, Merry tells him, "Cousin Brandybuck is going in front now" (*Towers* 62), because he has a better idea of the terrain, and leads them deep into the woods.

Both are later separated from their companions and at that time take formal service with a King, Pippin with Denethor and Merry with Théoden. Although they are taken on as squires, they both do great deeds in the war— Merry hamstringing the Witch-king, and Pippin acting decisively to save Faramir's life from Denethor's madness. By the time of the great feast at the Field of Cormallen, they are advanced in rank and are "knights of the City and of the Mark" (*Return* 233).

As they ride home, looking like "riders upon errantry out of almost forgotten tales" (*Return* 274), Gandalf hints at changes in the Shire and tells them: "You must settle its affairs yourselves; that is what you have been trained for. Do you not yet understand? . . . [Y]ou will need no help. You are grown up now. Grown indeed very high; among the great you are, and I have no longer any fear at all for any of you" (*Return* 275). On the travelers' return to the much-changed Shire, Merry and Pippin soon take charge of organizing the resistance, with Pippin riding off to muster the Tooks and Merry directing operations in Hobbiton. In later years, Merry becomes Master of Buckland and Pippin becomes Took and Thain. Along with Sam, now mayor of the Shire, they became counsellors to the king and his representatives in the Shire. Their *cursus honorum* has prepared them for leadership of their people.

Sam Gamgee

Sam too is prepared by his leadership experiences to take a role in governing the Shire. Throughout most of *The Lord of the Rings*, Sam is the perfect follower; and it is said that one cannot be a leader without first learning how to follow. A World War I training manual quotes General Pershing as saying, "if a soldier has been taught the imperative necessity of carrying out orders he will feel himself equal to giving them" (*Camps, Billets, Cooking,* preface). While Sam and Frodo often act like equals after their flight from the Company, when a decision needs to be made about their journey, Frodo makes it. The dynamics of leadership are unbalanced when Gollum joins them; Sam's place as Frodo's chief adviser is taken by his rival. However, when Gollum betrays and abandons them, the balance is briefly restored.

Sam's first short-lived experience of the responsibility of leadership comes when Frodo runs ahead "in a fey mood" (*Towers* 334) after their escape from Shelob's tunnel; Sam has to fight off Gollum and then kill the monstrous spider on his own. He thinks that Frodo is dead, and must make his own decision about going on with the quest or avenging Frodo's death. When he learns that Frodo has survived Shelob's attack and has been captured by the orcs, he has to rescue his helpless and despairing master and make all the arrangements for their escape. When he gives the Ring back to Frodo he becomes a follower again, but one more confident in his ability to act alone.

But it is not long before Frodo's growing weakness forces him to allow Sam to take the lead for good. Frodo gives his sword, Sting, to Sam, and soon after tells Sam he must lead the way because his hope is gone. Sam realizes what his task is: " 'So that was the job I felt I had to do when I started, . . . to help Mr. Frodo to the last step and then die with him? Well, if that is the job then I must do it.' . . . But even as hope died in Sam, or seemed to die, it was turned to a new strength. . . . With a new sense of responsibility he brought his eyes back to the ground near at hand, studying the next move" (*Return* 211). After the destruction of the Ring, when Frodo no longer cares about surviving, Sam leads him away from Mount Doom.

Merry and Pippin are the main leaders of the resistance during the Scouring of the Shire, and in fact Merry restrains Sam several times, but then sends him off to Farmer Cotton's to raise the village. Sam is very active in the restoration of the Shire, especially in planting trees, and is much admired by the other hobbits for organizing reforestation and gardening projects around the country. When Frodo takes leave of Sam at the Grey Havens, he tells Sam, "You will be the Mayor, of course, as long as you want to be," (*Return* 309), and indeed he is elected seven times. Sam's leadership experience is deeply rooted in his service to his master, and not in the leadership of men in battle. It is fitting that his position in the Shire should be one of nurturing, renewal, and service to his fellow hobbits.

Gandalf

Gandalf has a complex military leadership role in Middle-earth, serving sometimes as a leader, sometimes as a champion, at other times as a gadfly, and even on occasion as a statesman. The Istari, or wizards, were originally sent to Middle-earth by the Valar near the beginning of the Third Age. Their task was to "advise and persuade Men and Elves to good, and to seek to unite in love and understanding all those whom Sauron, should he come again, would endeavour to dominate and corrupt." They were sent in bodies "weak and humble" and forbidden "to seek to rule the wills of Men or Elves by open display of power" (*Unfinished* 389). Gandalf specifically was "the Enemy of Sauron, opposing the fire that devours and wastes with the fire that kindles, and succors in wanhope and distress" (*Unfinished* 390–91). In one of several versions of "The Quest of Erebor" in Tolkien's notes, Gandalf specifically refers to himself as a captain and "a member of a Council of War," and describes himself trying to guess whether Sauron would attempt to reoccupy Mordor or attack Rivendell and Lórien first (*Annotated Hobbit* 370).

At times he serves as leader of the Fellowship, and Elrond apparently envisaged this role for him in Rivendell. But when Gandalf stands on the Bridge of Khazad-dûm, as David Bratman has pointed out (Bratman), he is acting

not as a general or leader but as a champion. Compare his actions in defending a contested bridge to those of Beorhtnoth—Gandalf's only goal was the
defense of the other members of his Company and the larger world in general,
and he had no desire for glory or renown. His ego did not enter into the
equation, and it would have been disastrous to allow the enemy any advantage
out of an unbalanced sense of honor or fairness. Beorhtnoth, on the other
hand, held his honor above all else and allowed the enemy to cross the easily
defensible bridge in spite of his duty to those he was defending and to his
followers. His actions were both tactically and ethically wrong. Gandalf's act
calls to mind instead the Spartan stand at Thermopylae, where Leonidas held
the Persian forces at bay long enough for the other Greeks to retreat and
regroup. Or perhaps more pertinent, the defense of the Sublician Bridge by
Horatius, who fought off the Etruscans alone until the Romans behind him
could throw down the bridge, and who fell with the bridge but miraculously
managed to swim to safety.

Later Gandalf is the messenger flying before the storm to Rohan—"Storm-
crow," or "Láthspell, Ill-News," as Wormtongue names him, accusing him of
bringing trouble with him (*Towers* 117). Then he is the spiritual healer who
awakens Théoden and spurs him to action, and the *deus ex machina* who
leads Erkenbrand's cavalry to the Battle of Helm's Deep. At the siege of Minas
Tirith he is everywhere at once, it seems, standing as a champion against the
Witch-king, attempting to bring Denethor to his senses, taking charge of the
city when its lord dies and his heir lies feverish in the Houses of Healing.
After the battle, Aragorn suggests that "Gandalf should rule us all in the days
that follow and in our dealings with the enemy" (*Return* 138), and from that
point the wizard acts as commander in chief and the spokesperson of the
Western forces in negotiating with the Mouth of Sauron. His labors are many
and varied, and at his coronation Aragorn asks that Gandalf set the crown
on his head, "for he has been the mover of all that has been accomplished,
and this is his victory" (*Return* 246).

Gandalf is not an easy leader to follow, with his mercurial changes of role
and his need for swift movement, nor does he particularly seek out leadership
or need followers to help him accomplish his work. However, there are times
when his labors require him to lead with a firm hand and deep wisdom.

OBEDIENCE AND DISOBEDIENCE

Many elements of the plots of *The Hobbit* and *The Lord of the Rings* hinge
on disobedience to a commanding officer and its consequences. While there
are several examples of characters simply not doing what they are told, sometimes an order is disobeyed because it is wrong, or because the commanding
officer is not on the spot and is unaware of a change in the situation, or
because the character perceives some higher good that supersedes the order.
Particularly among the Rohirrim, captains in the field feel a responsibility to

think for themselves, take the initiative, and improvise when necessary. And in Tolkien's world, disobedience quite frequently has a eucatastrophic effect in the end.

Victor Davis Hanson, in his book *Carnage and Culture: Landmark Battles in the Rise of Western Power*, theorizes that the success of Western armies against non-Western foes can be attributed in part to a delicate balance between the willing submission of citizen-soldiers to discipline and drill on the one hand, and on the other, the encouragement of initiative and independent thought and action in battle. A World War I book about the British military system puts it this way: a soldier's life "entails the voluntary daily subjection of the individual will for the good of others" (Atkinson, foreword). This balance, with its roots in the democratic culture of ancient Greece, produces a flexible and motivated force adaptable to a variety of conditions. For example, Hanson credits the victory of the American forces at the World War II battle of Midway to the fact that

American military personnel at all ranks were unusually innovative, even eccentric, and always unpredictable. Most were unafraid to take the initiative to craft policy when orders from superiors were either vague or nonexistent—in a fashion completely antithetical to the protocols of operations in the imperial fleet, which in turn mirrored much of the prevailing values and attitudes inherent in Japanese society. The result was that Americans improvised when plans went awry, [and] resorted to new and innovative methods of attack when orthodoxy was unproductive. (*Carnage* 355–56)

Another element of the equation is the protection of soldiers' rights and responsibilities as citizens within the legal framework of the military. A soldier will not feel free to risk taking the initiative if the military structure in which he functions (and in turn, the society that supports it) punishes improvisation harshly and unfairly. Hanson describes the great advantage the Roman army gained after it relaxed the requirements for citizenship and military service in response to its defeat by Hannibal at Cannae:

This revolutionary idea of Western citizenship—replete with ever more rights and responsibilities—would provide superb manpower for the growing legions and a legal framework that would guarantee that the men who fought felt that they themselves in a formal and contractual sense had ratified the conditions of their own battle service. . . . [A]s citizens, they would see their military service as a contractual agreement rather than ad hoc impressments. (*Carnage* 122)

Centuries later, the British army of the late 1800s operated under the same legal framework:

The British army . . . had a written code of punishment and laws. Individual troopers more or less knew what was expected of them, assumed a relatively uniform and predictable application of justice throughout the ranks, and considered their own persons sacrosanct from arbitrary execution. For the most part, they followed orders from a sense of justice rather than mere fear. . . . [E]ven the queen could not execute a single soldier without at least a hearing or trial. (*Carnage* 321)

A World War I training guide explains the necessity for military law to the new recruit: "For the proper carrying out of the duties of the Army it is necessary to have a code of laws to a certain extent distinct from the civil code. This is due to the fact that many things which in civil life would either be no crime at all, or, at any rate, merely a breach of contract, must in military life be looked upon very severely" ("The Major" 65).

The oath of the *ephebes*, the young recruits of Athens, sums up this Western attitude toward military service as a contractual relationship, with obligations on both sides: "I will offer my ready obedience at any time to those who are exercising their authority *prudently*, and to the established laws" (quoted Hanson, *Carnage* 328, emphasis added). To be effective and capable of both disciplined drill and field initiative, soldiers need to know that there is a fair and reasonably democratic structure of legal rights, responsibilities, and promotions and rewards supporting them. In Middle-earth, the allies have this supporting structure: note for example Pippin's oath to Denethor and Denethor's oath in response. Pippin swears "to speak and to be silent, to do and to let be, to come and to go" at the steward's command, and Denethor in turn swears to reward "fealty with love, valour with honour, [and] oath-breaking with vengeance" (*Return* 28). Although it is not described in depth, a system of martial justice is implied by the fact that the legal consequences of two episodes of military disobedience are depicted. The orcs of Mordor and Orthanc, however, fear arbitrary execution, internal spies, and the unpredictable wrath of their commanders—they are slaves, not citizen-soldiers.

The one major act of military disobedience in *The Hobbit* occurs shortly after the Elves and Men have begun their siege of the Lonely Mountain. Thorin has been unable to find the Arkenstone in the dragon's hoard, and vows vengeance on anyone who "finds it and withholds it" (*Hobbit* 279). Unbeknownst to him, Bilbo had picked up the stone days ago and hidden it in his bedding. Bilbo creeps out of the dwarves' camp by night and offers the Arkenstone to Bard and the Elvenking as a bargaining chip to use in preventing battle with the Dwarves. While it does not have the decisive effect Bilbo had hoped, the parlay delays battle just long enough that the Men, Elves, and Dwarves are all on the battlefield prepared to fight when the Goblin and Warg armies attack. If they had not been ready to fight, or had already fought their own battle, the Goblins and Wargs would have overwhelmed them, captured the Lonely Mountain, and used it as a base to conquer Laketown, northern Mirkwood, and much of Wilderland. Bilbo's disobedience was essential to the eucatastrophic timing of the Battle of Five Armies.

The action in *The Lord of the Rings* is on a war footing from the time the Company leaves Rivendell, and during the events at Parth Galen, three acts of military disobedience occur that have long-term eucatastrophic effects. Aragorn calls the Company together to discuss their plans. Frodo asks for time alone to consider his decision, and while Aragorn does not give a specific order, he does say clearly, "you shall be alone. We will all stay here for a while" (*Fellowship* 412). But Boromir sneaks off and confronts Frodo, trying to take the Ring from him. Boromir's act has several consequences. First, it makes Frodo's path clear to him—he must get away from the Company before the Ring tears it apart, and he must go on alone to Mordor. Second, when Frodo runs from Boromir, he winds up at the Seat of Seeing, Amon Hen, and sees "signs of war" all over Middle-earth (*Fellowship* 416). In his vision he narrowly escapes being seen by Sauron, and is warned by the voice of Gandalf to take off the Ring. All these events serve to harden his will and lighten his heart—he knows clearly what he must do and has found the will to do it. Without Boromir's surrender to temptation, he might have delayed even longer and been captured by Saruman's Uruk-Hai. Third, Boromir's reappearance, and his edited story of his argument with Frodo, sends the other hobbits into a panic. They disregard Aragorn's orders to wait, and scatter to look for Frodo. Merry and Pippin go in one direction; Legolas and Gimli, usually obedient followers, are affected by their frenzy and run off in another. Aragorn sends Boromir after Merry and Pippin and chases Sam himself. When Aragorn catches up to him, he orders Sam to follow him, but Sam realizes what Frodo is planning and heads back down to the shore in time to persuade Frodo that he should accompany him. Without Sam, Frodo's mission could never have been accomplished; quite likely Gollum would have killed him in the Emyn Muil and taken the Ring.

Merry and Pippin's disobedience also has long-reaching consequences. The orcs quickly capture them, and Boromir's attempt to rescue them provides him an opportunity for redemption. Aragorn's decision to follow them with Legolas and Gimli brings him to Rohan in time to forge a relationship with Éomer and bring Gandalf to Edoras for the healing of Théoden. And when Merry and Pippin escape into Fangorn (because of Grishnákh's disobedience to Uglúk), they are the "small stones that [start] the avalanche" (*Towers* 99)—they wake Treebeard and the Ents, who turn their wrath against Saruman.

As Tom Shippey has pointed out, the Riders of Rohan, "while disciplined in a way, do not have the rigid codes of obedience of a modern army, or a modern bureaucracy. . . . They are freer to make their own minds up, and regard this as a duty. They surrender less of their independence to their superiors than we do" (*Century* 96). Éomer is already being disobedient to his king when he meets Aragorn: "Indeed in this riding forth I went without the king's leave" (*Towers* 39). His *éored* is not undisciplined—we first see them in an impressive close-order cavalry drill as they encircle Aragorn and his companions—but his second-in-command has no reservations about questioning his orders in his presence. Éomer asks a central question showing the

value he places on his own independence of thought and action: "How shall
a man judge what to do in such times?" and Aragorn answers, "As he ever
has judged" (*Towers* 40–41). Éomer's discussion with Aragorn confirms the
decision he has already made: that he should trust "the deed which my heart
would do" and let the strangers borrow horses and search for their friends
rather than come immediately with them to Meduseld. He asks only that they
return the horses to Théoden's house: "Thus you shall prove to him that I
have not misjudged" (*Towers* 41). Éomer has a responsibility to explain his
disobedience to his commander, which he willingly accepts. This sequence is
unfortunately abbreviated in Peter Jackson's movie, and much of its meaning
is lost.

Another example from Rohan is the interview with the door-warden when
Aragorn, Legolas, Gimli, and Gandalf come to Edoras. Shippey shows how
this echoes almost exactly a similar incident in *Beowulf*, where the Danish
coastguard challenges then passes Beowulf and his men, and later a door-
guard makes them leave their arms at the door (*Century* 94–96). In *Beowulf*,
the coastguard speaks to the warriors:

> Astride his steed, the strand-ward answered,
> clansman unquailing: "The keen-souled thane
> must be skilled to sever and sunder duly
> words and works, if he well intends.
> I gather, this band is graciously bent
> to the Scyldings' master. March, then, bearing
> weapons and weeds the way I show you.
>
> ("Beowulf" 35)

Shippey explicates his words further: " 'A sharp shield-warrior must be able
to decide, from words as well as from deeds' (for, unstated, any fool can
decide from deeds—it is deciding before anything has happened which is the
test of intelligence)" (*Century* 95). The doorward Háma makes a decision to
allow Gandalf to keep his staff in spite of Wormtongue's orders: "Yet in doubt
a man will trust to his own wisdom. I believe you are friends and folk worthy
of honour, who have no evil purpose" (*Towers* 116). His disobedience allows
Gandalf to strike down Wormtongue and revitalize the king.

Later, Faramir shows similar trust in his own judgment when he allows
Frodo and Sam to pass through Ithilien. As he tells Sam, "I am commanded
to slay all whom I find in this land without the leave of the Lord of Gondor,"
but he goes on to say, "I do not slay man or beast needlessly, and not even
gladly when it is needed" (*Towers* 273). Faramir obviously agrees with Napoleon Bonaparte that "blind obedience . . . is due only to a superior present
on the spot at the moment of action" (quoted Ridgway 10). Faramir again
makes his own decision when Gollum is caught fishing in the pool of Henneth
Annûn, and spares him at Frodo's wish in spite of his orders. On his own

authority, Faramir gives Frodo freedom to travel anywhere in the realm of Gondor. Because of Faramir's disobedience, Frodo and his companions are free to continue their journey, and Gollum is still alive to play the part he must play before the end. Faramir is also able to tell Gandalf what Frodo planned to do, so that the Captains of the West will know how important it is to keep Sauron's attention focused outside the borders of Mordor.

But Faramir serves a difficult and inconsistent master in his father. When Faramir asks Denethor if he has done ill to garrison Osgiliath, Denethor in a single speech in turn implies that he ought to be able to think for himself, that he has turned away from his father's advice, and that he only does what Gandalf wants. " 'If what I have done displeases you, my father,' said Faramir quietly, 'I wish I had known your counsel before the burden of so weighty a judgement was thrust on me.' 'Would that have availed to change your judgement?' said Denethor. 'You would still have done just so, I deem' " (*Return* 86). In reaction to his father's mood and his brother's death, Faramir bows to his father's will and goes to the garrison at Osgiliath against his own assessment of the situation, and is nearly killed in the retreat. Seeing his only remaining son near death because of his own orders is too much for Denethor and he gives way to despair. In this case, Faramir's obedience against his own judgment led to unnecessary death and suffering—yet still, some good came of it when Faramir met Éowyn in the Houses of Healing.

Éowyn presents a particularly strong example of a eucatastrophic result of radical disobedience to both military orders and social rules. She is explicitly commanded by her uncle the king to take charge of his people before the Battle of Helm's Deep (*Towers* 128), and when she would go with Aragorn on the Paths of the Dead, he reminds her that she accepted this charge (*Return* 57). But she breaks her pledge and disobeys her orders when she joins the muster of Rohan riding to Minas Tirith. Merry, too, is forbidden by the king to join the Rohirrim, but Éowyn takes Merry on her horse, compounding her insubordination. As she says, "Such good will should not be denied" (*Return* 78). Their presence is essential, for it is through their actions that the Lord of the Nazgûl is slain.

Another major example of military insubordination is taking place at nearly the same instant. Denethor in his suicidal despair plans to burn himself and Faramir alive, and as a last act releases Pippin from his service. But Pippin refuses to be released (*Return* 99). He flees the tomb of the Stewards, attempts to countermand Denethor's orders to his servants, and tells Beregond, on guard duty at the door, that he must "choose between orders and the life of Faramir" (*Return* 101). Beregond leaves his post and fights off the porter and the servants, killing several of them. Blood had never been shed in that place before, and Beregond is called outlaw, traitor, and renegade (*Return* 128). However, as Gandalf points out to the other guards: "But think, you servants of the Lord, blind in your obedience, that but for the treason of

Beregond Faramir, Captain of the White Tower, would now also be burned"
(*Return* 131).

What is the reaction of the commanding officers to these various acts of
disobedience? In *The Hobbit*, Thorin threatens to throw Bilbo off the wall
until Gandalf makes him release the hobbit, but eventually they make peace
with each other at Thorin's deathbed. In *The Lord of the Rings*, Aragorn
blames no one but himself for the confusion and disaster at Parth Galen; the
fog of war was on all of them, in a way.

Éomer had been imprisoned for disobedience on the advice of Wormtongue
(not banished, as in Peter Jackson's movie); as Théoden said, "He had re-
belled against my commands." But showing a fine sense of justice, Théoden
sends the doorwarden Háma to free him: "The guilty shall bring the guilty to
judgement" (*Towers* 120). Yet he punishes neither one of them in the end,
realizing that their disobedience was to the traitor Wormtongue's orders only.
Éowyn and Merry also, disobedient to the king of Rohan, are not punished
in any way. Initiative is apparently acceptable in Rohan's military, particularly
if the result is victory.

Justice in Gondor is sterner. Faramir is publicly shamed by his father, who
forces him to accept his will in council (*Return* 90); he punishes himself in
trying to fulfill his father's orders. Denethor orders his attendants to slay the
renegade Beregond on the spot. However, Aragorn is fair and even merciful
to Beregond. The guard must be removed from his post and reduced in rank
for what he has done, but he is allowed to serve in battle with the men of
the City, and eventually he is given a different posting by the new king. Nothing is said about Pippin's disobedience in searching for Gandalf.

These events and their eucatastrophic consequences bring up the question
of free will in Middle-earth. Is each act of disobedience fated, designed to
bring the characters where they need to be at a certain time? Certainly the
will of the author says it shall be so, and of course, all these "what-ifs" are
at this level only a game played with the information Tolkien has given us.
But he has given us a world that hangs together so well at all levels that it is
possible to play these games. And in the underlying mythology, disobedience,
fate, and eucatastrophe all play a part; even Melkor's disobedience is foreseen
in Ilúvatar's plans and subsumed by them. Ilúvatar takes the discordant notes
of Melkor's melody and weaves them into his own themes: "no theme may be
played that hath not its uttermost source in me, nor can any alter the music
in my despite" (*Silmarillion* 17).

CONCLUSION: LEADERSHIP AND THE WAR OF THE MACHINES

If Aragorn is Tolkien's ideal leader, then what is he saying about military
leadership? First and foremost, he says that a leader must be prepared to
lead from in front. A leader should also gain experience by moving up through

the ranks, as Aragorn did when he served in disguise in Gondor and Rohan. A leader who expects to move into a position of political leadership should have an understanding of fighting with all the means at his disposal; in Aragorn's case, infantry, cavalry, and naval warfare, and even covert intelligence, were all areas where he had experience.

A leader should develop a leadership style that involves consulting with his commanders on a regular basis, and those commanders should be picked neither for sycophancy nor for outstanding heroic achievement, but for the ability to work with each other and with their commander, and for proven leadership skills. He should keep the needs of his troops uppermost in his mind, and make sure the wounded are cared for, the dead buried with honor, and victories celebrated with ceremony and dignity. Those who break the rules should be dealt with fairly and mercifully, and rewards should be given for outstanding performance. Patience and humility should be two of the leader's outstanding virtues—patience not to claim too much too soon, and humility to show solidarity with the average soldier. And a leader must also "[believe] in a cause which [transcends] themselves and their own desires or ambitions" (Stokesbury 151).

But is Aragorn really Tolkien's ideal? For all the anachronisms mentioned above, he is not that different from ancient heroes. We never see him doubting the wisdom of war or considering it philosophically—he simply accepts that it is a normal part of the duty of a king. As Hanson says of the Greeks at the time of Xenophon, they did not operate "on a belief that war was either abnormal or amoral" (*Carnage* 4), and for all we see of Aragorn's thoughts he appears to feel the same way. As with Alexander, there is no distinction "between his roles as king and war-leader" (Keegan, *Mask* 312).

Faramir has a more modern and thoughtful attitude toward war, and is perhaps a more realistic model to emulate for the twenty-first-century reader. It is possible that he speaks with Tolkien's own voice when he says, "I do not love the bright sword for its sharpness, nor the arrow for its swiftness, nor the warrior for his glory. I love only that which they defend" (*Towers* 280). Yet even suffering from these doubts about the very value of war, he is as beloved and charismatic a leader as Aragorn and as effective and skilled in battle; he has the same leadership style and characteristics, but thinks (or at least speaks) more deeply about why he fights.

It is also important to note that leadership among the allies in Middle-earth is decentralized and decisions are generally reached by discussion and consensus rather than submission to the will of a single leader. For example, the Council of Elrond makes its decision as a group, every member of the Company has a chance to speak before entering Moria, and all the leaders of the allies consult together before the march against Mordor. Paradoxically, this style of consultative leadership means that a leader like Aragorn can take command quickly and decisively in a crisis, and count on the rest of the group to follow him. Because his peers have discussed other situations with him and understand how his mind works, they know they can trust his judgment when there is no time for discussion.

Hal Colebatch discusses the difference between this type of leadership and that of Sauron and Saruman in his book *Return of the Heroes*: "[A] king is a legitimate head in the natural order of things, whose position and role have something of sacrifice about them. A tyrant is one who has seized power for self-aggrandisement, a gangster writ large, but more dangerous than any gangster if he is operating on a spiritual or ideological level. The gangster is satisfied with robbing and perhaps killing; the ideological tyrant wants souls as well, and there is no limit on his appetite" (51). Théoden sums it up in his forthright way when he tells Saruman: "Were you ten times as wise you would have no right to rule me and mine for your own profit as you desired" (*Towers* 185). The right to rule is earned only by securing the consent of the governed through discussion and consultation, and those ruled still have the right to think for themselves.

Are Tolkien's ideals of Northern heroism and personal leadership still applicable in the postnuclear era? The modern way of war—highly technical; controlled from a distance; and with an emphasis on real-time communications, precise "surgical strikes" from the air, and above all low casualty counts (especially on "our side")—makes personal leadership in battle seem obsolete. Should a leader risk his expensive technical and analytical training out in the field, where he is subject to the fog of war? Is he not more effective in a heavily shielded command post where he can get a good overview of the battle as a whole and direct each unit where it will do the most good? A modern leader may say that he saves more of his men's lives by commanding from his situation room, but without close attention to building relationships with field soldiers, he runs the risk of attenuating the human element and intellectualizing what is at heart an emotional bond.

Military historian James Stokesbury comments on how technology has changed leadership in modern warfare:

In the twentieth century, the tasks of leadership at the highest levels of authority have become strangely complicated. On the one hand the simple growth of the population has made in increasingly difficult for a leader to touch all his potential followers; on the other, the development of modern communication methods has made it easier for a leader to project at least an image of himself to vast numbers of people. . . .

Such problems were in their infancy, and but imperfectly perceived, at the time of the First World War. Until 1914 men were convinced that modern masses could meet and overcome any challenge by the application of modern technology. There was then what looks like a charmingly naive confidence that anything might be achieved. . . .

That complacent confidence had evaporated by 1917. It had been slaughtered on the "corpsefield of Loos," blown apart on the slopes of Vimy Ridge, and ground into the mud on the Somme and Verdun. (148–49)

John Keegan lists a set of "imperatives of command" that defined leadership in the prenuclear age:

kinship, by which a leader surrounded himself with intimates identifiable by his followers as common spirits with themselves . . . *sanction*, the reward—or punishment—
of followers according to a jointly accepted value system . . . *example*, the demonstra-
tion of the personal acceptance of risk by the authority who requires others to bear
it at his behest . . . *prescription*, the explanation of the need of risk-taking by the
leader, in direct speech, to his followers . . . *action*, the translation of leadership into
effect, of which victory was the desired result. (*Mask* 343–44)

But in Keegan's analysis, nuclear warfare has overturned all of these imperatives. The sense of *kinship* between leaders and led is destroyed by the
secrecy and isolation needed to keep nuclear weapons hidden and secure.
Sanction has little meaning since, as he puts it, "the proper management of
a nuclear system will generate no occasion for either punishment or reward,
or none at any rate that can be readily revealed." *Example* is "denied by
nuclear logic"; those most vulnerable are on the front lines, while the leaders
are protected in bunkers and flying fortresses. *Prescription* is farcical when
the leader is in no danger; the leader has no moral right to demand sacrifice
and courage of those who bear all the risk when he bears none. And *action*
is "denied by the necessity to avoid all outcomes in nuclear confrontation
whatsoever" (*Mask* 344).

Keegan calls for a type of "post-heroic leadership"—intellectual, detached,
moderate, and analytical—and sees the Cuban Missile Crisis of 1962 as the
first example of this paradigm. Analysis of the Russian speed of deployment
provided a timetable for decision making, built to prevent hasty and ill-
considered action; the executive committee formed to advise the president
worked without hierarchical leadership and reached decisions by discussion
and consensus. Keegan identifies three "velocities" that have to be managed
in a military situation: "velocity of events, velocity of response, and velocity
of human decision-making" (*Mask* 348)—and points out that while the velocity of events and response continue to accelerate, the speed of human
decision making cannot be altered. In his analysis, heroism historically served
the purpose of deflecting risk from the people in general to the heroic leader
who accepted it on their behalf. However, nuclear war threatens everyone
and the leader can no longer take on risk for others by heroic action. In fact,
Keegan's conclusion is that "what is asked first of a leader in the nuclear
world is that he should not act, in any traditionally heroic sense, at all" (*Mask*
351). Tolkien actually does echo this sentiment in a letter to his son Michael
during World War II: "it is to sloth, as much or more than to natural virtue,
that we owe our escape from the overt violences of other countries. In the
fierce modern world, indeed, sloth does begin almost to look like a virtue"
(*Letters* 55).

Keegan in conclusion rejects entirely the heroic ethic for the postnuclear
age, the ethic that Tolkien is both so reactionary in adhering to and yet of
which he is so critical. Did Tolkien have an understanding of how the imper-

atives of command are invalidated by the demands of nuclear strategy, which carry the war of machines to its inevitable conclusion? He saw the possibilities quite clearly; in a letter to Christopher just after the bombing of Hiroshima he deplores the "utter folly" of scientists "calmly plotting the destruction of the world, while man's "moral and intellectual status is declining" (*Letters* 116). Even earlier in the war, he observes, "we are attempting to conquer Sauron with the Ring. And we shall (it seems) succeed. But the penalty is . . . to breed new Saurons, and slowly turn Men and Elves into Orcs" (*Letters* 78).

One of the reasons Tolkien viewed mechanized war as a great evil is that it allows leaders to avoid personally sharing the dangers of the led and thereby validating their leadership. As noted earlier, he was quite scathing about child-less leaders who observed World War II "from the vantage point of large motor-cars" (*Letters* 89). Tolkien's fiction and criticism show that he would prefer to keep some of the best aspects of more modern military leadership: for example, leaders who are modest and close to their men; the consultative leadership style, not loving war for itself but only for what it defends; glory ranked well below duty as a motivation. But he would also keep the best of the old heroic style: personal responsibility and assuming risk on the behalf of others. Maintaining this balance cannot be particularly easy for military leaders in the nuclear era.

The Ring may not be an allegory for the Bomb, but it does have symbolic applicability. It is the weapon by which either side could totally destroy the other—and in it are also the seeds of the spiritual destruction (at the very least) of the victor. Tolkien's answer to these overturned imperatives is to destroy the Ring—to get rid of the temptation to use a device that negates personal heroism so utterly. But it is not so easy to turn back the clock and eliminate atomic weapons from the arsenals of the world.

Chapter 6

"The Dull Backwaters of the Art of Killing": Training, Tactics, Strategy, and Battlefield Communication

> These grey days, wasted in wearily going over, over and over again, the dreary topics, the dull backwaters of the art of killing, are not enjoyable.
> —Carpenter, *Tolkien* 78

What did Tolkien's war experiences and reading teach him about tactics and strategy? How did his military training affect his depiction of warfare? In this chapter, I will look at several of the major battles in *The Hobbit* and *The Lord of the Rings* and analyze the strategies and tactics used by both sides. Just as with Tolkien's depictions of modern heroism in an archaic world, the anachronisms point out Tolkien's criticisms of both ancient and modern ways of making war; as Alex Lewis has pointed out, "Tolkien's battles owe more to the nineteenth and twentieth centuries than to the Middle Ages and Medievalism" ("Arma" 10). I will pay particular attention to the roles of battlefield communication and intelligence in each battle because of Tolkien's background as a signaling officer.

Before the war, Tolkien might have gained some casual familiarity with the basics of classical tactics and strategy through his reading. As a student of Greek and Latin at King Edwards School, he is likely to have read Xenophon, Tacitus, Polybius, Caesar, Arrian, and so on before learning Anglo-Saxon and discovering sources in the literature of northern Europe, such as those concerning the Battle of Maldon. But it is difficult to acquire skill in strategy and tactics through reading and study of historical examples alone (especially if one is not reading with that purpose in mind); formal training, frequently updated, and experience are better teachers.

Ongoing training is essential to a country's military readiness. During

World War I, "The western front ate up young front-line officers partly because of the lack of training and education of senior officers and their staffs"
(Higham 49). Younger officers who had started their training after 1902 had
the advantage of a modernized, post–Boer War education at Sandhurst and
other military academies and through the Officer Training Corps attached to
the public schools, but their elders and commanders were still most familiar
with the now-outdated tactics developed during the Peninsular War and
proven in colonial actions (Higham 48–49). The early years of the war dec-
imated this well-trained core of younger officers and left men hurried through
their training to take their place. One soldiers' manual written in 1916 states
that recruits normally trained for three months to a year before the war, but
now "the time is very considerably shortened" ("The Major" 45). A book on
the British army system for the American soldier describes the course of
training Tolkien would have gone through. The officer candidates are first
trained in small cadet camps. "After the new officers are qualified to take
command they are moved to other small camps and watched and guided while
they drill the recruits. Then the unit is moved to France where the last in-
tensive touches are given" (*Camps, Billets, Cooking* preface).

Tolkien touches on his training experiences in several of his letters. Writing
to Edith Bratt from Oxford in October and November 1914, he mentions
drilling with the University Officer Training Corps, marching in the rain on
a Saturday and spending "ages" cleaning his rifle afterward (*Letters* 7). At
first he called drill "a godsend," even though it was combined with his regular
academic responsibilities, saying it had preserved him from the "Oxford 'slee-
pies' " (Carpenter, *Tolkien* 73). In July 1915 he began officer training with
the Lancashire Fusiliers and learned to drill recruits in platoon formation
(*Tolkien* 77). In August he was doing "trench drill" and attending lectures on
"the dull backwaters of the art of killing" (*Tolkien* 77–78). In November
1915 he wrote about bomb-throwing practice with dummies and dealing with
drill in extremes of heat and cold (*Letters* 8), and in March 1916 he mentioned reviewing military lecture notes (*Letters* 8). Training exercises continued at the base camp in Étaples after he arrived in France (Carpenter, *Tolkien*
81) and even closer to the front, where the troops had physical training and
bayonet practice (*Tolkien* 82). Back in England during his long recovery from
trench fever, he started additional signaling training (*Tolkien* 95). According
to his daughter, Priscilla, Tolkien learned horseback riding during his basic
officer training (Armstrong 31); he would also have learned some basic ru-
diments of cavalry drill during his few brief months with King Edward's Horse
in 1912 (Carpenter, *Tolkien* 58).

Small pocket books about military drill and training were widely available
during the Great War. In 1914 His Majesty's Stationery Office authorized
Harrison and Sons to print handbooks on army accounts, ballooning, camel
corps training, chiropody, cooking, drum and flute duty, hygiene, law, tele-
scopic sights, X-rays, and a long list of other military topics (*Signalling* [1]–

[23]). Another London firm published *Soldiers on Service* in 1915, a practical handbook on how to prepare for going to the front. With chapter headings like "Feet, Care of" and "Sea Voyage, Arrangements on Board," this small book was designed to prepare both officers and Other Ranks for embarkation to France and the trenches. Officers were given £50 to buy their kit and limited to 35 pounds of baggage. The list of suggested items for the field kit spans two and a half pages, and includes the advice that "one can scarcely have too many socks and handkerchiefs" (Wyndham 11). One can easily picture Sam stowing his kit about his person as suggested by the author: "In Pockets: Clasp-knife . . . handkerchief . . . field-dressing, matches or tinder lighter, pipe and tobacco. . . . In Haversack: Knife, fork, spoon, mug. . . . In Holdall: Hussif (with needle and thread), soap, boot-laces . . . razor, shaving-brush. . . . In Valise: . . . muffler, knitted waistcoat" (Wyndham 34). Another book includes a recipe for Irish stew very similar to Sam's "herbs and stewed rabbit"—except that Sam had to just wish for the "taters" (*Camps, Billets, Cooking* 173).

Drilling a platoon of new recruits was part of the training of young officers, one that would have taken up much of Tolkien's time during the latter half of 1915, until he began to specialize in signaling. A 1917 pamphlet designed to "assist Platoon commanders in training and fighting their Platoons" (*Instructions* 3) advises officers in basic attack and defense fighting in trench-to-trench combat and open warfare. General tactical principles are listed: aim at surprise, reconnoiter before movement, post sentries, guard your flanks and attack your enemy's flanks, send information back to your company commander, and hold what you gain (*Instructions* 9–10). Platoon commanders were expected to develop the offensive spirit and bloodthirstiness in their men.

A pocket book on bayonet fighting published in 1916 details one of the training methods used in the Anzac and British Expeditionary Forces. The instructor combines what appear to be techniques from quarterstaff fighting, fencing, and jiu-jitsu, and rather euphemistically speaks of "delivering 'point' " to a downed opponent or "bringing the knees smartly up opponent's lower parts" (McLaglen 12–13). The grip Gollum uses to force Sam to drop his sword outside Shelob's lair is described in detail in this book (McLaglen 12). As the author says, "since the invention of modern artillery it has been intimated on the highest military authority that warfare would be conducted in future at long range. This war proves the absolute falsity of that as a complete statement of the case. Little did military experts think that a great modern war would turn into siege warfare" (McLaglen 3–4). Siegfried Sassoon recalls his bayonet training at Flixécourt in the spring of 1916, a few months before Tolkien, taught by a "massive sandy-haired Highland Major" with "homicidal eloquence" and "genial and well-judged jokes" (*Memoirs of an Infantry Officer* 14–15). By the time Tolkien was being drilled in the bayonet in France, it was well established as an essential skill for trench warfare.

Tolkien's specialized training in signaling included "Morse code, flag and disc signalling, the transmission of messages by heliograph and lamp, the use of signal-rockets and field-telephones, and even how to handle carrier-pigeons" (Carpenter, *Tolkien* 78). Signaling manuals written in 1914 instruct the soldier in the use and care of semaphore flags, binoculars, telescopes, and signalling lamps; the message form and how to use it; keeping records of messages sent and received and using ciphers; how a signaling team works together in the field; how to organize and locate a station for maximum efficiency and secrecy; dispatch riding by horse, motor, or ordinary cycle; training of men by the signaling officer; map-reading and map-making; and laying cable and using telephones (*Signalling*; *Training Manual—Signalling*).

Map-making seems to have been one of the skills Tolkien most enjoyed learning, judging by the many maps of Middle-earth on which he lavished so much time and effort. One map he drew during World War I survives and is reproduced in *The Tolkien Family Album*; it shows an area of trenches, drawn after October 17, 1916, based on information from prisoners and aerial photographs (Tolkien and Tolkien 40). Although Carpenter does not mention it, it is almost certain that Tolkien learned military map-making during his officer training, if he was assigned to create such a map. This is another specialty where training manuals were widely available, teaching skills such as orienting the map, surveying contours, sketching, and using standard signs and abbreviations (e.g., Barnes; Stuart; Grieves).

While the authors of *J.R.R. Tolkien: Artist and Illustrator* had access to a great deal of material drawn in Tolkien's childhood, they do not indicate that he drew any maps before those used in *The Hobbit*. Hammond and Scull compare these maps to medieval maps, because of Tolkien's stylized representations of topography and his use of a woodcut-like technique for The Lonely Mountain (94). However, the style Tolkien used for his working maps also owes something to the map-making skills he learned as a signaling officer. The final version of the map of Wilderland, as published in *The Hobbit*, looks entirely medieval—even the dotted line indicating a road is a convention dating back at least to woodcuts of the 1500s (Harvey, *Medieval* 80, 84). But the earlier sketch reproduced in *The Annotated Hobbit* shows topographical contour lines within Mirkwood (*Annotated Hobbit* plate 4), which were not invented until the 1730s and not used widely until a century later (Harvey, *History* 182). The "first Silmarillion map" also uses contour lines (*Shaping* plates ii–v), as do other early maps included in the twelve-volume *History of Middle-earth*. Tolkien considered his son Christopher more talented at map-making and eventually called on his skills to redraw the maps for *The Lord of the Rings* for publication (*Letters* 177). Christopher Tolkien's large area map and map of the Shire are consistent with medieval maps and use perspective drawings to indicate mountains and forests, but the detail map of Gondor, Rohan, and Mordor in *The Return of the King* uses contour lines.

While maps are important and mentioned frequently in *The Hobbit* and

The Lord of the Rings, leaders are never depicted consulting them before a battle, nor does anyone appear to have sketched a copy of a map to carry on the journey. In a nice added touch in Peter Jackson's *The Two Towers*, Faramir is shown consulting a map to determine where Sauron is most likely to strike. Rivendell is a repository of many maps, and Aragorn and Gandalf are said to have consulted them before the Company sets out. Merry and Frodo also looked at them, but Pippin doesn't retain a clear memory of them, and of course "maps conveyed nothing to Sam's mind" (*Fellowship* 299).

Tolkien offers little background on how the soldiers of the various forces in Middle-earth were trained. Aragorn's military education is summarized in the appendices—he apprenticed himself under an alias to several military leaders in Middle-earth and rose through the ranks (*Return* 337–44, 70–71). It is logical to deduce from the way the Rohirrim encircled Aragorn and his companions at their first encounter that they were accustomed to close-order cavalry drill. They ride "with astonishing speed and skill," and halt "without a word or cry" (*Towers* 34). As Barbara Armstrong has pointed out, "A great deal of experience is needed for a troop to do this, steering with the left hand and carrying lances in the right. Few places other than cavalry riding schools would see such a manoeuvre in this century" (30–31).

It is likely that in most of the cultures of Middle-earth, education in strategy came in the form of storytelling—passing down the wisdom and folly of earlier leaders orally, just as the Greeks did with *The Iliad*. We see a glimpse of this in *The Hobbit*, when the dwarves sit in the tunnel leading to Smaug's lair and discuss "dragon-slayings historical, dubious, and mythical, and the various sorts of stabs and jabs and undercuts, and the different arts devices and stratagems by which they had been accomplished" (*Hobbit* 241). The first movie of Peter Jackson's trilogy interpolates a scene where Boromir spars with Merry and Pippin on the road to Moria (*The Lord of the Rings: The Fellowship of the Ring* scene 25); it is reasonable to assume that the more knowledgeable members of the Company would instruct the inexperienced hobbits in self-defense tactics at the very least, although there is no support for this in the text. Tolkien apparently did not always find his training sessions interesting and useful, so perhaps it is only natural that he did not bother to depict military training in his books. He admits to working on his histories of the gnomes "at lectures in cold fogs," among other places where a good officer should be paying attention, and writes to Christopher that his World War II camp experiences sound just as "exasperating" as his own were (*Letters* 78).

There is very little description of formal battlefield communication techniques in Tolkien's works, which is perhaps surprising considering his background. It is risky to assume that because a thing is not mentioned, it is not there, but given his distaste for modern warfare, it is entirely possible Tolkien did this deliberately. Perhaps his experiences had also convinced him of the untrustworthiness of signaling under field conditions. However, the reliable use of signaling devices to convey coded information is ancient; Sun-tzu's *Art of War*, most likely written in the sixth century B.C.E., quotes an even older author who says, "When voice cannot be clearly heard, drums and gongs are used; when eyesight cannot clearly observe, battle standards and flags are used" (Sun-tzu 72).

Both sides use horns and trumpets for sounding a charge or rallying a scattered force, and during the Battle of the Pelennor Fields, trumpets in Minas Tirith sound a retreat (*Return* 122). Some of these horns have long histories, like the one Boromir sounds upon leaving Rivendell, or the one given to Merry "as a memorial of Dernhelm and the horns of the Mark at the coming of the morning" (*Return* 256). One horn-call that conveys specific information is the Horn-cry of Buckland, used by Fatty Bolger when Crick-hollow is attacked by the Black Riders (*Fellowship* 188) and again by Merry to rouse the hobbits during the Scouring of the Shire (*Return* 286). Because this horn-call has a very specific meaning, it might be inferred that there are other calls with specific meanings as well, at least among the hobbits.

Banners and flags in Middle-earth are apparently used to indicate the leader's position in battle but nothing else—Tolkien does not describe them being used to convey coded signals or directions to the troops. Théoden's banner-bearer is actually named and his death is mentioned. The banner of Rohan attracts the attention of the chieftain of the Haradrim at the Battle of the Pelennor Fields, and when Théoden hews down their leader and his flag, the Southrons flee in terror. Théoden identifies the leader with his banner as he lies dying—"I felled the black serpent" (*Return* 118). The banner of Rohan is given to Éomer as symbol of the passing of the kingship. The White Tree banner wrought by Arwen for Aragorn is a symbol of her belief in him and his cause, but this is not a meaning with particular relevance on the battlefield. However, the banner does proclaim one important symbolic meaning when it is first displayed on the captured corsairs—the allies plan to restore the kingdom of Gondor, and this ship bears the man who will be their leader.

Several groups also use drums for communication. The orcs in Moria drum in the depths; after Pippin throws a pebble down the well, their noise sounds "disquietingly like signals of some sort" (*Fellowship* 327). Their drums and horns alert the Company to the impending attack in the Chamber of Mazar-bul. The Woses in Druadan Forest actually do seem to encode information in their drumbeats: "Thus they talk together from afar," as one of the Riders comments (*Return* 105). Drums are used to signal the orcs and mountain-trolls wielding the battering ram Grond at the gates of Minas Tirith (*Return* 102).

The beacon flares on the peaks between Minas Tirith and Rohan convey no specific information; they simply show that Gondor is in need of help from its allies (*Return* 19). Errand-riders are sent out at the same time to expand on the message of the beacons and bear the Red Arrow to Meduseld. While flashes of light or puffs of smoke have long used beacons to convey coded messages, the signalers of Gondor seem to use them for one predetermined message only. As Gandalf explains to Pippin, at one time the kingdom of Gondor had used the *palantíri* to communicate with her allies (*Return* 20); in ancient times at least there had been the possibility of real-time communication across a distance.

However, Sauron has long since corrupted the remaining *palantíri* to his will, and uses them to communicate with Saruman and influence Denethor. He also uses the Nazgûl as airborne messengers and gatherers of information. (It is interesting to note that in *The Hobbit*, Thorin and Dain use birds in a similar fashion, and at this point in the story the Dwarves are being depicted as less than sympathetic characters.) Sophisticated battlefield communication can allow commanders to stay out of the front lines and direct their troops from safety (which Tolkien depicted as morally questionable), but it can also give them access to essential information about the tide of battle and other fronts of the war. Why did the allies have no kind of efficient battlefield communication equipment, given Tolkien's war training and the level of technology they appear to have had? It seems clear that the absence of even the simplest low-tech coded message signaling among the allies reinforces Tolkien's opinion that battles should be led from in front, where the commander can gather intelligence and act on it simultaneously. The loss of the *palantíri*, and the fact that nothing has been developed to take their place, also emphasizes that Gondor and her allies have declined from their former greatness during their long resistance to Sauron.

John Keegan sees the problem of real-time intelligence as a serious limiting factor in personal leadership and command:

Particular knowledge—of the enemy's whereabouts, strength, state, capabilities and intentions—is . . . the material on which effective command thrives. . . . [I]n pre-industrial society, particular knowledge was generated in quantities small enough to be handled by an individual, but reached him at a speed not much faster than armies moved and so tended to be out of date when received. . . . [O]nce industrial technologies—of which the telegraph was the first—allowed intelligence to outpace the movement of armies, its volume at once increased to exceed the capacity of any one man to collect and digest it. . . . [T]he delegation of information-processing to subordinates imposes a remove between the commander and his besetting realities. . . .

Château generalship—in some sense, an acceptance of the logic of circumstance—was one reaction to this development. (*Mask* 326)

As Keegan readily admits, "The problem of 'real time' intelligence probably defies solution" (*Mask* 327). Keegan has pointed out elsewhere that the speed of human decision making cannot be altered, even though the velocity of events and the reporting of those events continues to accelerate—"the human mind and tongue work no faster in 1987 . . . than in 334 BC" (*Mask* 348).

Having too much information to assimilate hampers decision making as surely as having no real-time intelligence at all. Tolkien's approach to this dilemma is to show his allied leaders in the field making effective on-the-spot decisions with limited information, while the enemies, who have access to more information with less time lag through the *palantíri* and the Nazgûl, overlook crucial points and make poor decisions. The allies understand that they must make up for limited real-time information by outthinking and outmaneuvering the enemy, by considering possibilities he cannot comprehend, and by trusting each other to act effectively even when out of communication range.

INDIVIDUAL BATTLES

In looking at the individual battles in *The Hobbit* and *The Lord of the Rings*, we should keep in mind that playing "what-if" exercises with a work of fiction is at its foundation merely an enjoyable mental exercise. The author is omnipotent and will of course make the battle turn out however he wants. But "what-if" games give us a tool for finding instances of the influence of Tolkien's real-life experience, literary background, historical milieu, and moral views. And Tolkien's own attitude toward his work—that he was writing feigned history—grants his readers a certain amount of leeway in analyzing the battles as if they were real. In this section, I will look at two battles from *The Hobbit* and four from *The Lord of the Rings*.

The Defense of Laketown

The first set-piece battle in *The Hobbit*, as distinct from ambushes and skirmishes like that with the spiders in Mirkwood, is the defense of Laketown against the attack of the dragon Smaug. Shippey notes how the battle of Bard and the Lake-men against Smaug reads more like a World War I battle than a Dark Ages one because of its emphasis on collective action and discipline (*Century* 40). Bard, the hero of the battle, reacts in a modern way when he realizes the dragon is coming: "what Bard does is not prepare his own armoury, like Beowulf, but start to organize a collective defense, like a twentieth-century infantry officer" (*Century* 40). As he points out, "Though victory does in the end turn on a single man and an ancestral weapon, the vigour of the description comes from collective action, from forethought and organization; in a word, from discipline" (*Century* 40). This is a Dark Ages world with anachronistic military values (and one can read them as anachronistic in the sense of being either modern values or older ideals abandoned, at least in heroic literature, during the Middle Ages). Individual heroism in Middle-earth can mean organizing the defense of a town or holding steady against an attack, as well as killing a dragon single-handedly. If Bard had reacted like Beowulf instead, the rear guard would have lost morale, collapsed, and fled in panic instead of providing cover for the fleeing townspeople.

This sort of heroism, in which value is placed on leadership, discipline, clear thought in a crisis, strengthening troop morale, holding one's ground, and being the last to abandon a position, is distinct from the values of individual heroism, where personal honor, reputation, and individual action outweigh any duty to one's followers—the sort of heroism Tolkien criticized in Beorhtnoth. As Keegan pithily stated, "Heroes observed a code of honour but not of social responsibility" (*Book of War* x). Hanson offers a framework that helps to illuminate Tolkien's thoughts on the shortcomings of Dark Ages "Northern" courage in battle:

From the Greeks onward, Westerners have sought to distinguish moments of individual courage and obedience to leaders from a broader, more institutionalized bravery that derives from the harmony of discipline, training, and egalitarian values among men and officers. Beginning with the Hellenic tradition, Europeans were careful to organize types of purported courage into a hierarchy, from the singular rashness of bold individual acts to the cohesive shared bravery along a battle line—insisting that the former was only occasionally critical to victory, the latter always. (*Carnage* 325)

Tolkien drew a map of Long Lake showing the location of Esgaroth and other local features, apparently for his own use (Hammond and Scull 134). Communication and intelligence play a key role in getting crucial information to Bard, when the thrush perches on his shoulder in the heat of battle and tells him about Smaug's weak spot.

Battle of Five Armies

The Battle of Five Armies resembles the sort of classic example used in lectures to cadets. William Green suggests that it demonstrates the kind of military strategy Tolkien might have learned about in his officers' training (Green 105–6). Thorin's dwarves have plenty of time to prepare a strong defensive position, which they have reinforced at key weak points. Expecting a siege, they have sent for reinforcements. The Men and Elves also have sufficient time to set up a comfortable camp and are well rested and provisioned; they are negotiating from the strong point of controlling all access to the mountain. When Dain's dwarves arrive on the scene, Bard notes a weakness in their thinking—"Fools! . . . to come thus under the Mountain's arm! They do not understand war above ground, whatever they may know of battle in the mines" (*Hobbit* 291). He positions archers and spearmen above the path the dwarves must take to join their kinsmen.

Then everything changes. The armies of the Goblins and the Wild Wolves attack from around the unguarded eastern spur of the mountain. Gandalf has just enough time to rearrange the troops to take advantage of the terrain in an attempt at a classic pincers movement. The Elves are arrayed on the southern spur; the Men and Dwarves on the eastern, and some make a feint of resistance at the head of the valley to lure the Goblins in, so the allies can pour down on them from above. But their own tactics are turned against them when some of the goblins climb above them and attack from even higher points. It takes help from two unexpected allies—the Eagles and Beorn—to turn the tide of battle.

Bilbo's attitude throughout is out of place in a heroic, medieval battle. He first tries to prevent the battle from taking place but only succeeds in delaying it (and as I have said earlier, this is a eucatastrophic failure because all the parties are in the field and prepared to fight when the Goblins attack). He is an anachronistic observer, viewing the carnage with eyes more akin to those of the modern reader than to his contemporaries. He puts on his Ring and takes his stand among the Elves on Ravenhill, high above most of the fray. He mourns that among the dead are "many a fair elf that should have lived yet long ages merrily in the wood" (*Hobbit* 296), and thinks to himself, "Really it is enough to make one weep, after all one has gone through. . . . I have heard songs of many battles, and I have always understood that defeat may be glorious. It seems very uncomfortable, not to say distressing. I wish I was well out of it" (*Hobbit* 297). Afterward he observes, "Victory after all, I suppose! . . . Well, it seems a very gloomy business" (*Hobbit* 299). Although he enjoys telling stories about it later, he sees very little that is splendid and wonderful in the battle at the time.

Thorin's map is essential to the plot of the book as a whole, and the reader's familiarity with the Lonely Mountain from this map will make the battle easier to understand. The ravens carry intelligence between Thorin and Dain, though somewhat unwillingly, since Roäc advises against war (*Hobbit* 279). But the ravens bring no warning about the Goblins and Wolves, who traveled "by tunnel or under dark" (*Hobbit* 293); and although Gandalf had an idea something was brewing (*Hobbit* 285), he gave no specific warning. The Men and Elves use trumpets for basic signaling and banners to indicate leaders' positions, and the Goblins carry banners as well. When Thorin bursts out of the mountain, he gives a trumpet call to help rally the allies to him.

In the *Hobbit* battles, we see Bard's more modern style of heroism preferred to Thorin's stiff-necked heroic stubbornness, and Bilbo's antiwar attitude preferred to the bloodthirsty behavior around him. However, in *The Lord of the Rings*, it is the older heroic style and values that are favored over the anachronistic modern mass-warfare tactics of Sauron and Saruman.

Helm's Deep

The first major battle in *The Lord of the Rings* is the Battle of Helm's Deep. In this battle, we see traditional heroism and tactics opposed to modern, mechanized war:

[T]he battle of Helm's Deep presents a stark contrast between two styles of portraying war: a heroic battle romance, on one side, and the nightmarish reality of modern mass warfare on the other. The fighting of the forces of the West celebrates individual heroism. . . . The Orcs fight in the latter tradition: their masses swarm forward like "a great field of dark corn" and they die in unacknowledged and anonymous droves: slow to react, mindless, and persistent. (Black 63–64)

Individual heroic actions of the defenders are described in detail: Éomer and Aragorn leading the first charge, Gimli and Legolas and their grim competition, Théoden riding out on Snowmane, Erkenbrand and Gandalf appearing in the nick of time, and Éomer and Gimli fighting rear guard on the retreat back to the caves. In contrast, there is no indication that the orcs and Dunlendings even have leaders; all actions are described in terms of mass movements. The orcs are "thick as marching ants," the valley is "boiling and crawling with black shapes," and they charge over and over again "like the incoming sea" (*Towers* 137–38). And when Aragorn comes out to parley, no individual orc voice speaks to him; all the responses are in the form of "they cried," "they answered," "they jeered" (*Towers* 145). Paul Fussell cites a widely distributed work of British propaganda during World War I that contrasts "our soldiers," taught the value of individual effort by playing football, with the German soldier, whose "whole training from childhood upwards has been to obey, and to obey in numbers" (quoted *Great War* 26).

Siege is wasteful—only a commander who can afford to be profligate with his troops and resources can hope to win. Sun-tzu recommends against siege: "[The] worst [strategy] of all is to besiege their city fortifications. Besiege city fortifications only when no other option is left" (49). His reasoning is that the preparation of siege engines takes too much time and too many resources, and he calculates that one-third of the besiegers will be destroyed, win or lose. (The attack on Orthanc by the Ents is the only account of a siege initiated by the allies. But the Ents are their own siege weapons; their unique ability to crack stone makes them ideally suited for siege work.) Saruman can be terribly wasteful of his troops, since he can always breed more orcs. They are like machines—as easy to use and throw away as weapons, shields, ladders, or grappling hooks. As for the Dunlendings, they are allies of convenience and unimportant to his long-range plans.

Saruman's forces use modern technology against an ancient fortress, but their development of gunpowder is still primitive enough that they cannot easily bring it down. In late medieval Europe, the development of the cannon would eventually render such fortifications obsolete, but for now Saruman can only use his gunpowder to try to breach the walls by detonating explosives in direct contact with them.

The most memorable examples of battlefield communication in this sequence are the various battle cries: "Gúthwinë! . . . Gúthwinë for the Mark!"; "Andúril! . . . Andúril for the Dúnedain!"; "Baruk Khazâd! Khazâd ai-mênu!"

(*Towers* 139); "Helm for Théoden King! . . . Forth Eorlingas!" (*Towers* 146). The orcs give no battle cries, but use trumpets to direct their charges. The sounding of Helm's horn, and an answering blast from Erkenbrand, rally the men of Rohan. It is semantically significant that the instrument used by the Rohirrim, although very similar to a trumpet, is identified by a word implying a device closer to nature in that it copies the shape of an animal's horn, even when made of metal. The Rohirrim, who live close to the land, are opposed by Saruman, the cunning man of science and modernity. As for military intelligence, the Rohirrim send scouts ahead of their march, and Théoden warns that the secrets of Helm's Deep may have been spied out by Saruman (*Towers* 135), which appears to be true in that the orcs know where to creep in through the culverts to place their blasts.

This has always seemed to me to be the hardest battle to understand without a map, and I find Karen Wynn Fonstad's map of this encounter particularly useful (148–49). Tolkien drew a detailed map and a perspective view for his own use in plotting this battle (Hammond and Scull 165), but it was never redrawn for possible inclusion in the published book.

Battle of the Pelennor Fields

The Battle of the Pelennor Fields even more obviously pits the ancient heroic style of the Western allies against Sauron's modern battle tactics. Given the strategic and psychological importance of Minas Tirith, it is obvious why Sauron's heaviest blow should fall there. Since Minas Tirith lies at the northeast corner of Gondor on a narrow strip of land between the end of a steep mountain range and a wide river, controlling the city would effectively divide Gondor and Rohan, making it easier to conquer them separately (Bell 25). At the time of the battle, the enemy already held the islands of Cair Andros and Osgiliath, which lie north of Minas Tirith in the same narrow river valley, giving him safe passage down the western flanks of the Ephel Duath. Sauron sent the Corsairs of Umbar up the Anduin to Pelargir to tighten the noose still further and push the Gondorians back up into the mountains of the Ered Nimrais. As the ancient symbolic center of the Gondorian Empire, if Minas Tirith fell it would be a severe, perhaps even fatal, blow to the morale of the West—like Paris occupied by the Nazis.

The defenders of Minas Tirith expect to be besieged after the fall of Osgiliath, and prepare by sending the noncombatants to safety in the hills. Though the soldiers fear hunger (*Return* 96), the wains that come into the city during its evacuation undoubtedly bring in supplies (*Return* 36). The Houses of Healing prepare to receive the wounded rather than the ill. The defenders have a wide diversity of armor and weapons: some of the troops that enter into the city wear mail, and are armed variously with swords, spears, battle-axes, or bows and arrows; some are mounted and some on foot (*Return* 43–44). There are a few pieces of plate armor mentioned—Prince Imrahil, for example, wears a polished metal vambrace, or forearm protector. The men of Rohan wear mail and metal helms and carry shields, and are armed with swords, bows, and pikes. Pippin, as an esquire of the Steward, wears chain mail of blackened steel, and Merry wears a leather jerkin and a small helm. There are catapults upon the outer walls of Minas Tirith, but none as large as those used by the enemy, who carefully keep their equipment out of range of the defenders' shot (*Return* 96).

Sauron, on the other hand, combines more advanced siege equipment and other devices of mechanized war with a ruthless disregard for the safety of his own troops. (He has no noncombatants to consider.) The orcs tear down the wall defending the northern approaches to the city with "earth-thunder" (*Return* 108). After the men of Minas Tirith are forced to abandon the enclosed fields of the Pelennor, Sauron's troops burn the fields and dig trenches outside of bow-shot of the walls, which they fill with fire, "though how it was kindled or fed, by art or devilry, none could see" (*Return* 95). They set up their siege-engines behind the trenches, and use their huge catapults to throw burning shot and the heads of the men they have killed into the city (*Return* 96). Siege-towers roll and crawl across the field, crashing and burning; none are reported reaching the wall of the city. But the great battering ram Grond, forged by the technologies of Mordor, brings down the city gates.

Sauron also uses the unconventional tactics of terror—the Nazgûl fly low over the city like vultures and terrify the inhabitants. Sauron fortunately does not grasp all the possibilities of the Nazgûl or use them as effectively as he could; they do not drop incendiary devices on the city, keep surveillance on the Corsairs to see how soon they might arrive at the battle, or watch for the approaching Rohirrim. The enemy forces are all the more terrifying because they are exotic and unfamiliar: the bearded Easterlings with their axes, the black Southrons armed with scimitars and poisoned darts and riding *mûmakil*, the great war-elephants with towers on their backs; the Variags of Khand and the troll-like men of Far Harad; the Orcs who are completely "Other."

In this battle, the forces of Sauron have a clear leader and chain of command, and both the Witch-king and his lieutenant Gothmog actually take part in the battle. While this gives the enemy more of a recognizable face and identity than the leaderless masses at Helm's Deep, still the orcs are "reckless of their loss" (*Return* 98) and advance to attack "driven as by a madness" (*Return* 102). The Witch-king tramples the fallen as he rides to the gate; he "cared not greatly what they did or how many might be slain" (*Return* 101). As Kevin Black has pointed out: "Grond is a massive machine, and orcs swarm around it to keep it running, making it almost seem alive. But though it depends on orc labor to operate, the orcs are considered to be the most expendable parts of the mechanism, and are wasted and replaced without any consideration. The good of the machine is held as all-important, and the value of life is completely degraded in comparison" (65).

The tactics of Minas Tirith are those of defense—no other course is open to them until Rohan's cavalry charge divides the enemy's forces enough that sorties can be launched from the city under the command of Prince Imrahil. When Aragorn's forces unexpectedly land at the quays, the tide is turned and the enemy caught between the hammer and anvil. Éomer's cavalry charge nearly backfires on him when his flying wedges plunge too deep into the enemy forces and are surrounded; he is attempting to rally his forces and join with Imrahil when Aragorn arrives. "His fury had betrayed him," as Tolkien puts it, and Sun-tzu warns sternly that "in having short tempers, [commanders] can be humiliated" (77).

Both intelligence and signaling, and their lack, play important parts in this battle. Aragorn finds out about the corsairs during his confrontation with Sauron in the *palantír*; by understanding the implications of what he has seen and acting boldly and decisively on this information, he changes Sauron's sure victory to ruin. Denethor also sees the corsairs in his *palantír*, but his reaction is defeatist; his actions in response end in disaster and delay. Because the errand-riders were killed on their way back from Rohan, he also does not know that Théoden is coming to help, and this adds to his despair.

Concealing his banner until the last minute was a calculated risk on Aragorn's part. It made the enemy army overconfident, thinking their own reinforcements were arriving, and guaranteed that the enemy would not molest him on his flight up the river. The benefit of their consternation would be enormous: "Imagine the feelings of a soldier seeing friendly ships come into port and disembark an enemy army when there seemed to be no sign that the ships had been fought over and no way for the enemy to get near them" (Bell 26–27).

However, Aragorn ran the risk of throwing the allied forces into confusion and rout. When Theseus returned from Crete after slaying the Minotaur, he forgot to change his black sails for white ones. His father, despairing, threw himself from the Acropolis to his death. In Aragorn's case, the men of Minas Tirith immediately conclude that the towns downriver have fallen to the enemy and sound the retreat (*Return* 122). But for the most part Aragorn must have known the other field commanders and how they would be likely to react to seeing apparent enemy reinforcements—that Éomer and the Rohirrim, for example, would fight all the harder. Sauron showed the corsairs to Denethor thinking they were his own ships; both distant leaders were deceived because they were not gathering intelligence on the spot in the field, but instead depending on a device that could only show them part of the truth. If Sauron had looked just a little further downriver with his *palantír*, he would have realized something had gone very wrong with his plans; but he was apparently quite sure that black-sailed ships approaching Minas Tirith could only mean one thing.

Another example of the use of intelligence by the allies in this battle occurs during the ride of the Rohirrim. The wild men of Druadan Forest, who have as little reason to love the orcs as the Rohirrim, provide them with valuable information about enemy numbers and troop movements. They offer to guide the horsemen by secret paths through the woods. Ghân-buri-Ghân derides the orcs at work destroying the Pelennor wall for setting so poor a watch that he can easily spy on them. Théoden and Éomer make frequent use of their own scouts as well, and are careful to plan their movements according to their reports. It was scouts from Rohan who found out that the orcs had booby-trapped the main road to Minas Tirith with trenches and stakes, and that the errand-riders of Gondor had been killed.

One of the most moving signals in the entire work is the sound of the horns of Rohan, echoing from the mountain as if in answer to the cock's crow. The Rohirrim use a number of battle cries, but the most chilling is simply "Death" after Théoden's fall (*Return* 119). Trumpets are used in Minas Tirith to sound a charge or retreat (*Return* 93–94), and Aragorn used trumpets captured from the enemy to announce to the Shadow Host that their oath was now fulfilled (*Return* 152).

Tolkien made several working sketches of the city while writing the chapters of Book Five. Fonstad points out that Tolkien's sketches reproduced in *The War of the Ring* do not match his description of the "vast pier of rock" that cut in two "all the circles of the City save the first" (*Return* 24): "As this distinctive feature was absent from Tolkien's drawings, its effect on the pattern of the walls can only be surmised" (Fonstad 138). However, a very rough sketch in the later *J.R.R. Tolkien: Artist and Illustrator* does show how he intended this "ship-keel" of rock to look (Hammond and Scull 174).

Attack at the Gates of Mordor

This is the battle where the grand strategies of Mordor and the West finally clash, although it is the shortest battle of all, ending almost as soon as it is joined. The preliminaries to this battle are actually far more important than the battle itself. Sauron's long-range goal, as Paul Lloyd has pointed out, is "the complete conquest and domination of Middle-earth" (3). His immediate strategic goals are to "prevent his enemies from uniting;" to "overawe" and divide his opponents by offering friendship to some; and to win allies (including Saruman) by "promises of loot" or other benefits (Lloyd 4). The overarching goal of the West hinges on the destruction of the Ring, and is simply the permanent elimination of Sauron as a threat. As Gandalf said at the Council of Elrond, "[I]t is not our part here to take thought only for a season, or for a few lives of Men, or for a passing age of the world. We should seek a final end of this menace" (*Fellowship* 280). Anything less is simply a stopgap measure. Although the allied leaders are well aware that another evil may eventually arise to replace Sauron, they see it as their duty to attempt to defeat him, "that those who live after may have clean earth to till" (*Return* 155).

The preliminaries start with the Last Debate of the Captains of the West, a top-level strategy meeting similar to the Council of Elrond. As Lloyd suggests, "the forces of the free peoples have in Gandalf the Grey a strategist of the highest order, a truly dangerous enemy for Sauron" (5). And what is most dangerous about Gandalf is his understanding of the mind of Sauron. He knows how Sauron will react if the allies follow his advice and march in force to the Gates of Mordor—he will try to "trap the fly and take the sting" (*Return* 158). More important, he can see how to use this knowledge to support their strategy, which is to distract Sauron from looking inside his own territory long enough for the Ringbearer to fulfill his quest and destroy the Ring. Sauron must be given no opportunity to consolidate his thoughts and resources after the loss at Minas Tirith. He must be made to think that the forces of the West have the Ring and plan to use it, and that this is why they dare to march on Mordor in such pitifully small numbers. But the force must still be large enough to compel him to take it seriously as a threat in itself and bring all his strength to the Black Gates. The allied strategy is to keep him guessing, off balance, his attention focused in the wrong place, and to sacrifice themselves if need be.

Sun-tzu places great value on deception, or as one translator calls it, "unpredictable flexibility" (136). Gandalf's strategy is exactly the opposite of what Sun-tzu would normally recommend in such a situation: he plans to attack an enemy more then ten times his size, in a fortified position, after marching his troops deep into unfriendly territory, with no expectation of winning. But in the broader strategic picture his actions are an example of weakening the enemy through deception: "seem humble to fill them with conceit" (Sauron must be made to think that it would be easy to crush this pitiful attack and take the great leaders of the West prisoner); "be far but appear near" (make this attack seem the main thrust, while the actual attack takes place in obscurity deep within Mordor); "show gains to lure them" (maintain the illusion that the allies have the Ring and plan to use it at the Gates) (Sun-tzu 41). The allied strategy was fraught with danger: "Much has been written, and justly, about the self-sacrificial courage of Frodo and Sam in the last stages of their journey through Mordor. But few or none have remarked on the equal if less solitary unselfish daring displayed by the seven thousand men whom Aragorn and his peers lead up to the Black Gate to challenge the ten times ten thousands inside" (Kocher 157).

Gandalf knows his enemy, which is one of Sun-tzu's strongest precepts. "By perceiving the enemy and perceiving ourselves, there will be no unforeseen risk in any battle" (Sun-tzu 52). "Perceiving" in this context translates as knowledge, anticipation, and prediction (161). In Sauron's conceit and his lack of understanding of Gandalf's mind lies his danger: unable to see any possible reason but foolhardiness for the allies' attack, he falls into the trap they have laid. Sauron's "strategic ineptitude" is one of the greatest advantages the West has; as Lloyd points out, Sauron continually picks the "least imaginative, least effective, and most costly of all types of attack, one that throughout history has appealed to the mediocre commander: a direct frontal assault on the opponent's strongest position" (5). When the West apparently adopts this plan of attack against Mordor, he readies for it in an entirely conventional manner—it is a form of attack he understands. Sauron is not a chess player; he exhibits a "basic inability to consider all possible moves by his opponents" (Lloyd 6).

In this battle, we can see another parallel between Aragorn and Alexander in their strategy for dealing with a powerful entrenched enemy. After the Battle of Issus, where Darius was defeated, the Persian king, like Sauron, withdrew deep into his own country. "Ultimately, he knew, Alexander must come to him, in the heartland of the empire, and he was prepared to use space and time to offset the advantage of superior operational ability that the young king demonstrably possessed." Darius's strategy was "that of letting distance exhaust the enemy until 'overstretch' in unfamiliar terrain exposed his elite formations to a decisive counterstroke" (Keegan, *Mask* 84). However, he underestimated Alexander's "superior operational ability" and his strategy backfired on him; the Macedonian took an unanticipated route and defeated Darius at Gaugamela, deep within his own territory, then quickly subdued the rest of the Persian Empire.

Unlike Alexander, Aragorn's primary aim was to distract Sauron from the Ringbearer's mission, not to win the battle, so Aragorn did not strike out in an unexpected direction in an attempt to conceal his army's movements. Instead he announced his intentions at regular intervals, taking the most direct and visible route to Mordor in order to keep Sauron's eye riveted to his army—and Sauron, unable to imagine Aragorn and Gandalf's deeper strategy, obligingly cooperated. All nine of his Nazgûl, instead of keeping a wary eye out for deception, hovered over the army and were there at the Gates to greet them.

Allied tactics at the Black Gate were entirely defensive; it would be difficult to imagine anything else such a small force could do except find the most defensible position available, and like the Macedonian phalanx of Alexander, stand in "the closest possible formation, shoulder to shoulder, armed with weapons that kept the enemy at the greatest possible distance" (Keegan, *Mask* 37). They make themselves weaker, however, by dividing their force between the two slag-hills; was this more deception on Aragorn's part, or simply a requirement of the terrain? The hills were not large, and perhaps only half of his army could fit on each one. Sauron's tactics are correspondingly simple: soften the target with artillery (arrows) and terror (Nazgûl), and then send in the heavy infantry (trolls and orcs). But after the Nazgûl are called back into Mordor, the allies start an offensive, and phalanxes of spearmen prepare to charge.

Drums and horns signal the movements of the forces of Mordor; the men of Gondor use trumpets and the voices of heralds to announce their challenge on the road and at the Gates. Note that in this battle the semantic values of "trumpet" and "horn" are inverted from their use in the Battle of Helm's Deep. Here the conflict is not between nature (Rohan) and science (Saruman), but between civilization (Gondor and her allies) and primitive brutality (orcs and the uncivilized humans of the East and South).

Again in this battle we see the dangers of relying on incomplete intelligence. Sauron has obtained the mail shirt and elven-cloak taken by the orcs in Minas Morgul and the sword Frodo discarded. He uses them to taunt the allies and send them into despair, but he does not understand what they mean. The reader, knowing more of Frodo and Sam's story, will note that the Mouth of Sauron only mentions one hobbit (the last the reader knew, both were still alive) and wonder if Gandalf, at least, is being very clever, playing for time and allowing the enemy to think he holds all the cards. His request to see the prisoner (singular) hints at this. If Sauron had taken both hobbits and what one of them carried, the game would have been over already, and if he only had one he would have had little difficulty finding out about the other and tracking him down. Logically, saying he has one prisoner and showing the mail shirt, cloak, and sword to the allies is very likely to mean that he does not have the Ring and does not even know it is in his own country. Given time to interpret this intelligence, the allies would have seen what a good sign this actually was, but with battle looming, they had no time for analysis. Sauron, probing to find out who among the allies held the Ring, gave away valuable information about his own capabilities, had they but time to see it.

Could Sauron really have been as inept as he appeared in these two battles? Or did he simply operate under an entirely different set of rules and assumptions, where the waste of personnel and matériel and the loss of individual battles were unimportant, and the only thing that mattered was his personal survival in the extremely long term? Perhaps he was seeing this war as just one round of a vast eternal chess tournament, and did not realize it was actually the deciding game. It is a frequent assumption in storytelling that the evil are stupid and unimaginative, and history written by the victors often paints the losers in this light; biographies of Hitler, for example, often depict him as a limited thinker and primitive strategist. But might there be some basis for this in fact? In one chapter of Herrnstein and Murray's controversial *The Bell Curve*, the authors analyzed the IQs of criminal offenders, both incarcerated and self-confessed. They found criminal offender IQs averaged about eight points below the mean of the general population, even for those who reported themselves as getting away with their crimes, and chronic offenders averaged even lower. These findings held true regardless of the socioeconomic status of the criminals (235). The authors speculate that one possible reason, out of many contributing factors, for this link between low IQ and criminal behavior is that lack of foresight is often associated with low IQ (240). Those with higher IQs have a greater ability to think ahead, visualize the consequences of their actions, and imagine the possible reactions of others to them. Sauron could not imagine anyone having different goals than his and therefore could not envisage the radically different strategy required to achieve these goals.

Battle of Bywater

The Battle of Bywater differs enormously from the other battles in *The Lord of the Rings*. As I pointed out in Chapter 3, the language used to describe it is spare and journalistic rather than operatic, in keeping with the circumstances. It is also the only battle won without a *deus ex machina*—no thrush whispering in anyone's ear, no cavalry charge in the nick of time, no Ring going into the fire or eagles flying to the rescue. The Shire is an occupied territory that turns on its occupiers, using all the weapons and tactics at its disposal. The rules of chivalry and the uses of war can be suspended; victims of such sordid oppression are justified in using any means necessary to free themselves from a dishonorable enemy. It is fitting that the hobbits, anachronisms in Middle-earth already, should use unconventional tactics, guerrilla warfare, and civilian resistance to free their country. But what else can the small and weak do against their opponents' strengths?

As in France under the occupying Germans during World War II, the ruffians retain some hobbit shirriffs to keep order among the others, and a few of these become collaborators—"sneaks" who betray their fellows to the chief (*Return* 279), who "like minding other folk's business" and even "spy-work" (*Return* 281). Frodo makes a distinction between those who have really gone over and those who obey out of fear, but insists that no hobbits should be killed (*Return* 285).

The four companions, like Merry and Pippin in Fangorn, are the sparks that set the rebellion aflame. Once the hobbits are roused to action, they know what they must do and have no moral qualms about it. Frodo, who wishes it were not necessary to fight, raises the only objection, but pragmatic Merry knows a battle is unavoidable. The courage of the Hobbits is in a way a criticism of the courage of Beorhtnoth: they are honorable in offering their enemy a chance to surrender and they refuse to kill unnecessarily, but they do not offer to even the odds or give up any of their advantages. That would be to betray those they are defending. Honor lies in group actions in defending the Shire, not in individual heroics. Shire historians memorize a list of all who took part in the battle, not just the leaders (*Return* 295).

The first engagement is an evening ambush using Farmer Cotton as bait. Hiding their strength, the hobbits count on being underestimated and use it to their advantage. Two hundred hobbits kill one man and take twenty prisoners. "Seems almost too easy," says Farmer Cotton (*Return* 291), but no one suggests it was not fair. Using such a superior force guaranteed a minimum of bloodshed on both sides, which was one of their goals. The second engagement is the Battle of Bywater; the hobbits carefully choose their location and herd the ruffians into an ambush. The odds are a bit more even—

around 300 hobbits to 100 men—and there are far more casualties. But the Hobbits, through strategic positioning of their troops, use of information from scouts, mopping-up crews in the surrounding woods, and superior unity and morale, minimize their own losses and achieve their goals.

Horns play a significant part in the Scouring of the Shire. When the travelers first face down Sharkey's men outside the Green Dragon, the fleeing men blow their horns to alert their companions (*Return* 285). Soon afterward Merry blows the horn of Rohan and rouses the village; the inhabitants pour out of their homes in response (*Return* 286). During the Battle of Bywater, Merry blows his horn to alert the archers in the woods that some of the ruffians have broken out and are headed cross-country (*Return* 295). Ted Sandyman blows a horn to warn Sharkey in Bag End about the marching hobbits, but Merry blows his in response and raises even more hobbits to join them.

What tactical lessons are taught by the hobbits' conduct of this war of liberation? First, that to be effective, war should be swift, accurate, and overwhelming. The hobbits liberated their country in one skirmish, one battle, and one small-scale confrontation with the defeated enemy's leadership. As Hanson argues, "The real morality in war hinges not on damage wrought but rather concerns the moral imperative to reduce the number of dead and so end the killing as quickly as possible. To accomplish that goal an army must attack in overwhelming strength and be imbued with a clear moral sense" (*Autumn* 31). The hobbits managed to do what had to be done while operating within Frodo's parameters of harming no hobbits and keeping bloodshed to a minimum.

A second lesson is that one should expect treachery from a defeated enemy even when offering mercy—but it must be offered in any case, because it is the moral thing to do. When Saruman attacks Frodo, he verifies that "illegitimate and murderous regimes, when they are at last stripped of their terror and the illusion of power, threaten even as they broker to save their own skins" (Hanson, *Autumn* 10).

CONCLUSION

Why did the West win in the end? To understand why the forces of Mordor, well equipped, vastly outnumbering the allies, and with a strong central command utilizing advanced communication and intelligence-gathering techniques, failed so utterly when Sauron fell, read this passage and substitute "Mordor" for the Aztecs, the Mycenaeans, the Persians, the Incans, the Soviets:

[T]he greatest cultural disadvantage of the Aztecs has often gone unnoticed: that of the age-old problem of systems collapse that threatens all palatial dynasties in which political power is concentrated among a tiny elite. . . . The abrupt destruction of the

Mycenaean palaces (ca. 1200 B.C.), the sudden disintegration of the Persian Empire with Darius III's flight at Gaugamela, the end of the Incas, and the rapid collapse of the Soviet Union all attest that the way of palatial dynasties is one of extreme precariousness to outside stimuli. Anytime a narrow elite seeks to control all economic and political activity from a fortified citadel, island redoubt, grand palace, or walled Kremlin, the unraveling of empire shortly follows the demise, flight, or discrediting of such imperial grandees—again in contrast to more decentralized, less stratified, and locally controlled Western political and economic entities. (Hanson, *Carnage* 218)

The same can apply to Saruman, both at the height of his power and in his reincarnation as Sharkey, headquartered in Bag End; or to the figure of Smaug, concentrating all of the apparatus of power of a palatial society into himself. The West at the time of the war was a loose federation of independent states temporarily allied but with no supreme commander; it was not until after the war that Aragorn was crowned, and even then his policy was to allow autonomous home rule in many areas of his kingdom, like the Shire and Fangorn Forest.

The leaders of the West understood quite well that Sauron's empire would fall apart with his destruction—the mission of Frodo, their secret underlying strategy, was to strike at the very heart of the central control of Mordor. It was the only way the relatively powerless West could hope to win, and by chance—or divine intervention—they held the only possible means by which they could accomplish their goal. They had to use all the tricks available to a weaker, smaller force, as the hobbits did in freeing their country: distraction of the enemy's attention, guerrilla warfare, using the enemy's strength against him, finding the enemy's vulnerability and exploiting it, nimbly outthinking the huge slow-moving behemoth, and knowing how it would all fall apart if the central command could only be destroyed.

And in the end their victory would only keep the world free for a little space of years, as Tolkien knew only too well: "Wars are always lost, and The War always goes on; and it is no good growing faint!" (*Letters* 116).

Chapter 7

"War Must Be, While We Defend Our Lives": Philosophy, Pathology, and Conclusions

"MAKE SURE OF THE MARK, BEFORE SHOOTING": THE WAR LETTERS

In earlier chapters I have focused primarily on war in Tolkien's fiction and criticism, the works he wrote for public consumption. But during World War II Tolkien wrote a number of letters to his sons Michael and Christopher while they were on active duty. It is in these letters that we see Tolkien's most intimate thoughts on war and what it meant to him personally.

Michael Tolkien was called up in the summer of 1940. In October of that year, Tolkien wrote to him about the "waste of time and militarism of the army," but suggested that he would learn a great deal, even though the war had interrupted his formal education. Tolkien says he hadn't minded "the tough stuff" during World War I as much as the fact that he had been called up at a point in his life when he had so much to learn and write (*Letters* 46). A letter to Michael in January 1941, when he was in the hospital recovering from a night training accident, speculates about the plans of the USSR, a possible attack by Hitler on England, and communists in Great Britain (*Letters* 47–48), showing the attention Tolkien paid to current events. The next letter to Michael in the published collection, written in March 1941, is a long essay on marriage, in the course of which Tolkien talks about his own experiences as a newly married soldier and the difficulties of his first few years with Edith (*Letters* 53).

Tolkien's letter to Michael in June 1941, when his son was in officer cadet training at Sandhurst, is one of the most revealing. In this letter, he says, "One War is enough for any man," and hopes Michael will not experience a second as he is doing. Tolkien implies that his son is more efficient and military than he was, but says that they both share "a deep sympathy and feeling for the 'tommy.' " He comments on how difficult it is to stay at home and do nothing while his son is in danger: "If only I could do something active!" Tolkien is proud of Michael's service: "It is something to be the father of a good young soldier," he says. In this letter he praises the German virtues of industry, bravery, obedience, and patriotism, and reveals his "burning private grudge" against Hitler for "[r]uining, perverting, misapplying, and making for ever accursed, that noble northern spirit" (*Letters* 54–56).

The remaining collected wartime letters are all to Tolkien's third son, Christopher, who was called up into the Royal Air Force in the summer of 1943. Tolkien wrote to him in November 1943, expressing his dissatisfaction with the government and his sympathy for anarchists. He encourages his son's morale by quoting a few lines from his own poem "Mythopoeia" and saying, "Have at the Orcs, with winged words, hildenæddran (war-adders), biting darts—but make sure of the mark, before shooting" (*Letters* 63–64). Tolkien continues in the same vein in his next letter, and adds, "if I was of military age, I should, I fancy, be grousing away in a fighting service, and willing to go on to the bitter end" (*Letters* 65).

The next several letters say little about war except to mention that the censor opened some of Christopher's letters home. But in April of 1944, Tolkien comments on Christopher's account of his life in camp in South Africa and compares it to his own experience of "trenchlife" during World War I. He again complains about the waste of war: "How stupid everything is!, and war multiplies the stupidity by 3 and its power by itself." He hopes for Christopher, as he did for Michael, that he will derive some benefit from his experiences in later days (*Letters* 71–73).

In a letter later that same April Tolkien comments, "The utter stupid waste of war, not only material but moral and spiritual, is so staggering to those who have to endure it. And always was (despite the poets), and always will be (despite the propagandists)—not of course that it has not is and will be necessary to face it in an evil world." He expresses the hope "May you, too, escape—strengthened." In spite of the stupidity and waste of war, Tolkien is telling his son that it may at times be necessary to fight, and that the individual soldier can grow and learn even in such a situation (*Letters* 75–77).

In a letter written the next month, Tolkien again talks about the stupidity of war and especially life in camp. He says, "the only cure (short of universal Conversion) is not to have wars" (*Letters* 78). Tolkien also mentions Faramir's speeches in Ithilien, which he was writing at the time, "with some very sound reflections no doubt on martial glory and true glory" (*Letters* 79). Tolkien comments a few letters later that in real life the orcs "are on both sides," but that "it does make some difference who are your captains and whether they are orc-like *per se*!" (*Letters* 82). He was under no illusions that the English or their allies were perfect.

In the next several letters Tolkien raises concerns about wartime propaganda, deploring the urge to demonize and dehumanize the Germans and the prevalence of a *"Delenda est Carthago"* bloodthirstiness in the press (*Letters* 89, 93). A January 1945 letter bemoans the fact that some people were gloating to hear of refugees, and that the only winners in the current war were likely to be the Machines (*Letters* 111).

In June of 1945 he tells Christopher that in spite of the fact that the war in Europe had ended, "Wars are always lost, and The War always goes on; and it is no good growing faint!" (*Letters* 116). He was horrified two months later to hear of the use of the atomic bomb against Japan—the "utter folly" of the scientists who designed it seemed to fulfill his worst fears about the War of the Machines (*Letters* 116).

One theme running through the letters to Christopher is Tolkien's deep-seated loathing for the use of aircraft in wartime. The April 18, 1944, letter is the first in which Tolkien mentions his feelings about the air force, saying, "I was always against your choice of service (on the ground it seems a war behind)" (*Letters* 72). In May he argues, "we are attempting to conquer Sauron with the Ring" (*Letters* 78). Air bombing was notoriously inaccurate and not as useful as had been hoped in eliminating specific military targets and, by this point, was being used more and more as part of a strategy of terror aimed at breaking the will of the enemy, rather than his means. In July he speaks again to the use of airplanes in war, tracing the "Giant Bomber" back to Daedalus and Icarus, but says, "I will forgive the Mordor-gadgets some of their sins, if they will bring [this letter] quickly to you" (*Letters* 88).

In December of 1944, Tolkien again shows his disgust with the air force:

I fear an Air Force is a fundamentally irrational thing *per se.* I could wish dearly that you had nothing to do with anything so monstrous. It is in fact a sore trial to me that any son of mine should serve this modern Moloch. But such wishes are in vain, and it is, I clearly understand, your duty to do as well in such service as you have the strength and aptitude to do. . . . As long as war is fought with such weapons, and one accepts any profits that might accrue (such as preservation of one's skin and even "victory") it is merely shirking the issue to hold war-aircraft in special horror. I do so all the same. (*Letters* 105)

He felt that the navy, in which his publisher Stanley Unwin's son Rayner was serving, was "less irrational and wasteful" (*Letters* 112). In May of 1945 he says, "it is the aeroplane of war that is the real villain. . . . My sentiments are more or less those that Frodo would have had if he discovered some Hobbits learning to ride Nazgûl-birds, 'for the liberation of the Shire' " (*Letters* 115). But in the letters Tolkien unfortunately never makes explicitly clear on what basis he despises the airplane, implying in one letter that it is no longer as relevant as in World War I, in another that it exemplifies the hubris of the scientific inventor, in yet another that it is a god to which the young are sacrificed. To Tolkien, air warfare may have been a symbol of all that was worst about modern war: the ability to kill from a distance without even seeing the face of your enemy, the lack of discrimination between combatant and noncombatant, and above all a thing being done simply because it could be done—not because it should be done.

"THE SCOURING OF THE SHIRE" AND PACIFISM

The place in Tolkien's fiction where the conflicting attitudes expressed in his letters are most obvious is the problematic chapter "The Scouring of the Shire." This chapter has seemed anticlimactic and out-of-place to many readers, a shabby letdown from the glorious magnificence of the adventures in the southern kingdoms. But reading it as Tolkien's final word on the subject of war brings that which was remote, and only a concern of great kingdoms safely far away, home to the defenseless Shire. It forces the reader to confront how he or she would react in a similar situation. The unprovoked and almost unopposed occupation of the peaceful Shire points out certain shortcomings of the pacifistic response to violence and injustice, and reveals the root of the pacifist's catch-22: "The unwillingness to kill or injure may be part of the pacifist's very being, but what happens to his 'respect for life' defense when his refusal to fight causes loss of lives which could have been saved?" (Phillips 104).

If there is any sort of war that a pacifist might be able to accept, it should be the war that liberates a peaceful people from brutal oppression. Yet Frodo objects to the use of any force at all. His close friends, whom the reader knows as equally admirable and moral people, are of the opinion that force must be used. Whose judgment should we as readers trust: Frodo, sanctified by his sufferings, or the practical Merry and Pippin, veterans of battle and orc-capture, and companions to the great military leaders of their time? In a letter to a reader, Tolkien professes that "Frodo's attitude to weapons was personal" and that "he had . . . reached the conclusion that physical fighting is actually less ultimately effective than most (good) men think it" (*Letters* 255). But Tolkien leaves the question of who is right unanswered; the efforts of Merry and Pippin free the Shire, but Frodo's influence keeps the bloodshed to a minimum, and it is only Frodo who has the moral authority to offer Saruman the chance of redemption essential to the balance of the story.

The "Scouring" presents what Nan C. Scott calls "the pacifist's ultimate dilemma" in Frodo's pacifism and Merry's opposition to it: "If evil exists in the world, the weak must be defended against it, or die. Just being shocked and sorry won't save the Shire. . . . Like many pacifists [Frodo] feels an increased love and pity for all living creatures; unable to act in their defense by slaying even one of them, he can only move from agony to agony in a world so flawed" (29).

It is certainly appealing to think that a pacifist's approach could end a conflict, and indeed the two prime examples of the success of nonviolent action have been Mahatma Gandhi's liberation of colonial India and the civil rights movement's use of passive resistance in the United States in the 1960s. Phillip Helms theorizes that Tolkien was strongly influenced by Gandhi because of his interest in South Africa, the country where both were born; that this interest is reflected in Frodo's pacifism; and that Frodo's plans to liberate the Shire peacefully failed only because they were "inadequately understood by his companions" (Helms 35). But there is no basis for this theory in any of Tolkien's letters or his biography.

Helms felt that "[t]he situation of the occupied Shire at the time of the Scouring is strongly analogous with that of India under the *raj*" (35), but I do not think this is true. In the case of both colonial India and mid-twentieth century America, the "enemy" being resisted was a society governed by rule of law, which had, even at its most cynical, a vested interest in appearing civilized to the rest of the world. Their intent in denying rights to these groups was not evil at its base, just very deeply misguided, although individual members of each society might have had evil motives in supporting continued oppression. These societies could be reasoned with, but needed to be shamed into action; and the success of nonviolent resistance in these cases "[owes] more to the self-imposed restraint of the adversary than the efficacy of the method" (Coates 115). An enemy like Saruman cannot be shamed by these means; he has already rejected the norms of civilization. As Hannah Arendt pointed out, "If Gandhi's enormously powerful and successful strategy of nonviolent resistance had met with a different enemy—Stalin's Russia, Hitler's Germany, even prewar Japan, instead of England—the outcome would not have been decolonization, but massacre and submission" (43). When faced with such an enemy, "[w]hether one raises a sword eagerly, like Boromir, or regretfully, like Faramir, it would appear that raise it he must or die" (Scott 25). The success of Gandhi's means in these particular limited cases might lead to the hope that they will work in all cases, but this is very unlikely to be true.

Why did Frodo become a pacifist? "Frodo, who begins by wishing that Bilbo had killed Gollum, and who, even in Moria, brings a fair degree of enthusiasm to fighting Orcs" (Scott 28), who cut off the Barrow-wight's hand and bravely stood in front of his friends at Weathertop and raised his sword to the Ringwraiths? Scott sees it as a result of his sufferings and burdens, but even more of his growing feelings of pity (28–29). I feel that one key element of his sense of pity, his empathy, or deep ability to understand the feelings and motivations of others, had the effect of sensitizing him to the point where he could not raise a hand against another being. Frodo was taught by Gandalf to see the terrible responsibility inherent in deciding whether another person deserves to live or die, and his own natural insight and sympathy were enhanced and tormented by the Ring's demand that he dominate others. Frodo's imaginative nature allowed him to see himself in another's shoes all too clearly. Imagining harming another being was too close to imagining harming himself, too close to giving in to the Ring (even after its destruction, the memory of the Ring was a torment), and far too close to claiming that terrifying godlike power of deciding if another should live or die.

Those who know Frodo only from the Peter Jackson movies, however, may have an entirely different image of the hobbit. The key Barrow-wight incident is completely eliminated, gone with the framing Tom Bombadil sequence. The first time we see Frodo fighting for his life is at Weathertop, and here he does not stand protectively in front of Merry and Pippin, who in the book fall to the ground in terror, and Sam, who "shrunk to his side" (*Fellowship* 207). Instead, while Frodo does draw his sword first, he is hidden behind all three of the other hobbits, who bear the brunt of the Ringwraiths' first attack (*The Lord of the Rings: The Fellowship of the Ring* scene 15). Frodo does not brandish his sword in defiance of the Ringwraiths after crossing the Ford of Rivendell, as in the book; instead, lines and actions similar to his are given to Jackson's version of Arwen, who carries the nearly comatose Frodo across the river on her horse like a sack of potatoes (*The Lord of the Rings: The Fellowship of the Ring* scene 17). In Moria again the other hobbits stand in front of Frodo and try to protect him (*The Lord of the Rings: The Fellowship of the Ring* scene 29), whereas in the book, Frodo feels "a hot wrath blaze up in his heart" and leaps forward to strike a blow that even Aragorn admires (*Fellowship* 339). These may all seem to be minor changes in the staging of each event, but taken cumulatively, they present a very different Frodo from the one in Tolkien's books. Jackson has eliminated an important element of Frodo's character arc, his gradual evolution into a pacifistic character, by making him appear not just reluctant to fight but inept and almost cowardly from the start. In fact, with *The Two Towers*, Jackson seems almost to reverse this important character arc—in the Osgiliath sequence he has Frodo actually threaten to kill Sam with Sting, an event as stunningly at odds with Tolkien's text as Jackson's revision of Faramir.

One character in *The Lord of the Rings* lives a life close to the pacifistic ideal: Tom Bombadil. In a letter to Naomi Mitchison, Tolkien describes Bombadil as a pacifist who has renounced any interest in controlling anything outside himself, then goes on to say of pacifism: "[T]he view of Rivendell seems to be that it is an excellent thing to have represented, but that there are in fact things with which it cannot cope; and upon which its existence nonetheless depends. Ultimately only the victory of the West will allow Bombadil to continue, or even to survive. Nothing would be left for him in the world of Sauron" (*Letters* 179). This kind of pure, almost mystical pacifism requires complete withdrawal from the world and a lack of any desire to influence it. Note Goldberry's reaction when Frodo asks her who Tom Bombadil is: "He is the Master of wood, water, and hill," but these things do not belong to him because "That would indeed be a burden" (*Fellowship* 135). Tom is simply the Master, but as Gandalf says, what he is master of, essentially, is himself (*Fellowship* 279). The Ring has no effect on him because

Tom allows nothing outside himself to influence him. Even rain will not fall on him if he does not want it to; he cannot stop the rain, nor would he wish to, because he is not its Master, but his head is his own and he can keep it dry if he so wills. However, most people do not have the ability to renounce the desire to control events around them, and can find no other way to exist except to live in the world and be influenced by what happens there.

Éowyn, like Frodo, turns to pacifism after experiencing sustained military action and being severely wounded in battle. Although she makes a strong argument against pacifism to the Warden, reminding him that someone must be prepared to defend those who cannot fight, because of her love for Faramir she decides that she "will be a shieldmaiden no longer, nor vie with the great Riders, nor take joy only in the songs of slaying. I will be a healer, and love all things that grow and are not barren" (*Return* 243). In her case it is joy and healing, not pain and bitter loss, which turn her away from fighting. In some ways this is an unsatisfactory conversion because it is only described in emotional terms and no rational reason is given for her change; Faramir certainly does not ask her to give up being a shieldmaiden. While not implausible, her change of heart is not adequately explained, particularly for female readers who see a role model in Éowyn.

"I AM WOUNDED, WOUNDED; IT WILL NEVER REALLY HEAL": SHELL SHOCK AND OTHER PSYCHOLOGICAL WOUNDS

One of the grimmest lessons *The Lord of the Rings* teaches about war is that some of the mental wounds it causes never heal in this world. Frodo is Tolkien's prime example of the heartbreaking effects of war on certain minds. As Bruce Leonard has pointed out, Tolkien "described the chronic pain and 'the memory of the fear' that are characteristic of [posttraumatic stress disorder], before PTSD was widely recognized as a clinical phenomena" (2).

It is possible that the first recorded case of "war neurosis" occurred at the Battle of Marathon in 490 B.C.; Herodotus reported that a soldier suddenly lost his sight in the midst of battle without any sign of being wounded (Babington 7). But while there are similar isolated incidents recorded down though the centuries, it was during World War I that military doctors suddenly began to notice a large number of cases of men suffering from a peculiar constellation of symptoms: "withered, trembling arms, paralyzed hands, stumbling gaits, tics, tremors and shakes . . . numbed muteness, palpitations, sweaty hallucinations and nightmares" (Leese 3); "startled reactions, hyper-awareness, insomnia" (Leed 95); and "nervous mannerisms such as blinking or grimacing . . . loss of speech, the development of a stammer, deafness, or paralysis of one or more limbs" (Babington 46). Many of these symptoms sound like the effect of the Black Breath of the Nazgûl, or like Frodo's sufferings after the attack with the Morgul-blade on Weathertop.

One military doctor who observed this phenomenon firsthand was Charles Moran. His memoir, *Anatomy of Courage*, published in 1945, recounts his observations on courage, fear, and men's reactions to the stresses of war (Moran). Like many doctors during the war, he first saw shell shock as a failure of manly courage: "As far as Moran was concerned, mastery of fear in conditions where fear was a natural response to the constant threat of annihilation, was a primary component both of manhood and of duty" (May 97). John T. MacCurdy, an American doctor who studied shell shock among British troops before the American forces went to Europe, sometimes took a dim view of shell shock patients as well; if one showed a "disinclination to return to the front," he had to be shown that this was "essentially a selfish desire to avoid his responsibility as a citizen" (85). Moran soon grew to have a more sympathetic outlook, after living through a close bombardment himself (May 99). His conclusion was that every person had a certain amount of courage, which under stress wore away and was not replaced. When it was gone, all that was left was will power. May describes the way the definition of courage had been revised by the war and the phenomenon of shell shock: "it shifted from episodic physical heroism to stoical endurance, and adjustment to powerlessness" (97).

Why did war stress take this form during World War I? Joanna Bourke summarizes the work of MacCurdy, who theorized in 1918 that "modern warfare was more psychologically difficult than warfare in the past because the men had to 'remain for days, weeks, even months, in a narrow trench or stuffy dugout, exposed to constant danger of the most fearful kind . . . which comes from some unseen source, and against which no personal agility or wit is of any avail.' . . . It was their enforced passivity that was emotionally incapacitating" ("Effeminacy" 58). Anthony Babington also attributes part of the cause to the fact that battles were of "much shorter duration" during earlier wars; Agincourt took just a few hours, Waterloo only one day for most participants, and Gettysburg lasted three days. But battles during the First World War could go on for weeks or months (10). Hans Binneveld adds loneliness as a factor—soldiers were fighting in smaller, more open groups, with less close contact with a mass of comrades in arms, and frequently could not even see their enemies; they were "an anonymous threat" (41). He also thinks that delayed reactions to battle stress may come from the release, after homecoming, from the pattern of "the alternation of intense pressure with periods of rest" (183). Carl May puts it this way: "Personal courage was often rendered meaningless in an industrialized war where the enemy was often unseen and was normally spatially remote, and where artillery destroyed the very landscape in which the soldier found himself" (96). Bourke sees the static nature of trench combat as a major factor: "combat fatigue . . . was frequently due to the blocking of elemental 'fight or flight' responses" (*Intimate History* 237). A soldier who was fixed in one place and could not see an enemy to fight was in the grip of a difficult inner conflict.

This may help explain why Frodo is the only character who exhibits such a strong delayed reaction to his experiences: Frodo's experience of the war was different from everyone else's and more akin to modern war in its unrelieved stress. After entering Mordor, he was in effect threatened continually by an invisible enemy for ten days and nights without relief, and in fact, his sense of being under the constant observation of an unseen enemy dates back to the moment he put on the Ring on Amon Hen. He exemplifies Binneveld's lonely soldier, being unable to share the burden even with Sam. All the other characters experienced a more traditional pattern of war, with battles lasting a day and a night at most and divided in space and time from other confrontations. Faramir, shuttling rapidly between Osgiliath and Minas Tirith, or Aragorn, flying from Helm's Deep to Pelargir to the Pelennor Fields, might have approached Frodo's level of battle fatigue, but neither of them had to bear the kind of burden Frodo did.

Frodo's condition after his return to the Shire was complicated by guilt as well; many who suffered from shell shock also experienced "depression, taking the form of a feeling of hopelessness and shame for their own incompetence and cowardice" (Babington 46). In a draft of a letter to a reader in 1963, Tolkien says that at first Frodo felt no guilt for his fall into temptation, as "he expected to die very soon. But he did not, and one can observe the disquiet growing in him" (*Letters* 327). He suffered from "unreasoning self-reproach: he saw himself and all that he done [*sic*] as a broken failure" (*Letters* 328). Tolkien also felt that Frodo was tempted by two things: the prideful wish to be thought a hero, and regret and desire for the destroyed Ring (*Letters* 328). Hiding all this from his friends, it is no wonder he suffered.

Frodo exhibits few of the classic physical symptoms of shell shock as observed in World War I, except during the flight from Weathertop to Rivendell. But after his return to Hobbiton, his behavior almost perfectly fits the modern diagnostic criteria for posttraumatic stress disorder, a broader disorder applicable to more than just battle fatigue. He "has been exposed to a traumatic event," which included "actual or threatened death," and his response included "intense fear, helplessness, and terror." The climactic struggle at the Cracks of Doom resulted in Gollum's death and Frodo's injury, and in his hopelessness, he was unable to do anything of his own free will to try to escape the conflagration afterward. The event is "persistently reexperienced" in several ways: "recurrent and intrusive distressing recollections of the event" and "recurrent distressing dreams of the event" ("Posttraumatic Stress Disorder" 467–68). On the anniversary of his wounding at Weathertop, Gandalf notices Frodo's distress; he says, "The wound aches, and the memory of darkness is heavy on me" (*Return* 268). On other anniversaries he is described as seeming "half in a dream" (*Return* 304) or seeing "things far away" (*Return* 305). Leonard describes this as "a disconnection where the trauma replaces the present [and] what is now real seems unreal to the sufferer" (3).

Frodo experiences a "numbing of general responsiveness": he shows a "markedly diminished interest or participation in significant activities"; he has a "feeling of detachment or estrangement from others" and a "sense of a foreshortened future" ("Posttraumatic Stress Disorder" 468). In less than a year after the travelers' return, he "dropped quietly out of all the doings of the Shire" (*Return* 305), resigned the post of deputy mayor, and began putting his papers in order, as if he expected to die soon. Seeing him through Sam's distracted eyes, while Sam is caught up in the life and work of the Shire, we do not know if Frodo has trouble sleeping or difficulty concentrating, but as Leonard points out, Frodo talks several times about seeking "rest" (5). However, we do know that the disturbance has had a delayed onset and lasted more than a month, and that it has caused "clinically significant distress" and "impairment in social . . . functioning" ("Posttraumatic Stress Disorder" 468).

Even given the fact that they did not experience the war in quite the same way as Frodo, why did the other hobbits, who grew up in the same peaceful society and had no prior exposure to war except in stories, have such an easy time returning to their normal lives? Did they suffer less because they lacked Frodo's imaginative nature? To Tolkien, "the hobbits represent the combination of small imagination with great courage which (as Tolkien had seen in the trenches during the First World War) often led to survival against all chances. 'I've always been impressed,' he once said, 'that we are here, surviving, because of the indomitable courage of quite small people against impossible odds' " (Carpenter, *Tolkien* 176).

Moran speculated that one contributing factor to the outbreak of shell shock was the fact that the draft brought the kind of men into the army who, having a strong imagination, might have avoided military service in previous years. He felt it was possible that "the armies of long ago were recruited, broadly speaking, from men who did not feel fear. . . . Their imagination played no tricks. They drew no picture of danger for their own undoing. . . . Phlegm, that was the yokel's virtue as a soldier; it was the distinctive quality of his race" (Moran 4). It is not that Merry and Pippin and Sam did not feel fear, because they did; but they did not dwell on it obsessively before or after the battle. Fraser offers a different take on this, less dismissive of the feelings of "yokels": "The celebrated British stiff upper lip, the resolve to conceal emotion which is not only embarrassing and useless, but harmful, is just plain common sense" (89). Confessing fear, or dwelling on it, was "simply not done, partly out of pride, but far more from the certainty that nothing could be better calculated to sap confidence, in one's self, in one's comrades, and among those at home" (35).

Many of those who suffered from the stress of World War I were urged to try to forget their experiences; in British society, "[i]n the 1920s the war was officially forgotten by not being talked about" (Leed 91). In earlier cultures, telling war stories was something warriors did as part of their established role: "The retelling aspect of war comes from the tradition of sagas and stories that celebrate brave deeds in dark times" (Spencer and Soule 63), and "[t]raditionally, successful warriors were enjoined to sing and boast of their killings or paid others to do so" (Leed 88). But twentieth-century wars were fought by "citizen-soldiers," who were expected to "set aside their soldierhood," forget their military training, and return to normal life (Leed 88). And many men managed to do so without any difficulty, of course.

Of those who could not forget, the more fortunate, like Siegfried Sassoon, found doctors like W.H.R. Rivers who practiced the "talking cure" and encouraged them to examine their experiences rather than try to forget them (Babington 108). Many were placed in institutions, some far more helpful than others. Babington quotes an article in *The Lancet* describing an institution very like the Workhouse to which Niggle is assigned, especially after the doctor prescribes "Complete rest—in the dark" (Tolkien, "Leaf" 99). The rooms had "plain grey walls with no pictures or ornaments or anything else to attract or distract the tired men, to whom complete and absolute rest of the body and mind is the first essential of recovery" (Babington 55). After several weeks of this treatment, they were moved to a second hospital reminiscent of Niggle's "next stage" of open blinds, sunshine, and life in the Forest with Parish ("Leaf" 102): "a comfortable private house with a spacious garden . . . well-furnished sitting-rooms with beautiful pictures on the walls . . . they could play billiards or croquet" (Babington 55). Here they could talk with each other and take meals together, instead of living in silent austerity as in the first hospital. In six weeks, they were thought to be fit to return to the Front.

It is the talking, with doctors and with other veterans especially, which is the key; telling the tale grants the teller some control over and ownership of his memories. Andrew Spencer and Brandon Soule suggest "an addendum to Tolkien's realistic view of war: if you fight in a war, then you are entitled to tell the stories afterwards" (63). They speculate that, for the hobbits especially, "[t]he experience just isn't complete until the stories have been told and the songs have been sung" (63). Bilbo certainly found this important in handling his memories of the Battle of Five Armies: "It was a terrible battle. The most dreadful of all Bilbo's experiences, and the one which at the time he hated most—which is to say it was the one he was most proud of, and most fond of recalling long afterwards, although he was quite unimportant in it" (*Hobbit* 294). Merry and Pippin too "cut a great dash in the Shire with their songs and their tales" (*Return* 305). As Spencer and Soule suggest, "Being stuffed into the rank armpits of Grishnákh is no doubt a frequently repeated story of the two young Conspirators, of the same ilk as Bilbo's Battle of Five Armies" (64). *Telling* the stories is a reflection and extension of Tolkien's theme of being *in* a story. One of Tolkien's letters to Christopher juxtaposes both sides of storytelling: "You are inside a very great story! I think also that you are suffering from suppressed writing" (*Letters* 78). One should both recognize that one's experiences form part of a story and tell that story as well. Deborah Tannen, well known for her theories on gender and communication, sees this tale-telling as an essential part of male behavior in our culture. In describing how male members of a family she observed talked about accidents they had had on their bicycles, she observed, "[n]ot only was doing dangerous things part of being a man, but so was crashing—and telling about it before an audience of other men and appreciative women" (136).

Frodo writes about his experiences in the Red Book he leaves to Sam, but does not talk to anyone directly about them, keeping his pain hidden. Leonard observes that "it is curious that Frodo did not seek support from Sam, his fellow Mordor vet" (4), but it was part of Frodo's personality to avoid distressing his friends, and he would be unlikely to want to burden Sam with his troubles when his friend was fully occupied with the regreening of the Shire and making a life with Rosie. Frodo only says privately to Gandalf, "I am wounded with knife, tooth, sting, and a long burden. Where shall I find rest?" (*Return* 268). Compare this to Alexander the Great's speech to the mutineers at Opis—"I have been wounded by the sword, shot with arrows, struck from a catapult, smitten many times with stones and clubs—for you, for your glory, for your wealth" (quoted in Keegan, *Mask* 58). Frodo bears his wounds silently, in private. He "undertook his quest out of love . . . and also in complete humility" (*Letters* 327), was wounded for the salvation of Middle-earth, and claims nothing in return; and in fact knows he must soon leave everything behind. What Frodo says in the end is "I tried to save the Shire, and it has been saved, but not for me. It must often be so, Sam, when things are in danger: some one has to give them up, so that others may keep them" (*Return* 309). Shippey points out the similarity between this speech and the inscription on the Imphal-Kohima monument to the dead of the World War II battles on the India/Burma border:

> When you go home tell them of this and say
> For your tomorrows we gave our today.

(quoted in *Century* 156)

TOLKIEN AND JUST WAR DOCTRINE: "WAR MUST BE, WHILE WE DEFEND OUR LIVES"

Tolkien's fiction, criticism, and letters make it clear that he greatly desired peace, but on the other hand felt that war was sometimes necessary, despite his disgust with modern military means. Tolkien was not a pacifist in the political sense, that is, in the sense of "using pacifism as a moral tool to effect nonviolent political change" (Phillips 6), and he did not appear to agree with pacifists that their philosophy would ensure peace. Tom Bombadil lives a life of pure pacifism, but his existence may at any time depend entirely on the efforts of those willing to defend him. Frodo's rejection of the use of violence during the Scouring of the Shire is shown to be admirable but impractical, as the success of Merry and Pippin's methods demonstrate. Éowyn's response to the pacifistic philosophy of the Warden of the Houses of Healing is somehow more convincingly written than her sudden conversion a few pages later: "It needs but one foe to breed a war, not two, Master Warden. . . . And those who have not swords can still die upon them" (*Return* 236).

It is also clear that Tolkien did not see war as a splendid thing in and of itself. While Tolkien regarded war as something which on occasion was unavoidable, he did not glorify war as such; although there are moments during the Battle of the Pelennor Fields that rival the highest ancient heroic battle poetry, they are more than balanced by other passages on the evils of war. He was certainly well aware of the shortcomings of modern warfare in particular, and of the dangers of too much pride in military valor. For himself and his sons, he saw participating in their country's wars as a duty to be fulfilled to the best of their ability, but not an occasion for boastfulness or for surrendering one's conscience to the state.

How can one desire peace and yet at the same time see war as sometimes the only course that can be taken? How can Tolkien's contradictory attitudes be reconciled? A philosophical system called "just war doctrine" provides a way to balance these positions. Under this system, an acceptable war is defined as "a morally justified arbitrament of arms aimed at resolving by means of discriminate and proportional force an injustice which is incapable of resolution by other means" (Phillips 61). Someone who subscribes to the theory of just war

insists on the moral determination of war where that is possible, and on the moral renunciation of war where it is not. In opposition to the militarist, the just war theorist consistently affirms the moral primacy of peace over war, resisting the cult of violence and the drift into total war. . . . In opposition to the pacifist, the just war theorist resists the blanket moral condemnation of war and of all things military, affirming the potential moral instrumentality of war. (Coates 97)

The roots of *bellum justum* can be found in Plato's *Republic* and its rules of war. The system was developed further by the Romans and by Augustine, and evolved during the Middle Ages as a church doctrine providing a moral basis for Christians to participate in war. *Bellum justum* has continued to adapt to changes in warfare, and is applicable even in our century of nuclear conflict, insurgency, and terrorism. The Catholic Church revived its interest in just war doctrine in the late 1800s, in response to the weapons and tactics of modern war, and refined its position further in the years after World War I through various bishops' councils and papal encyclicals.[1]

It seems to me far more likely that Tolkien, as a devout Catholic, would follow this theological and philosophical debate within his own church, than be as influenced by Gandhi as Philip Helms has suggested (31). While Tolkien's published works do not mention just war doctrine specifically, the opinions he expressed in his letters and criticism and brought to life in his fiction show, if not the direct influence of the theory at least an independent arrival at the same conclusions. In fact, several paragraphs of a letter written to W. H. Auden but never sent deal with the moral necessity of using right means in support of good causes and with the fact that individual examples of moral behavior in the service of a bad cause cannot make that cause good, which is a sophisticated extension of just war reasoning (*Letters* 243). During the typical Inklings meeting, "reconstructed" by Humphrey Carpenter from letters, notes, and other unpublished writings, there is a discussion of pacifism and war, during which Tolkien says that even the winners in wartime have no right to exterminate the losers, another example of just war argument (*Inklings* 149).

Very simply put, just war doctrine states that "a war to be just must be initiated and led by a proper authority, must be fought for a just cause with right intentions, and must not use illicit means" (Teichman 46). *Bellum justum* is generally divided into two components: *jus ad bellum*, which deals with when it is morally allowable to resort to war, and *jus in bello*, which defines the moral conduct of war after it has been initiated. To be morally justifiable, a war must be "undertaken with the intention of bringing about peace" (Phillips 12), and the party declaring war should meet all of the appropriate standards at all times or the war becomes unjust. Among these standards are that there must be a reasonable expectation of success. The nation declaring war must also believe that it "will result in the realization of greater moral good than would result if the war were not fought" (Mattox 31). There has been a steady evolution of moral justifications since the Middle Ages, and some causes that were once thought just are no longer considered to be so.

The two main principles of *jus in bello*, or the conduct of war, are proportionality ("[t]he quantity of force employed or threatened must always be morally proportionate to the end being sought in war") and discrimination ("[f]orce must never be applied in such a way as to make non-combatants and innocent persons the intentional objects of attack") (Phillips 13). Tolkien's objection to the use of war aircraft, if rooted in the inaccuracy of bombing raids, would have its theoretical basis in the principle of discrimination.

An analysis of the quest of Thorin and Company and the subsequent Battle of Five Armies in *The Hobbit* shows the applicability of the theoretical framework of just war to Tolkien's work. There is a great deal of moral ambiguity throughout *The Hobbit* to begin with, and the way the quest fits the tenets of *bellum justum* emphasizes this theme. First, was marching on the Lonely Mountain with the intent of dislodging Smaug a last resort? Yes, if their cause were accepted as moral; it would have been impossible to negotiate with this dragon, although Farmer Giles of Ham was able to do so with a quite different worm. Was this small war declared by a legitimate authority? Yes; Thorin was the rightful king of the dwarves he led, albeit a king in exile. Was it morally justifiable? It depends on the context of the age. Recovery of ancestral lands and property might or might not seem worth a war to our time, but in a medieval world, it would be perfectly acceptable. However, the quest was not undertaken with any specific thought of creating a lasting peace or stopping the dragon's depredations on Laketown, so the overall motives are questionable; and indeed, revenge, an unacceptable motive, was in Thorin's thoughts. Did Thorin have a reasonable expectation of success? Considering the fact that he planned to sit on the doorstep until an idea came to him, no, but this is one of the more difficult precepts of just war to fulfill. Was Thorin planning to adhere to proportionality and discrimination in his war on Smaug? Again, his lack of planning leaves this question open.

What about the subsequent march of the Men of Laketown and the Elves of Mirkwood on the supposedly deserted Lonely Mountain? The Mayor and the Elvenking were legitimate authorities. Their ostensible motive was to seek supplies, or treasure that could be used to buy supplies, to help the displaced townspeople survive the winter, but there was also a strong element of greed involved, which makes their motives less admirable. Was marching on the mountain their last resort? It was the only nearby source of such help, the Elvenking having already aided them as much as possible. But their actions after discovering the dwarves still alive are questionable. Were the Men within their rights to demand reparations for the damage to their town? Here we enter the murky waters of third-party bystanders, neutrality, ultimate responsibility, and unintentional collateral damage. While Bilbo, the practical hobbit, is willing to consider such claims fairly, the spell of the dragon-gold is working on all the other parties. One almost heaves a sigh of relief at the return to moral clarity when the Goblins and Wargs attack. It is always easy to justify a war of defense against unprovoked aggression.

There is substantially less moral ambiguity concerning the War of the Ring. The lands of the West are clearly under unprovoked attack aimed at destroying their sovereignty, an unjust motive on Sauron's part. Is war a last resort? Yes; negotiating with Sauron is useless because of his ultimate goal of total world domination. Is the war declared by legitimate leaders? There really is no formal declaration of war on the part of the West until Aragorn marches on the Gates of Mordor, but at least all the Western armies involved seem to be led by their own legitimate leaders. But then this has been a defensive war up to this point and therefore no declaration was required from the West. Does the West have any hope of winning? A slim one, but given Sauron's goal, they have little choice but to resist him in any way they can. What about right intentions? The aim of the West is freedom for all peoples from the domination of Sauron and defense against his aggression, but there is a strong element of hatred for the orcs bound up in it. A desire for vengeance or extermination is not considered a right intention.

This returns us to the question of the orcs and whether they have redeemable souls or not. During the first Crusades, when just war theory was being rewritten in support of the Church's goal of retaking Jerusalem, Pope Urban II said that those who "killed excommunicated people were not guilty of murder" and that "killing an infidel was not a sin" (Teichman 54). This attitude, translated to Middle-earth's terms, would allow the forces of the West to kill orcs without a second thought, just as the Crusaders slaughtered Jews on their way to Jerusalem, but be required to offer the chance for surrender to the Men fighting on Sauron's side. This does seem to be how the West saw the orcs; in a note on Auden's review of *The Return of the King*, Tolkien says that one of the reasons Denethor was flawed by his political view of life was that "one may be sure he did not distinguish between orcs and the allies of Mordor" (*Letters* 241).

What about *jus in bello*? Does the West practice discrimination? The question does not appear to arise, as Sauron does not seem to have had any noncombatants present at any of his battles. There were unwilling slaves in Mordor who presumably might come to harm in the final cataclysm of Mount Doom, but any collateral damage would be limited to those within range; the "great slave-worked fields . . . by the dark sad waters of Lake Núrnen" in southern Mordor (*Return* 201) would probably be safe. What about proportionality? The West must defend itself with all its strength against a superior foe; it is Sauron's power that is disproportionate.

Another *jus in bello* issue that sometimes arises is the place of deception in a just war. There might be more or less latitude for practices such as spying and ambush, depending on the era; for example, John Mark Mattox points out that Shakespeare is very careful to portray Henry V in the play of the same name winning the Battle of Agincourt "without stratagem / But in plain shock and even play of battle" (quoted Mattox 49). On the other hand, at least one theologian argued during World War I that "the use of ambushes to kill the enemy was legitimate because it displayed the allegedly Christian traits of forethought and prudence" (Bourke, *Intimate History* 261–62). However, the whole strategy of the West during the War of the Ring hinged on one key deception: convincing Sauron that they had the Ring and were planning to use it against him. And there is a further moral dilemma here: the plan of destroying the Ring is in effect a clandestine assassination attempt aimed at the enemy leader. It is questionable whether it is moral to use such deception, but the tenet of proportionality may permit it since it is the only way the West could hope to succeed against disproportionately larger forces using immoral means. Their means might therefore be interpreted as a proportional reaction to Sauron's means.

While Sauron uses immoral means, he is well aware of the principles of just war and tries to manipulate the Allies' adherence to them during the parley with the Mouth of Sauron (*Return* 164–67). The Messenger's intent is to tempt Gandalf and Aragorn to stray from the path of just war because the enemy has clearly already done so and obviously plans further treachery. The scene illustrates the principle that one must adhere to all the tenets of *bellum justum* at all times or one's part in the war becomes unjust. The Messenger's first words point out the fact that Aragorn has not been crowned yet and therefore is technically without authority to declare war or negotiate. When Aragorn stares him down, he attempts to protect himself by calling on the *jus in bello* rule that heralds "were supposed to be protected and given safe conduct" (Teichman 56): "I am a herald and ambassador, and may not be assailed!" (*Return* 165). The herald then shows the tokens supposedly taken from the imprisoned hobbit, and tells them of Sauron's plans to torture his captive. But under the principles of just war, a prisoner once removed from combat has immunity; as Phillips argues, preventing someone from taking further part in battle removes the "combatant" from the "man"; the "man" therefore becomes a noncombatant and should be protected from harm (35–37). Sauron's proposed treatment of the hobbit violates just war principles and angers the Allies, but they hold firm. Next, the Messenger names terms that the Allies can only reject, as they would create a false peace worse than the war and thus be against *jus ad bellum* doctrine. Again they keep to the moral high ground and allow him to return to Mordor unharmed though humiliated.

It is also enlightening to analyze the Scouring of the Shire through just war doctrine. The cause of liberating the Shire from its occupiers is overwhelmingly just. Frodo makes sure that honorable intentions and means will be used—that as little killing as necessary will take place and that the men will have a chance to surrender. But from what do Merry and Pippin derive their authority to lead the hobbits in revolt? It is true that they are heirs to the Thain and the Took, respectively, but they seem to simply step into their roles by virtue of being the first to propose the hobbits take action. The other hobbits unquestioningly accept their right to lead. But it may only be possible for someone not in obvious power to lead a revolt in an occupied territory; those legitimately in power have usually been removed or suborned as early in the occupation as possible, as happened in the Shire. *Jus in bello* is followed scrupulously by the hobbits. It may appear at first that it is not proportionate for the hobbits to so vastly outnumber the men in their two battles, but this irresistible force is precisely what is needed to achieve their goal of a nearly bloodless coup. In this case, threatening with overpowering force was the moral thing to do. As Hanson argues, "overwhelming violence in response to great evil, while tragic, is not therein evil" (*Autumn* 103). The hobbits follow the *jus in bello* principle of prisoner immunity; all the Men taken prisoner were quickly removed from combat and held securely until it was over.

Does just war theory have room for the Rohirrim, who "sang as they slew" (*Return* 113)? Many readers, pacifist or not, are uncomfortable with this passage and point to it as an example of Tolkien's supposed delight in war. This joy in battle seems to go against the tenets of right intentions and proportionality, but Timmons points out that what Tolkien is showing us is that "some battles *are worth fighting* and one *should take joy* in defeating a wicked

adversary" ("We Few" 6). Fraser notes this phenomenon from his experiences
in Burma during World War II: "A few really enjoy [battle]; I've seen them
(and I won't say they're deranged, because even the most balanced man has
moments of satisfaction in battle which are indistinguishable from enjoyment,
short-lived though they may be)" (87). Timmons argues that

> none of the expressions of joy and glory are gratuitous. There is never any boasting,
> overt bravado, or exulting in the fallen or defeated. Both after the victories at Helm's
> Deep and Minas Tirith, mercy and care are shown towards some of the wretched allies
> of Saruman and Sauron. There is joy in a victory over evil, not in death and destruc-
> tion. Similar to Armistice Day and Victory in Europe Day, the celebrations are for
> the *end of war*. The glory achieved is well-deserved because the cause was just. Joy in
> battle might disturb modern sensibilities. But, clearly, in LOTR, no true-hearted war-
> rior kills chiefly for pleasure. ("We Few" 14)

The whole subject of whether or not the Allies can use the Ring against
Sauron is a just war issue. All internal dissension in the West hinges on
whether it is right to use this fortuitously obtained weapon, and a character's
answer to this question is the key to his or her attitude on just war. In this
way, the Ring can be read as clearly applicable to the philosophical and moral
problems raised by the atomic bomb. Planning from the start to use the Ring
would be a violation of the principle of right means: "[a] nation would not be
entitled to engage in a war that it intended to fight using immoral means.
This would be so even though it had just cause for going to war and had noble
intentions" (Fotion and Elfstrom 108). Protestant theologian Reinhold Nie-
buhr's argument against the bomb arises from the tenet of proportionality:
"this weapon could never be a moral instrument of coercion in the cause of
justice because of the greater injustice its use would bring" (Johnson 337).
Phillips approaches the problem through the discrimination argument: the
possession of atomic bombs "is a standing threat to non-combatants in a way
that the possession of conventional weapons is not, for the latter *can* be used
justly, the former can be used *only* unjustly" (Phillips 80). A recent article in
National Geographic put this very succinctly: "In a very real sense, whenever
weapons of mass death are unleashed, all humanity is downwind" (Simons
35). Tolkien himself argues against the militaristic view taken by Clausewitz
(who did not believe in just war) that means determine policy: "if a thing *can*
be done, it *ought* to be done" (Phillips 124). Tolkien contends that this "most
widespread assumption of our time" is "wholly false" (*Letters* 246).
All of this applies to the Ring as well: even the strongest and most moral
person who tried to use the Ring would find that he or she was not strong
enough to refrain from the temptation to unjustly enslave the rest of the
world. Those who appear to adhere most strongly to the tenets of just war
feel the least temptation to claim the Ring; Aragorn and Faramir, for example, see the moral dangers of using the Ring very clearly from the start.

Those of a militaristic mind, like Boromir, or those who believe in Clause-witzian realpolitik and scorn ethics in war as a dream for fools, like Saruman or Denethor, desire the Ring for the power it would give them and think that they could control it. Those who desire peace above all else are tempted by the Ring's power to allow them to impose their will on the world for good purpose—but the Wise, whether Gandalf or Samwise, see the trap of power for what it is. Only those who can remove themselves entirely from wanting to influence the outside world, like Tom Bombadil in his private nirvana, are completely unaffected by the Ring.

CONCLUSION: TOLKIEN'S MESSAGE

Tolkien was deeply influenced by both his war experiences and his study of heroic northern European literature. He was a thoughtful observer of "War, and the pity of War" (Owen), and understood the unhappy balance between the occasional necessity for war on the one hand, and on the other, the price it exacts from the bodies and souls of participants. The key to his philosophy is just war theory, its sometimes sterile logic tempered by his understanding of what we now call posttraumatic stress disorder, his wide reading in history, his views on the art of leadership, and his distrust of modernity (particularly what Fussell called "that contempt for life, individuality, and privacy, and that facile recourse to violence that have characterized experience in the twentieth century" [*Great War* 322]).

Understanding Tolkien's approach to war is crucial to fully understanding his works, particularly *The Lord of the Rings*, as a whole. Many critics and readers have viewed Tolkien as simplistically pacifist or war-loving, by reading shallowly and ignoring Tolkien's seeming self-contradictions, or simply disregarded the presence of war in the works altogether. What they miss by reading this way is a well-thought-out, comprehensive, and realistic philosophy of war.

World War I was a seminal event in Tolkien's life. He witnessed incredible carnage and impossible heroism, and lost most of his best friends in battle. He went through rigorous technical training in his specialty, as well as combat training designed to provoke hate and bloodthirstiness. His taste for fairy-stories was awakened, and he began to write in earnest, filling notebooks with his tales of the gnomes as an escape and a way of translating his experiences. Yet the war did not turn him into an ironic writer, as it did so many others of his generation; he retained his undespairing but realistic outlook in spite of all the war could do.

World War II taught him the frustrations of a parent, too old for active duty, forced to watch his sons risking their lives in a war that was, from the point of view of 1918, never supposed to happen. In "The Homecoming of Beorhtnoth Beorhthelm's Son," he emphasizes the youth of the slain: "It's a wicked business / to gather them ungrown" ("Homecoming" 7). This second war in his lifetime was even more bitter than the first, as he helplessly observed the inexorable advance of modernity and the machine culminate in the atomic bomb. Like Sassoon, Tolkien worried about the "slavedom of mankind to the machine" ("Litany of the Lost"). In Tolkien's view, only one thing was "triumphant" as World War II came to an end: "the Machines," and he wondered plaintively, "What's their next move?" (*Letters* 111).

The heart of the morality of leadership, for Tolkien, was the willingness of a leader to take the same risks as those he leads—to lead from the front rather than from behind. Leadership is an important part of the maturation process for many of his characters, and one may assume it was for him as well. In *Beowulf: The Monsters and the Critics* and in "The Homecoming," Tolkien makes clear that leaders have an overwhelming responsibility, toward both those they lead and those they protect, that should outweigh any consideration of personal glory and renown.

Tolkien's dislike of all modern war and preference for earlier models of military conflict can be understood by using just war theory. While *bellum justum* can be applied to modern war, it is a much better fit for earlier modes of combat and makes them seem less morally ambiguous in comparison. Just war strikes a realistic and morally sustainable balance between militarism (or "war for its own sake") on the one hand, and pure pacifism on the other, which may have appealed to both Tolkien's desire for moral clarity and his questioning of ancient heroic literature. In the modern age of total war, it is harder to see right and wrong clearly, and there is an ever-present danger of descent into mutually assured destruction. As Tom Shippey explains, in Denethor, Tolkien has depicted a leader who would rather see the end of the world than have things turn out other than the way he desires; and "[b]y the time *The Lord of the Rings* was published, of course, it was for the first time in the history of the world possible for political leaders to say they would have 'naught,' *and make it come true*" (*Century* 173).

Tolkien's distaste for contemporary war can also be traced to his understanding of the causes and agonies of modern war neuroses. At the very simplest level, modern technology (in the sense not just of weapons but also of matériel) erases the differences between night and day, summer and winter, that in primitive times limited war to particular times and seasons and supported a natural rhythm of "a time for war and a time for peace." Trench warfare constrained and held back the fight-or-flight instinct, creating a disconnect between attacking and being attacked. As Adams asserts, when "[t]echnology kills randomly and meanly" (70), there is little the individual soldier can do to feel effective. Courage had to be redefined; heroic action was no longer paramount but was supplanted by dogged endurance, which Tolkien embodied in Frodo and Sam's journey across Mordor.

Tolkien warns us against the concentration of power and the will to dominate (to the point where all ethics are ignored): Sauron, Saruman, and the Ring itself illustrate a soul-destroying addiction to the power of controlling others. Tolkien also reminds us of the eucatastrophic nature of mercy, that transcending the hard rules of just war and military law, and freely offering mercy and pity, is an act of grace that may rebound in unexpected ways. As Nan Scott has pointed out, "But for four separate acts of mercy all the defenses of sword, shield, and tower would have been altogether futile, each victory utterly in vain" (29). Four times Gollum's life was spared—by Bilbo under the Misty Mountains, by Frodo in the Emyn Muil, by Faramir in Ithilien, and by Sam on the slopes of Mount Doom—and without these acts of mercy, Gollum would not have survived to enter the chamber of the Sammath Naur and do what he had to do.

It is these words, spoken by Faramir to Frodo in the woods of Ithilien, that express the essence of Tolkien's philosophy of war: " 'War must be, while we defend our lives against a destroyer who would devour us all; but I do not love the bright sword for its sharpness, nor the arrow for its swiftness, nor the warrior for his glory. I love only that which they defend: the city of the Men of Númenor' " (*Towers* 280).

NOTE

1. Joanna Bourke's *An Intimate History of Killing* includes a chapter, "Priests and Padres," on clerical attitudes toward combat during World War I, World War II, the Korean War, and the Vietnam War. Most of their statements supporting war draw on just war doctrine (*Intimate History* 256–93).

Appendix A

A Chronology of J.R.R. Tolkien's World War I Experiences

(Based on material from Latter vol. 1, 93–165, 349–53; Carpenter, *Tolkien* 58, 72–98; Tolkien and Tolkien 38–41; J.R.R. Tolkien, *Letters* 7–10, 420; Duffy; *The Lancashire Fusiliers*; Hammond and Scull; P. Tolkien.)

1912	Summer	The summer after his first year at Oxford, Tolkien enrolls in King Edward's Horse, a territorial cavalry regiment, and spends two weeks in camp near Folkstone in Kent, but resigns after a few months.
1914	June 28	Assassination of Archduke Ferdinand.
	August 4	British government gives orders for mobilization of the army.
	September 15	Beginning of trench warfare. By late summer his brother Hilary has enlisted as a bugler.
	Early October?	Tolkien signs up for officer training with deferred call-up; begins drilling with Oxford University Officers' Training Corps.
	November	Training at Rugeley Camp in Staffordshire.
	December	Last meeting of TCBS (Tolkien and friends' "Tea Club and Barrovian Society"); Christopher Wiseman in navy; Rob Gilson and G. B. Smith go to Somme.
1915	January 19–20	First German zeppelin attack on England.

March	Training continues (letter to Edith).	
May 7	Sinking of the Lusitania.	
June	Tolkien passes final exam with First Class honors. Takes up commission with Lancashire Fusiliers, Thirteenth Battalion (which was a draft-finding reserve unit, training reinforcements). Tolkien's brother Hilary serving in Royal Warwickshire regiment as a private; suffers minor shrapnel wounds several times at Passchendaele Ridge.	
July	Training camp begins at Bedford: platoon drill, lectures.	
August	Unit moves to Staffordshire, then to various other camps.	
1916 Early in year	Tolkien decides to specialize in signaling; begins training. Eventually appointed battalion signaling officer.	
March 22	Marries Edith in Warwick; Edith moves to Great Haywood, near the camp at Cannock Chase.	
May–July	British army prepares for major offensive at the Somme.	
May	Eleventh Battalion (Tolkien's later posting) captures "Crosbie Craters," then is withdrawn into divisional reserve.	
June 2	Embarkation orders arrive.	
June 4	Tolkien departs for London.	
June 6	Arrives at Calais and taken to base camp at Étaples. Transferred to Eleventh Battalion with many other officers.	
End of June	Battalion goes to the front by train as far as Amiens. Marches from Amiens to Rubempré in the rain.	
June 30	Moved closer to front (to Warloy)—held in reserve.	
July 1	Attack on the Somme begins; twelve battalions of Lancashire Fusiliers participate during the course of this four-and-a-half-month battle. Eleventh Battalion remains in reserve.	
July 4	Eleventh Battalion moved to Bouzincourt, then forward to Usna Hill redoubts.	

July 6	Moved to La Boisselle. Ovillers, July 7–10: "A" and "C" Companies of Eleventh Battalion sent to front with Seventy-fourth Infantry Brigade; "B" Company, in which Tolkien served, kept in reserve to carry rations and ammunition. 171 casualties.
July 7	"A" Company withdrawn from the line. "C" Company continues with brigade and takes objective, then pushes on 600 yards farther. Carrying parties from "B" and "D" Companies help them entrench.
July 9	"C" Company forced to withdraw.
July 11	Survivors of "A" and "C" Companies return to Bouzincourt, then three days of rest at Senlis.
July 14	Battle of Bazentin Ridge, July 14–17. Eleventh Battalion moves up to trenches at La Boisselle, attached to Seventh Infantry Brigade. Attacks Ovillers twice that evening; "A" and "B" Companies are part of the second attack. It fails due to uncut wire, machine gun fire.
July 15	Battalion returns to La Boisselle.
July 16	Bombing squadrons from Eleventh Battalion capture German garrison.
July 17?	Company returns to Bouzincourt, then on to Forceville. Tolkien finds letter from G. B. Smith about Rob Gilson's death on July 1.
August 19	Smith meets Tolkien at Acheux, and they visit for several days.
September 15	First use of tanks by British, on the Somme battle-front.
September 28	Schwaben Redoubt (Part of Battle of Thiepval Ridge). Nineteenth Division attacks the Schwaben Redoubt; "C" and "D" Companies of the Eleventh Battalion occupy the enemy's trenches and take prisoners. (Carpenter reports that Tolkien spoke to a captured German officer at this time, but his chronology places the storming of this redoubt before his meeting with Smith in August, so this may have occurred earlier with a prisoner from the July 16 action.)
October 16	Tolkien draws a trench map based on air photos and prisoner information shortly after this date.

October 27	Tolkien diagnosed with "pyrexia of unknown origin," or "trench fever," while billeted at Beauval.
October 29	In hospital at Le Touquet.
November 8	Embarked for England; taken by train to hospital in Birmingham.
November 18	End of Battle of the Somme.
Late December	Well enough to spend Christmas with Edith in Great Haywood. Learns that G. B. Smith died December 16.
1917 Winter	During convalescence writes "The Fall of Gondolin" and Edith copies it out. Posted temporarily to Yorkshire. Falls ill again; moved to sanatorium at Harrogate.
February 24	"Zimmerman telegram" passed on to United States by Britain.
April	Declared fit for duty; sent for additional signaling training. Possibility of becoming signaling officer for Yorkshire camp and staying out of combat.
April 6	United States declares war on Germany.
June	Had been promoted to full lieutenant; in command of an outpost of the Humber Garrison, near Roos in Yorkshire.
June 26	First U.S. troops arrive in France.
July	Tolkien fails signaling exam; falls ill again a few days later.
Mid-August	At Brookland Officer's Hospital in Hull. Edith still in Hornsea and pregnant; she returns to Cheltenham. While at Hull, Tolkien works on "The Children of Húrin."
November 7	Bolshevik Revolution in Russia.
November 16	John Tolkien born.
1918 Spring	Posted to Penkridge in Staffordshire.
May 28	Third Battle of the Aisne, May 27–June 6. Eleventh Battalion sustains enormous losses at Chemin des Dames; all are presumed taken prisoner or killed.

August 12	Eleventh Battalion is officially disbanded.
Late Summer	Tolkien becomes ill on his way to the Humber Garrison; returns to officers' hospital at Hull.
October	Discharged from hospital.
November 11	War ends. Tolkien granted permission to be stationed at Oxford until demobilized.

Daniel Grotta's biography adds that Tolkien was attached to the Third Reserve Battalion of the Lancashire Fusiliers when he left the hospital in April 1917, was finally released from military service on July 16, 1919, and formally relinquished his commission on November 3, 1920, retaining the rank of first lieutenant (58). Grotta says Tolkien never claimed the medals and ribbons he had won and did not apply for the disability award for which he was eligible, not wanting to be reminded of the war (58). Unfortunately, Grotta's biography is considered untrustworthy by many critics because of its factual errors. I have been unable to confirm Grotta's facts in Carpenter's official biography or other published sources, so I have not included them in the table.

Appendix B

A Chronology of J.R.R. Tolkien's Family's World War II Experiences

(Based on material from Carpenter, *Tolkien*; J.R.R. Tolkien, *Letters*; Tolkien and Tolkien; J.R.R. Tolkien, *Father Xmas*; Dear; Polsson; Hammond and Scull; Ready.)

1937	May 28	Neville Chamberlain becomes British prime minister.
	September 21	*The Hobbit* published.
1938	March 11	Germany invades Austria.
	November 9	Kristallnacht: attacks on Jews throughout Germany
1939	January	Tolkien asked if he would work in cryptological department of Foreign Office in event of war.
	March 8	Tolkien delivers "On Fairy-stories" lecture.
	March 27–31	Tolkien has four days training in cryptography at Foreign Office.
	Summer	John taking finals at Exeter.
	September 1	"Blackouts" begin in London.
	September 3	Great Britain and France declare war on Germany.
	September	Michael at age nineteen volunteers for the army but is told to wait and spend one year in university first.
	October	Tolkien informed he would not be needed as a cryptographer.

| November | John travels to Rome to study and train for priesthood. |
| December 19 | Tolkien reports that two of his assistants have been called up. |

1940

January	Rationing begins in UK.
May 10	Neville Chamberlain resigns; Winston Churchill appointed prime minister.
Spring	At some point John and the rest of his College in Rome evacuate to England and relocate at Stonyhurst in Lancashire; probably before June 10, when Italy declared war on France and the UK.
June 14	German troops enter Paris.
Summer	Two women evacuees billeted with the Tolkien family.
July 10	Battle of Britain begins.
August 24	German planes bomb London; Britain retaliates by bombing Berlin the next night.
October	Michael is in training as an antiaircraft gunner.
October 31	End of Battle of Britain.
Late 1940	Michael participates in defense of aerodromes during Battle of Britain; also serves in France and Germany; injured in an accident during night training, sent to hospital in Worcester.
November 14	German air raid on Coventry; Tolkien can see the glow of the burning city from his study in Oxford.

1941

January	Tolkien participating in air raid warnings as warden.
June 9	By this time, Michael is an officer cadet at the Royal Military College, Sandhurst. Also at this time, Tolkien is involved in organizing a syllabus for naval cadets reading English at Oxford. Tolkien says he is "permanently reserved" and does not even have time to be in the Home Guards.
(no date given)	Michael posted to Sidmouth, where the Tolkiens had often holidayed; tests in situ guns.
December 7	Japanese attack Pearl Harbor.

	December 11	Germany declares war on United States.
1942	(no date given)	Warehouse stock of *The Hobbit* burnt in London blitz. During 1942 Tolkien serves as an air raid warden, which requires occasional overnight stays at area Headquarters.
	January 1	UN Declaration signed by United States, USSR, UK, China. (First official use of term "United Nations.")
	June 4	Battle of Midway starts.
	October 22	Draft age in Britain lowered to eighteen; Christopher turns eighteen in November.
	December 7	*Lord of the Rings* up to chapter "Flotsam and Jetsam."
1943	April	Tolkien still involved in teaching cadets, as is C. S. Lewis.
	Summer	Christopher called up into the Royal Air Force.
	July 25	Mussolini resigns.
	October	Tolkien still serving as an air raid warden.
	November	Christopher in training camp at Heaton Park in Manchester.
	December 2	First atomic chain reaction at University of Chicago.
	Christmas	Last "Father Christmas" letter to Priscilla.
1944	January	Christopher posted to South Africa for pilot training; sails on S.S. *Cameronia*. Tolkien still performing air warden duties; recounts incident sharing watch with professor of Jewish studies. Also around this time Tolkien is consulted by a Polish officer for help in devising a technical vocabulary.
	April 13	Christopher arrives in South Africa shortly before this date and is in a camp in the Transvaal. Tolkien still involved with cadet program at Oxford.
	May 11	By this date, Michael has been invalided out of the army and is back at Oxford being tutored in history. He had been judged unfit for further military duty due to "severe shock to the nervous system due to prolonged exposure to enemy action."

June 6		D-Day—Allied invasion of Normandy.
June 13		Start of V-1 bombardment against England.
June		Christopher at a training camp at Kroonstad in Orange Free State.
August 25		Germans surrender Paris.
September 23		By this date, Christopher has moved to a camp at Standerton in the Transvaal. Blackouts ending in Oxford.
1945	January 30	Russians marching on Berlin.
	February 13	Air raid on Dresden.
	March 18	Christopher in transit to England.
	April 12	Roosevelt dies; Truman becomes president.
	April 30	Hitler commits suicide.
	May 8	V-E Day; war in Europe ends.
	May 15	Charles Williams (Inkling) dies.
	May 29	By this date, Christopher has returned to England and is stationed with the Royal Air Force in Shropshire, hoping for a transfer to the Fleet Air Arm in order to avoid becoming a physical training equipment officer.
	June 3	Tolkien to attend a stand-down of the Civil Defense this day.
	July 16	Atomic bomb tested at Alamogordo.
	July 26	Churchill resigns after losing election.
	August 6	Bombing of Hiroshima.
	August 9	Bombing of Nagasaki.
	September 2	Japanese surrender signed.
1946	February	John ordained in Oxford.
	Spring	Tolkien visits John at Stonyhurst.
	Summer	Tolkien and Edith visit John at Stonyhurst.
	July	Christopher by this date has transferred to Fleet Air Arm, and has returned to Oxford.

Works Cited

Adams, Michael C. C. *The Great Adventure: Male Desire and the Coming of World War I*. Bloomington: Indiana UP, 1990.

The American Library in Paris. 2002. 23 April 2002 <www.americanlibraryin paris.org>.

Anderson, Douglas A. "Tolkien after All These Years." *Meditations on Middle-earth*. Ed. Karen Haber. New York: St. Martin's Press, 2001. 129–51.

Aoki, Elizabeth. "We Can't Kick 'The Hobbit.' " *Boston Globe* 21 August 1988, sec. A: 1, 13–14.

Arendt, Hannah. *On Violence*. London: Allen Lane, 1970.

Armstrong, Helen. "It Bore Me Away: Tolkien as Horseman." *Mallorn* 30 (1993): 29–31.

Ashurst, George. *My Bit: A Lancashire Fusilier at War, 1914–1918*. Ed. Richard Holmes. Ramsbury, Eng.: Crowood Press, 1987.

Atkinson, J. *ABC of the Army: An Illustrated Guide to Military Knowledge for Those Who Seek a General Acquaintance with Elementary Matters Pertaining to the British Army*. London: Gale & Polden, 1914.

Auden, W. H. "Balaam and His Ass." *The Dyer's Hand and Other Essays*. New York: Random House, 1962. 107–45.

———. "Reading." *The Dyer's Hand and Other Essays*. New York: Random House, 1962. 3–12.

Babington, Anthony. *Shell-Shock: A History of the Changing Attitudes to War Neurosis*. London: Leo Cooper, 1997.

Barnes, John B. *Military Sketching and Map Reading*. 4th rev. ed. New York: D. Van Nostrand, 1918.

Beach, Edward A. *The Eleusinian Mysteries*. 1995. The Ecole Initiative. 5 June 2002 <http://users.erols.com/nbeach/eleusis.html>.

Bell, David. "The Battle of the Pelennor Fields: An Impossible Victory?" *Mallorn* 19 (1982): 25–28.

"Beowulf." Trans. Francis B. Gummere. *The Oldest English Epic: Beowulf, Finnsburg, Waldere, Deor, Widsith, and the German Hildebrand.* New York: Macmillan, 1909 [1914]. 1–158.

Bergonzi, Bernard. *Heroes' Twilight: A Study of the Literature of the Great War.* 1965. 2nd ed. London: Macmillan, 1980.

Best of Millennium Poll. 1999. Amazon.com. 17 October 2002 <www.amazon.com/exec/obidos/subst/features/c/century/best-of-millennium.html/>.

Binneveld, Hans. *From Shell Shock to Combat Stress: A Comparative History of Military Psychiatry.* Trans. John O'Kane. Amsterdam: Amsterdam UP, 1997.

Black, Kevin Roger. "Where the Shadows Lie: The Battle against Modernity in J.R.R. Tolkien's *The Lord of the Rings.*" Senior thesis. Princeton, 1995.

Bloom, Harold, ed. *J.R.R. Tolkien.* Philadelphia: Chelsea House, 2000.

———, ed. *The Lord of the Rings.* Philadelphia: Chelsea House, 2000.

Blunden, Edmund. "Report on Experience." *The Penguin Book of First World War Poetry.* Ed. Jon Silkin. London: Penguin, 1979. 113–14.

———. "Rural Economy." *Undertones of War.* London: Collins, 1965 (1928). 225.

Bourke, Joanna. "Effeminacy, Ethnicity and the End of Trauma: The Sufferings of 'Shell-Shocked' Men in Great Britain and Ireland, 1914–39." *Journal of Contemporary History* 35.1 (2000): 57–69.

———. *An Intimate History of Killing: Face-to-Face Killing in Twentieth-Century Warfare.* New York: Basic, 1999.

Bratman, David. "Through the Tolkien Jungle: From the Mountains to the Swamps." *Mythcon 33: Annual Conference of The Mythopoeic Society.* Boulder, CO: (unpublished), 2002.

Brogan, Hugh. "Tolkien's Great War." *Children and Their Books: A Celebration of the Work of Iona and Peter Opie.* Eds. Gillian Avery and Julia Briggs. Oxford: Clarendon, 1989. 351–67.

Brooke, Rupert. "Peace." *The Works of Rupert Brooke: With an Introduction and Bibliography.* Wordsworth Poetry Library. Ware: Wordsworth, 1994. 144.

Brothers Gentile. "The Death of Boromir." *The 1980 J.R.R. Tolkien Calendar.* New York: Ballantine, 1980. June.

Bujold, Lois McMaster. *A Civil Campaign.* Riverdale: Baen, 1999.

Burger, Douglas A. "The Shire: A Tolkien Version of the Pastoral." *Aspects of Fantasy: Selected Essays from the Second International Conference on the Fantastic in Literature and Film.* Ed. William Coyle. Westport: Greenwood, 1986. 149–54.

Campbell, Joseph. *The Hero with a Thousand Faces.* 2nd ed. Princeton: Princeton UP, 1973.

Campbell, Kim. *Tolkien Buzz Moves Books.* 12 July 2001. Christian Science Monitor. 17 October 2002 <www.csmonitor.com/durable/2001/07/12/p15s1.htm>.

Camps, Billets, Cooking: Sanitation, Organization, Routine, Guard Duties, Inspections, Ceremonial, Bivouacs. Ed. E. John Solano. American ed. New York: George U. Harvey, 1917.

Card, Orson Scott. "How Tolkien Means." *Meditations on Middle-earth.* Ed. Karen Haber. New York: St. Martin's, 2001. 153–73.

Carpenter, Humphrey. *The Inklings: C.S. Lewis, J.R.R. Tolkien, Charles Williams, and Their Friends.* Boston: Houghton Mifflin, 1979.

———. *Tolkien: A Biography.* Boston: Houghton Mifflin, 1977.

Clark, George. "J.R.R. Tolkien and the True Hero." *J.R.R. Tolkien and His Literary Resonances: Views of Middle-earth*. Eds. George Clark and Daniel Timmons. Westport: Greenwood, 2000. 39–51.

Coates, A. J. *The Ethics of War*. Manchester, Eng.: Manchester UP, 1997.

Colebatch, Hal. *Return of the Heroes: The Lord of the Rings, Star Wars, and Contemporary Culture*. Critical Issues no. 13. Perth: Australian Institute for Public Policy, 1990.

Craig, David M. "Queer Lodgings: Gender and Sexuality in *The Lord of the Rings*." *Mallorn* 38 (2001): 11–18.

Davis, Richard Harding. "The German Army Marches through Brussels, 21 August 1914." *Eyewitness to History*. Ed. John Carey. Cambridge: Harvard UP, 1987. 445–48.

Dear, I.C.B., ed. *The Oxford Companion to the Second World War*. Oxford: Oxford UP, 1995.

Drout, Michael D. C., and Hilary Wynne. "Tom Shippey's *J.R.R. Tolkien: Author of the Century* and a Look Back at Tolkien Criticism since 1982." *Envoi* 9.2 (2000) <http://members.aol.com/JamesIMcNelis/9_2/Drout_9_2.pdf>.

Duffy, Michael. *First World War.Com*. 2002. 18 April 2002 <www.firstworldwar.com/index.htm>.

Eksteins, Modris. "Memory and the Great War." *The Oxford Illustrated History of the First World War*. Ed. Hew Strachan. Oxford: Oxford UP, 1998. 305–17.

Ellison, John. " 'The Legendary War and the Real One': *The Lord of the Rings* and the Climate of Its Times." *Mallorn* 26 (1989): 17–20.

Ellmann, Mary. "Growing Up Hobbitic." *New American Review*. Vol. 2. New York: New American Library, 1968. 217–29.

Englander, David. "Mutinies and Military Morale." *The Oxford Illustrated History of the First World War*. Ed. Hew Strachan. Oxford: Oxford UP, 1998. 191–203.

Flieger, Verlyn. *A Question of Time: J.R.R. Tolkien's Road to Faërie*. Kent, OH: Kent State UP, 1997.

Fonstad, Karen Wynn. *The Atlas of Middle-earth*. Rev. ed. Boston: Houghton Mifflin, 1991.

Fotion, N., and G. Elfstrom. *Military Ethics: Guidelines for Peace and War*. Boston: Routledge & Kegan Paul, 1986.

Fraser, George MacDonald. *Quartered Safe Out Here: A Recollection of the War in Burma*. London: HarperCollins, 1995.

Friedman, Barton. "Tolkien and David Jones: The Great War and the War of the Ring." *Clio* 11.2 (1982): 115–36.

Frye, Northrop. *Anatomy of Criticism: Four Essays*. Princeton: Princeton UP, 1957.

Fussell, Paul. *The Great War and Modern Memory*. 25th anniversary ed. New York: Oxford UP, 2000 [1975].

———. *Wartime: Understanding and Behavior in the Second World War*. New York: Oxford UP, 1989.

Gilchrist, K. James. "Continuing Research on 2nd Lieutenant Lewis." *Seven: An Anglo-American Literary Review* 18 (2001): 47–50.

———. "2nd Lieutenant Lewis." *Seven: An Anglo-American Literary Review* 17 (2000): 61–78.

Goldthwaite, John. *The Natural History of Make-Believe: A Guide to the Principal Works of Britain, Europe, and America.* New York: Oxford UP, 1996.

Graves, Robert. *Good-Bye to All That.* New rev. ed. New York: Anchor Books Doubleday, 1998.

Green, William H. *The Hobbit: A Journey into Maturity.* Twayne's Masterwork Studies. Ed. Robert Lecker. Vol. 149. New York: Twayne, 1995.

Grieves, Loren C. *Military Sketching and Map Reading.* 3rd rev. and enl. ed. Washington, DC: United States Infantry Association, 1917.

Grossman, Lev. "Feeding on Fantasy." *Time* 2 December 2002: 90–94.

Grotta, Daniel. *The Biography of J.R.R. Tolkien, Architect of Middle Earth.* 2nd ed. Philadelphia: Running Press, 1978.

Hammond, Wayne G. *J.R.R. Tolkien: A Descriptive Bibliography.* Winchester, Eng.: St. Paul's Bibliographies, 1993.

Hammond, Wayne G., and Christina Scull. *J.R.R. Tolkien: Artist and Illustrator.* Boston: Houghton Mifflin, 1995.

Hanson, Victor Davis. *An Autumn of War: What America Learned from September 11 and the War on Terrorism.* New York: Anchor, 2002.

———. *Carnage and Culture: Landmark Battles in the Rise of Western Power.* New York: Doubleday, 2001.

Hartt, Frederick, and David Finn. *Michelangelo's Three Pietàs.* New York: Henry N. Abrams, 1975.

Harvey, P.D.A. *The History of Topographical Maps: Symbols, Pictures and Surveys.* London: Thames and Hudson, 1980.

———. *Medieval Maps.* Toronto: U of Toronto P, 1991.

Hauptman, Robert. *War, Literature & the Arts: An International Journal of the Humanities.* n.d. U.S. Air Force Academy. 15 October 2002 <www.usafa.af. mil/dfeng/wla/>.

Helms, Philip W. "The Gentle Scouring of the Shire: Civilian-Based Defense among the Hobbits." *Tolkien's Peaceful War: A History and Explanation of Tolkien Fandom and War.* Minas Tirith Evening-Star 1986. Eds. Philip W. Helms, Kerry Elizabeth Thompson, and Paul Ritz. Rev. ed. Highland, MI: American Tolkien Society, 1994.

Hemingway, Ernest. *A Farewell to Arms.* New York: Charles Scribner's Sons, 1927 (1957).

Herrnstein, Richard J., and Charles Murray. *The Bell Curve: Intelligence and Class Structure in American Life.* New York: Free Press, 1994.

Higham, Robin. "The Selection, Education, and Training of British Officers, 1740–1920." *The East Central European Officer Corps 1740–1920s: Social Origins, Selection, Education, and Training.* Eds. Béla K. Király and Walter Scott Dillard. War and Society in East Central Europe, vol. 24. Boulder: Social Science Monographs, 1987.

Holden, Stephen. "Film Portrayals to Stir the Soul." Rev. of *The Lord of the Rings,* dir. Peter Jackson, et al. *New York Times* 4 January 2002, sec. E, 1.

Horticulture. 2002. Commonwealth War Graves Commission. 5 June 2002 <www. cwgc.org/horticulture.htm>.

Instructions for the Training of Platoons for Offensive Action, 1917. London: Great Britain War Office, 1917.

Johnson, James Turner. *Just War Tradition and the Restraint of War: A Moral and Historical Inquiry*. Princeton: Princeton UP, 1981.

Jones, David Michael. *In Parenthesis: Seinnyessit E Gledyf Ym Penn Mameu*. Compass Books ed. New York: Viking, 1963.

Keegan, John. *The Book of War*. New York: Viking, 1999.

———. *The First World War*. New York: Alfred E. Knopf, 1999.

———. *An Illustrated History of the First World War*. New York: Alfred A. Knopf, 2001.

———. *The Mask of Command*. New York: Penguin, 1988.

———. *The Nature of War*. New York: Holt Rinehart Winston, 1981.

Knowles, Sebastian D. G. *A Purgatorial Flame: Seven British Writers in the Second World War*. Philadelphia: U of Pennsylvania P, 1990.

Kocher, Paul H. *Master of Middle-earth: The Fiction of J.R.R Tolkien*. Boston: Houghton Mifflin, 1972.

The Lancashire Fusiliers. n.d. 1 April 2002 <http://memorabilia.homestead.com/files/wm_makinson_lfs.html>.

Larkin, Philip. "MCMXIV." *Collected Poems*. London: Marvell Press, 1988. 128.

Latter, John Cecil. *The History of the Lancashire Fusiliers, 1914–1918*. 2 vols. Aldershot, Eng.: Gale and Polden, 1949.

Leed, Eric. "Fateful Memories: Industrialized War and Traumatic Neuroses." *Journal of Contemporary History* 35.1 (2000): 85–100.

Leeds University Verse 1914–1924. Ed. English School Association. Leeds, Eng.: Swan Press, 1924.

Leese, Peter. *Shell Shock: Traumatic Neurosis and the British Soldiers of the First World War*. Basingstoke: Palgrave Macmillan, 2002.

Le Guin, Ursula K. "Escape Routes." *The Language of the Night*. 1974. Ed. Susan Wood. New York: Berkley, 1979. 193–98.

———. "From Elfland to Poughkeepsie." *The Language of the Night*. 1973. Ed. Susan Wood. New York: Berkley, 1979. 73–86.

Leonard, Bruce. "The Post Traumatic Stress Disorder of Frodo Baggins." *Mythcon 27*. Boulder, CO: (unpublished), 1996.

Lewis, Alex. "Arma virumque cano: Of Wars Real and Imaginary." *Amon Hen* 138 (1996): 10–11.

———. "The Lost Heart of the Little Kingdom." *Leaves from the Tree: J.R.R. Tolkien's Shorter Fiction*. Ed. Thomas A. Shippey. London: Tolkien Society, 1991. 33–44.

Lewis, C. S. "The Dethronement of Power." *A Reader's Companion to* The Hobbit and The Lord of the Rings. New York: Quality Paperback Book Club, 1995. 37–42.

———. *Surprised by Joy: The Shape of My Early Life*. New York: Harcourt Brace, 1955.

Lloyd, Paul M. "The Role of Warfare and Strategy in *The Lord of the Rings*." *Mythlore* 3.3 (1976): 3–7.

The Lord of the Rings: The Fellowship of the Ring. Dir. Peter Jackson. Perf. Elijah Wood et al. 2001. DVD. New Line Productions, 2002.

MacCurdy, John T. *War Neuroses*. Cambridge: Cambridge UP, 1918.

"The Major." *When I Join the Ranks: What to Do and How to Do It*. London: Gale & Polden, 1916.

Maryles, Daisy. "The Ring Leaders (Behind the Bestsellers)." *Publishers Weekly* 17 December 2001: 17.

Mattox, John Mark. "Henry V: Shakespeare's Just Warrior." *War, Literature & the Arts* 12.1 (2000): 30–53 <www.usafa.af.mil/dfeng/wla/12-1/current.html>.

May, Carl. "Lord Moran's Memoir: Shell-Shock and the Pathology of Fear." *Journal of the Royal Society of Medicine* 91.2 (1998): 95–100.

McLaglen, Leopold. *Bayonet Fighting for War.* London: Harrison and Sons, 1916.

Miller, John J. "The Truth Beyond Memory." Rev. of *The Lord of the Rings,* dir. Peter Jackson. *National Review* 21 December 2001: 43–45.

Moran, Charles. *The Anatomy of Courage.* First American ed. Boston: Houghton Mifflin, 1967 (1945).

Munro, H. H. "Saki." "Birds on the Western Front, 1916." *Eyewitness to History.* Ed. John Carey. Cambridge: Harvard UP, 1987. 469–72.

Nelson, Charles W. "The Sins of Middle-earth: Tolkien's Use of Medieval Allegory." *J.R.R. Tolkien and His Literary Resonances.* Eds. George Clark and Daniel Timmons. Westport: Greenwood, 2000. 83–94.

Newton, Charles. "Underground Man, Go Home!" *College English* 37.4 (1975): 337–44.

Norman, Philip. *The Prevalence of Hobbits.* 2001 [1967]. Interview. New York Times. 1 July 2002 <www.nytimes.com/1967/01/15/books/tolkien-interview.html>.

Obertino, James. "Moria and Hades: Underworld Journeys in Tolkien and Virgil." *Comparative Literature Studies* 30.2 (1993): 153–69.

"Of Hobbits, War and Bush." Rev. of *The Lord of the Rings,* dir. Peter Jackson. *Commonweal* 11 January 2002: 5.

Otty, Nick. "The Structuralist's Guide to Middle-earth." *J.R.R. Tolkien: This Far Land.* Ed. Robert Giddings. London: Vision, 1983. 154–77.

Owen, Wilfred. "Preface." *The Collected Poems of Wilfred Owen.* Ed. C. Day Lewis. London: Chatto and Windus, 1966. 31.

Parker, Peter. *The Old Lie: The Great War and the Public-School Ethos.* London: Constable, 1987.

Partridge, Brenda. "No Sex Please—We're Hobbits: The Construction of Female Sexuality in *The Lord of the Rings.*" *J.R.R. Tolkien: This Far Land.* Ed. Robert Giddings. London: Vision, 1983. 179–97.

Petty, Anne C. *One Ring to Bind Them All: Tolkien's Mythology.* University: U of Alabama P, 1979.

Phillips, Robert L. *War and Justice.* Norman: U of Oklahoma P, 1984.

Polsson, Ken. *Chronology of World War II.* 2002. 10 June 2002 <www.islandnet.com/~kpolsson/ww2hist/>.

"Posttraumatic Stress Disorder." *Diagnostic and Statistical Manual of Mental Disorders: DSM-IV.* 4th ed., text revision ed. Washington, DC: American Psychiatric Association, 2000. 463–68.

Prior, Robin, and Trevor Wilson. "Eastern Front and Western Front, 1916–1917." *The Oxford Illustrated History of the First World War.* Ed. Hew Strachan. Oxford: Oxford UP, 1998. 179–90.

Ready, William. *The Tolkien Relation.* Chicago: Henry Regnery, 1968.

Representations of the Pietà by Michelangelo. 1996. Web Gallery of Art. 6 June 2002 <http://gallery.euroweb.hu/html/m/michelan/1sculptu/pieta>.

Ridgway, Matthew B. "Leadership." *Military Leadership: In Pursuit of Excellence.* (Originally published in *Military Review* 46.10 [October 1966]: 40–49.) Eds. Robert L. Taylor and William E. Rosenbach. 4th ed. Boulder, CO: Westview, 2000. 6–15.

Rosebury, Brian. *Tolkien: A Critical Assessment.* New York: St. Martin's, 1992.

Ryan, John S. *The Shaping of Middle-earth's Maker: Influences on the Life and Literature of J.R.R. Tolkien.* Highland, MI: American Tolkien Society, 1992.

Sale, Roger. *Modern Heroism: Essays on D.H. Lawrence, William Empson, and J.R.R. Tolkien.* Berkeley: U of California P, 1973.

Sassoon, Siegfried. "Glory of Women." *Collected Poems.* New York: Viking, 1949. 79.

———. "Litany of the Lost." *Collected Poems.* New York: Viking, 1949. 205–6.

———. *Memoirs of an Infantry Officer.* New York: Coward, McCann, 1930.

———. "Suicide in Trenches." *Collected Poems.* New York: Viking, 1949. 78.

Schulp, J. A. "The Flora of Middle Earth." *Inklings: Jahrbuch* (1985): 129–39.

Scott, Nan C. "War and Pacifism in *The Lord of the Rings.*" *Tolkien Journal* 15 (1972): 23–25, 27–30.

Senior, W. A. "Loss Eternal in J.R.R. Tolkien's Middle-earth." *J.R.R. Tolkien and His Literary Resonances: Views of Middle-earth.* Eds. George Clark and Daniel Timmons. Westport: Greenwood, 2000. 173–82.

Shakespeare, William. *Macbeth.* New York: Dover, 1993.

Shippey, Thomas A. *J.R.R. Tolkien: Author of the Century.* Boston: Houghton Mifflin, 2001.

———. "Orcs, Wraiths, Wights: Tolkien's Images of Evil." *J.R.R. Tolkien and His Literary Resonances.* Eds. George Clark and Daniel Timmons. Westport: Greenwood, 2000.

———. *The Road to Middle-earth.* Boston: Houghton Mifflin, 1983.

———. "Tolkien as a Post-War Writer." *Proceedings of the J.R.R. Tolkien Centenary Conference, 1992.* Eds. Patricia Reynolds and Glen H. GoodKnight. Altadena: Milton Keynes Tolkien Society, 1992. 84–93.

Signalling: Morse, Semaphore, Station Work, Despatch Riding, Telephone Cables, Map Reading. Imperial Army Series; Based on Official Manuals. Ed. E. John Solano. London: John Murray, 1914.

Simons, Lewis M. "Weapons of Mass Destruction." *National Geographic* (November 2002): 2–35.

Spencer, Andrew, and Brandon Soule. "Not to Strike without Need: Evaluation of the Dichotomy of J.R.R. Tolkien's Views on War." *Concerning Hobbits and Other Matters: Tolkien Across the Disciplines.* Ed. Tim Schindler. St. Paul, CO: U of St. Thomas, 2001. 61–65.

Stanton, Michael N. *Hobbits, Elves, and Wizards: Exploring the Wonders and Worlds of J.R.R. Tolkien's The Lord of the Rings.* New York: Palgrave, 2001.

Stewart, Douglas J. "The Hobbit War." *The Nation* 9 October 1967, 332–35.

Stokesbury, James L. "Leadership as an Art." *Military Leadership: In Pursuit of Excellence.* (Originally published in *Military Leadership,* eds. James H. Buck and Lawrence J. Korb, Sage Publications, 1981, 23–40.) Eds. Robert L. Taylor and William E. Rosenbach. 4th ed. Boulder, CO: Westview, 2000. 141–56.

Strachan, Hew. *The Oxford Illustrated History of the First World War.* New York: Oxford UP, 2000.

Stuart, Edwin R. *Map Reading and Topographical Sketching*. New York: McGraw-Hill, 1918.

Sun-tzu. *Sun-Tzu: The New Translation*. Trans. J. H. Huang. New York: William Morrow, 1993.

Swanwick, Michael. "A Changeling Returns." *Meditations on Middle-earth*. Ed. Karen Haber. New York: St. Martin's, 2001. 33–46.

Tannen, Deborah. *You Just Don't Understand: Women and Men in Conversation*. New York: William Morrow, 1990.

Tarn, W. W. *Alexander the Great*. Boston: Bacon, 1956.

Teichman, Jenny. *Pacifism and the Just War: A Study in Applied Philosophy*. Oxford: Basil Blackwell, 1986.

Timmons, Daniel. "Mirror on Middle-earth: J.R.R. Tolkien and the Critical Perspectives." Ph.D. diss. U of Toronto, 1998.

———. " 'We Few, We Happy Few . . . ': War and Glory in *Henry V* and *The Lord of the Rings*." *Mythopoeic Society Mythcon 33*. Boulder, CO: (unpublished), 2002.

Tolkien, J.R.R. *The Annotated Hobbit*. Ed. Douglas A. Anderson. 2nd ed. Boston: Houghton Mifflin, 2002.

———. *Beowulf: The Monsters and the Critics*. London: British Academy, 1936.

———. *The Book of Lost Tales. Part I*. The History of Middle-earth, vol. 1. Ed. Christopher Tolkien. Book Club; 1st American ed. Boston: Houghton Mifflin, 1984.

———. *The Book of Lost Tales. Part II*. The History of Middle-earth, vol. 2. Ed. Christopher Tolkien. Boston: Houghton Mifflin, 1984.

———. *Farmer Giles of Ham: The Rise and Wonderful Adventures of Farmer Giles, Lord of Tame, Count of Worminghall, and King of the Little Kingdom*. Eds. Christina Scull, Wayne G. Hammond, and Pauline Baynes, ill. Boston: Houghton Mifflin, 1999.

———. *The Fellowship of the Ring: Being the First Part of The Lord of the Rings*. 2nd ed. Boston: Houghton Mifflin, 1965.

———. *The Hobbit, or There and Back Again*. Boston: Houghton Mifflin, 1966.

———. "The Homecoming of Beorhtnoth Beorhthelm's Son." *The Tolkien Reader*. New York: Ballantine Books, 1966. 3–24.

———. "Leaf by Niggle." *The Tolkien Reader*. New York: Ballantine, 1966. 85–112.

———. *Letters from Father Christmas*. Ed. Baillie Tolkien. Rev. ed. Boston: Houghton Mifflin, 1999.

———. *The Letters of J.R.R. Tolkien: A Selection*. Eds. Humphrey Carpenter and Christopher Tolkien. 1st pbk. ed. Boston: Houghton Mifflin, 2000.

———. *Morgoth's Ring: The Later Silmarillion, Part One: The Legends of Aman*. The History of Middle-earth, vol. 10. Ed. Christopher Tolkien. Boston: Houghton Mifflin, 1993.

———. "On Fairy-stories." *The Tolkien Reader*. New York: Ballantine, 1966. 3–84.

———. "Princess Mee." *The Tolkien Reader*. New York: Ballantine, 1966. 28–30.

———. *The Return of the King: Being the Third Part of The Lord of the Rings*. 2nd ed. Boston: Houghton Mifflin, 1965.

———. *Roverandom*. Ed. Wayne G. Hammond. Boston: Houghton Mifflin, 1998.

———. *The Shaping of Middle-earth: The Quenta, the Ambarkanta, and the Annals*.

The History of Middle-earth, vol. 4. Ed. Christopher Tolkien. 1st Ballantine Books ed. New York: Ballantine, 1995.

———. *The Silmarillion*. 1st American ed. Boston: Houghton Mifflin, 1977.

———. *Smith of Wootton Major; Farmer Giles of Ham*. Book Club ed. Garden City, NY: Nelson Doubleday, 1976.

———. *The Two Towers: Being the Second Part of The Lord of the Rings*. 2nd ed. Boston: Houghton Mifflin, 1965.

———. *Unfinished Tales of Númenor and Middle-earth*. Ed. Christopher Tolkien. 1st American ed. Boston: Houghton Mifflin, 1980.

Tolkien, John, and Priscilla Tolkien. *The Tolkien Family Album*. Boston: Houghton Mifflin, 1992.

"Tolkien Mythology Comes to Vietnam." *Publisher's Weekly* 4 September 1967: 24.

Tolkien, Priscilla. "J.R.R. Tolkien and Edith Tolkien's Stay in Staffordshire 1916, 1917, and 1918." *Angerthas* 34 (1992): 4–5.

Training Manual—Signalling. Vol. 2. London: His Majesty's Stationery Office, 1914.

Tuchman, Barbara Wertheim. *The Guns of August*. New York: Ballantine, 1994.

———. *The Zimmermann Telegram*. 1st Ballantine Books trade ed. New York: Ballantine, 1985.

Ulansey, David. *Mithraism: The Cosmic Rites of Mithras*. n.d. 5 June 2002 <www.well.com/user/davidu/mithras.html>.

Valent, Paul. "Survivor Guilt." *Encyclopedia of Stress*. Ed. George Fink. Vol. 3. San Diego: Academic Press, 2000. 555–57.

Veldman, Meredith. *Fantasy, the Bomb, and the Greening of Britain: Romantic Protest, 1945–1980*. Cambridge: Cambridge UP, 1994.

Walpole, Hugh. "Mobile Hospital Unit with the Russian Army, Galicia, 2 June 1915." *Eyewitness to History*. Ed. John Carey. Cambridge: Harvard UP, 1987. 453–54.

Warner, Marina. "Fantasy's Power and Peril." *The New York Times* 16 December 2001, sec. 4: 5.

Whelan, Michael. "The Eagles Are Coming." *The 1980 J.R.R. Tolkien Calendar*. New York: Ballantine, 1978. November.

Williamson, Samuel R., Jr. "The Origins of the War." *The Oxford Illustrated History of the First World War*. Ed. Hew Strachan. Oxford: Oxford UP, 1998. 9–25.

Wilson, Edmund. "Oo, Those Awful Orcs!" *A Reader's Companion to* The Hobbit *and* The Lord of the Rings. New York: Quality Paperback Book Club, 1995. 55–64.

Wood, Ralph C. "Tolkien the Movie." Rev. of *The Lord of the Rings*, dir. Peter Jackson. *Christian Century* 2 January 2002: 35.

Wood, Tanya Caroline. "Is Tolkien a Renaissance Man? Sir Philip Sidney's *Defense of Poesy* and J.R.R. Tolkien's 'On Fairy-stories.' " *J.R.R. Tolkien and His Literary Resonances: Views of Middle-earth*. Eds. George Clark and Daniel Timmons. Westport: Greenwood, 2000. 95–108.

Wyndham, Horace. *Soldiers on Service: A Manual of Practical Information for Members of the Expeditionary Force*. London: Eveleigh Nash, 1915.

Young, Arthur P. *Books for Sammies: The American Library Association and World War I*. Beta Phi Mu Chapbooks no. 15. Pittsburgh: Beta Phi Mu, 1981.

Index

About the Author

JANET BRENNAN CROFT is Head of Access Services at the University of Oklahoma. Previously, she was Library Director at Martin Methodist College in Tennessee. Her articles have appeared in numerous scholarly journals.